4/21

Ben Fletcher
The Life and Times
of a Black Wobbly

Peter Cole

Ben Fletcher: The Life and Times of a Black Wobbly, Second Edition
Peter Cole
This edition © 2021 PM Press.

All rights reserved. No part of this book may be transmitted by any means without permission in writing from the publisher.

ISBN: 978-1-62963-832-4 (paperback)
ISBN: 978-1-62963-862-1 (hardcover)
ISBN: 978-1-62963-848-5 (ebook)

Library of Congress Control Number: 2020934738

Cover by John Yates / www.stealworks.com
Interior design by briandesign

10 9 8 7 6 5 4 3 2 1

PM Press
PO Box 23912
Oakland, CA 94623
www.pmpress.org

Printed in the USA.

Contents

WRITINGS AND SPEECHES BY AND ABOUT BEN FLETCHER

APPENDIX

Foreword

Robin D.G. Kelley

Fletcher is the real type of "Southern Nigger Agitator" with no education, poor grammar. He is about 5 ft. 9 in. in height weighs 185
lbs.; and is reputed by the police as a bad man or a gun fighter. He
did not display any of that to agent.
—Report by Agent Henry M. Bowen, FBI, Boston, July 4, 1917

Rereading Peter Cole's marvelous *Ben Fletcher: The Life and Times of a Black
Wobbly* amid a global pandemic has been something of a revelation. Of
course, "sheltering in place" in order to reduce community spread of the
COVID-19 virus is a far cry from the kind of confinement Ben Fletcher
experienced in Leavenworth Federal Penitentiary or what millions of
imprisoned souls currently endure—caged men and women unable to
escape the coronavirus and its potentially lethal consequences. But, truth
be told, my epiphany about Fletcher's life and significance derived not
from some lofty reflections on the meaning of freedom from a place of
confinement. The real source was Hollywood.

Like everyone else privileged enough to shelter in homes with internet and cable access, between Zoom talks, reading, writing, cooking,
and cleaning, we watched TV. In honor of May Day, I streamed *Reds*,
Warren Beatty's three-hour masterwork about the Russian Revolution
told through the romance of John Reed and Louise Bryant. I hadn't seen it
since its theatrical release, which would have been the early part of 1982.
A sophomore in college and diehard Marxist who had spent the previous
summer reading the first two volumes of *Capital* and all three volumes of
Lenin: Selected Works, I vividly recall tearing up as Reed and Bryant joined
the throngs of workers marching down the streets of Petrograd toward
the Winter Palace, singing the "Internationale" in Russian. But seeing it
again after all of these years, I suddenly remembered why I found the
film unsettling. For one thing, the radical Reed came across at times as
a xenophobe. In one scene, Reed argued against uniting his Communist
Labor Party with the rival Communist Party of America led by the Italian-
born Marxist Louis C. Fraina because the latter wasn't truly "American."

Reed: We can't merge with [Louis] Fraina. We can't deal with him on membership eligibility. He wouldn't accept half of our people. The man is gonna do nothing but alienate himself from any potential broad base of support. He's sociologically isolated, programmatically he's impossible to deal with . . .
Bryant: You mean he's a foreigner?
Reed: Don't do that, Louise.
Bryant: Six months ago, you were friends.
Reed: These people can barely speak English. They don't even want to be integrated into American life.

Even more troubling was the film's thorough whitewashing of the Left. Here was a considerable slice of American Communist history without Negroes or even a "Negro Question." One would never know from the film that John Reed was the first American to address the Communist International (Comintern) on "The Negro Question in America." Delivered on July 25, 1920, just three months before his untimely death, his speech excoriated US racism, condemned lynching and disfranchisement, and heralded a new revolutionary movement among black workers and intellectuals such as A. Philip Randolph and Chandler Owen, editors of the socialist-leaning *Messenger* magazine. Yet, while urging Communists to support black struggles for social and political equality, he argued that their main task should be "to organize Negroes in the same unions as the whites. This is the best and quickest way to root out racial prejudice and awaken class solidarity." The IWW, he insisted, had been doing this all along.[1]

In fact, Benjamin Harrison Fletcher should have shown up in *Reds*, and not just in cameo. Reed first met Fletcher in 1910, and like everyone in the IWW's circle, came to regard him as one of the most talented organizers the Wobblies ever produced. Even those hostile to the Wobblies acknowledged Fletcher's venerated status among American labor leaders. The *Messenger* dubbed him "the most prominent Negro Labor Leader in America." A target of the post–World War I "Red Scare," Fletcher also became one of the most prominent black political prisoners

---

1   John Reed, "The Negro Question in America: Speech at the 2nd World Congress of the Communist International, Moscow—July 25, 1920," *Second Congress of the Communist International: Minutes of the Proceedings, Vol. 1* (London: New Park Publications, 1977), 120–24. Lenin famously disagreed, insisting that black working people in the South constituted a "dependent and subject" nation whose fight for self-determination took on a revolutionary character.

in the country—second only to Marcus Garvey. Indeed, he was the only African American among the 101 Wobblies convicted of violating the 1917 Espionage Act, for which he served two and a half years in Leavenworth Federal Penitentiary. Even after his death in 1949, long after the heyday of the IWW and his leadership of the Marine Transport Workers Union, Fletcher was still a widely respected figure in the labor movement. A fairly conservative black-owned newspaper, the *Atlanta Daily World*, ran a glowing obituary calling Fletcher "one of the most brilliant Negroes ever associated with a leftist organization" and "highly respected for his scholastic ability and his oratorical efforts." The author's point that Fletcher was jailed because "mass hysteria swept the country and new laws, Criminal syndicalism made its appearance . . . as a weapon to prosecute supposed subversives" was not lost on readers living through a new and more virulent Red Scare.

But by the time *Reds* hit the big screen, the name Ben Fletcher had faded into obscurity. In fact, it was precisely the whiteness of *Reds* that led me to books such as Philip S. Foner's *American Socialism and Black Americans*, where that I first encountered Ben Fletcher. I found traces of him in Sterling Spero and Abram Harris's classic 1931 text, *The Black Worker*, in Robert Allen's *Reluctant Reformers*, in Melvin Dubofsky's massive history of the IWW, *We Shall Be All*, and obscure history journals.[2] But even these excellent sources could not fully capture his complicated experiences as an independent black socialist labor leader, the breadth of his intellect and strategic brilliance, his triumphs and disappointments, not to mention his razor-sharp wit and wicked sense of humor.

That all changed in 2007, when a young historian named Peter Cole published the first edition of *Ben Fletcher: The Life and Times of a Black Wobbly* with Charles H. Kerr, the iconoclastic publishing house then run by the late Franklin Rosemont and Penelope Rosemont. It was soon followed by his magnificent monograph *Wobblies on the Waterfront: Interracial Unionism in Progressive-Era Philadelphia* (University of Illinois

---

2   Sterling D. Spero and Abram L. Harris Jr., *The Black Worker: The Negro and the Labor Movement* (New York: Columbia University Press, 1931), 333–36; Robert L. Allen, *Reluctant Reformers: Racism and Social Reform Movements in the United States* (Washington, DC: Howard University Press, 1974); Melvin Dubofsky, *We Shall Be All: A History of the Industrial Workers of the World* (Chicago: Quadrangle Books, 1969); William Seraile, "Ben Fletcher: IWW Organizer," *Pennsylvania History* 46, no. 3 (July 1979): 212–32; Irwin Marcus, "Benjamin Fletcher: Black Labor Leader," *Negro History Bulletin* 35 (October 1972): 131–40. When I was in graduate school, I also got hold of Myland R. Brown's pioneering dissertation, "The IWW and the Negro Worker" (EdD, Ball State University, 1968).

Press, 2007), which not only provided the most thorough account of Fletcher's life but also placed him squarely at the center of dockworker organizing in the early twentieth century. And that meant reckoning with the dynamics of race and class, not to mention the potentialities and limits of direct action versus bread-and-butter unionism in an interracial but predominantly black labor movement. Fleshing out Ben Fletcher unsettled not only US labor history but also histories of American radicalism and Black Studies. We learn that Fletcher was more than a "Black Wobbly." He exemplified the "New Negro" of the post–World War I era but was never included among the era's celebrated intellectuals, artists, and activists despite having been lionized in the pages of the *Messenger*. Cole's scrupulous introduction and the collected writings by and about Fletcher reveal a radical vision that rejected both emigration and inclusion within the existing system in favor of revolution—meaning transforming all social, cultural, political, economic, and juridical institutions to the core. Fletcher understood that only workers' power could usher in a new society, and that required obliterating the color line, building a durable solidarity, but also attending to working people's immediate needs. As a consequence, he was frequently deemed too radical by some and too conservative by others—evidence of a praxis that exceeded the terms of syndicalism, socialism, anarchism, and industrial unionism. Rather, Fletcher might be best described as a radical pragmatist in that he paid attention to context, emphasized solidarity, and approached the work in an improvisatory and flexible manner—all without ever losing sight of the long-term goal: the emancipation of the working class from Capital.

He also had no choice. His survival depended on keen wits and a fugitive's acumen. He knew that as a *black* organizer of an interracial movement, he was especially susceptible to lethal violence. Company thugs, mobs, and cops wouldn't stop at roughing him up a bit. White men savagely murdered hundreds of African Americans with impunity, while Fletcher was locked up for promoting industrial unionism, interracial solidarity, socialism, and an end to war.[3] In a 1931 interview with

---

3   Between Fletcher's conviction in 1918 and release from prison in 1922, there were at least 309 recorded lynchings of black people. During the Red Summer of 1919, thirty-eight black people were killed in Chicago and over two hundred killed in Elaine, Arkansas. In 1920 in Ocoee, Florida, more than fifty black people were killed for attempting to vote, and in 1921, white mobs and police officers destroyed a large swath of Tulsa's black community and killed over three hundred people. No white person was prosecuted for any of these crimes.

the *Amsterdam News*, Fletcher recalled how he narrowly escaped a possible lynching for organizing dockworkers in Norfolk in 1917. "One night friends, fearing that my life was in danger, smuggled me aboard a northbound ship to Boston."[4] As soon as he arrived, he took a job in a soap factory and continued agitating for the IWW. When a cop spotted him distributing Wobbly literature, he was taken into custody and interrogated by an FBI agent. Upon questioning, Fletcher cunningly pretended to disavow his membership, convincing the agent that he "discovered the folly of this as he has been unable to secure or keep any kind of job since his connection as organizer of the I.W.W."[5]

As Cole points out, Fletcher was a funny man. His capacity to find humor in the direst of circumstances caught the attention of all who knew him, including IWW leader William "Big Bill" Haywood. Much of his humor turned on the absurdity of racism, which not only made him vulnerable to lethal violence, but also rendered him invisible. When he learned about the federal indictment against him, Fletcher promptly left Boston and returned to Philadelphia to await his arrest. He took a job at a roundhouse operated by the Pennsylvania Railroad, never concealing his identity. Five months had passed before agents tracked him down and arrested him. While out on bail, he received a summons to appear in court in Chicago on April 1, 1918. Delayed by a train accident, Fletcher arrived at the courthouse a couple of hours late.

> Making my way through the federal agents and police who swarmed the corridors I was blocked at the courtroom door by the chief bailiff, who inquired:
> "What do you want in here?"
> "I belong in here."
> "Oh, a wise boy from the South side want to see the show?"
> "No, I'm one of the actors."
> "Take that stuff away. You can't get in here."

He had to produce identification and his summons just to prove he was the one and only Benjamin Harrison Fletcher. It was enough to finally persuade the chief bailiff to let him enter. "And then I walked into the courtroom and into the Federal penitentiary."[6]

---

4   "Some People Are Taken to Jail, but Ben Fletcher Just Walked In," *Amsterdam News*, December 30, 1931.

5   Report by Agent Henry M. Bowen, FBI, Boston, July 4, 1917, Old German Files, FBI "Ben H. Fletcher" (#29434), RG 65, National Archives, digital copy.

6   "Some People Are Taken to Jail, but Ben Fletcher Just Walked In."

But organizing wasn't funny. By the time he left prison and returned to his work with the Marine Transport Workers Union, he encountered two big challenges. The first was an old problem: white workers whose loyalty to white supremacy undermined interracial solidarity and class struggle. While his enthusiasm for "One Big Union" never waned, he did complain in the pages of the *Messenger*, "Organized labor, for the most part be it radical or conservative, thinks and acts, in the terms of the White Race."[7] Of course, the Wobblies never paid special attention to the specific situation of African Americans, and they sought, too simply, to rise above the racism and ethnocentrism of the working class and its capitalist masters. To solve the class question, they argued, was to solve the race question—a position Fletcher endorsed.

The second challenge was the Communist Party, to which he became bitterly opposed. But not right away. He was willing to work with Communists, even after the two warring factions united in 1924 to become the Communist Party USA. In 1925, he was recruited as one of the principal speakers at the first American Negro Labor Congress organized by the CPUSA. According to lore, he was slated to lead the ANLC if not for his former Wobbly comrade Lovett Fort-Whiteman. Credited as the first black person to officially join the Communist Party, Fort-Whiteman jealously opposed Fletcher holding a leadership role in the Congress. Fletcher also complained that Communists were attempting to take over the IWW and the unions they had built. But as the CP's star rose into the 1930s, Fletcher clung to the rapidly declining IWW, even when it became a shadow of its former self. Neither anticommunism nor organizational loyalty kept him tethered to Wobblies. Rather, he held on to the idea of industrial unionism. He predicted in 1931, "Inevitably, the IWW will be revived . . . with the full exposure of the insincerity of the American Communists and the continued rationalization of industry which obliviates craft lines, making the trade unions of the AF of L obsolete and necessitating the building of industrial unions such as those of the Industrial Workers of the World."[8] We know he was partly right. While the IWW never achieved the status it enjoyed during the first two decades of the twentieth century, a few years after Fletcher made his prediction, the Congress of Industrial Organizations was formed.

---

7   Benjamin Fletcher, "The Negro and Organized Labor," *Messenger* 5, no. 7 (July 1923): 760.
8   "Some People Are Taken to Jail, but Ben Fletcher Just Walked In."

Ben Fletcher believed in the working class and its capacity to win. He never wavered from his belief that capitalism would come to an end but only an organized working class could end it. A truly organized working class would have to eliminate all vestiges of racism and xenophobia, redirecting our collective anger toward the capitalist class. His was not a blind optimism, a naïve belief that persuasive arguments could wipe away color prejudice and unite the proletariat. Rather, he knew our survival depended on the overthrow of capitalism, and he had lived through an era when it appeared that the working class had capital by the throat. The state's decision to throw him in jail, along with over one hundred of his fellow Wobblies, was evidence of a terrified ruling class. But that meant working people had to be ready to take power. He said as much in a letter to Milwaukee socialist Miss Othelia Hampel, penned from his cell in Leavenworth. Written on New Year's Eve 1919, bookending what was arguably the most revolutionary year in American history if not the world, he wrote, "We are living in momentous times. . . . None of us are gifted with the power [of] 'clairvoyancy' as to be able to fortell [sic] the day or the hour, therefore the first and most important duty is for all of us to prepare ourselves for the final chapter in the life of Capitalism."[9]

---

9   Ben Fletcher to Othelia Hampel, December 31, 1919, quoted in Arthur T. Bagley Report to H. H. Stroud, Esq., January 1, 1920, Old German Files, FBI "Ben H. Fletcher" (#29434), RG 65, National Archives, digital copy.

Preface to the Second Edition

It is quite rare for a book to receive a second life—that is, a second edition—so why publish another version of *Ben Fletcher*? To put it kindly, Ben Fletcher is far from a household name. To put it more bluntly, 99.9999 percent of people never have heard of him, so surely one edition of a book on him should suffice, right? While it is undeniable that few have heard of him, Fletcher was one of the country's greatest black radicals ever, and today a great many people are increasingly interested in and hungry for inspirational, educational (hi)stories of such folks. Indeed, as more people question capitalism and come to understand its intertwining with white supremacy, the history of a working-class, black socialist and unionist is of great interest.

The Charles H. Kerr Publishing Company published the first edition of *Ben Fletcher*, and the University of Illinois Press published my book *Wobblies on the Waterfront: Interracial Unionism in Progressive-Era Philadelphia* (both in 2007). Yet after their publication, I continued to learn more about Fletcher and the union he helped lead, Local 8. Once these books were published, not surprisingly in retrospect, numerous people with connections to or deep interest in Fletcher and Local 8 found me and shared what they knew. Related to that, I also discovered new information about Fletcher's life. Due to the expansion of the internet and digitization of old records, many "new" documents are waiting to be found, if the researcher looks in the right places and gets lucky. As a result, this edition includes many additional documents that did not appear in the original book.

In addition, in the thirteen years since publication of the first edition, much has changed in the United States and world. One important way is the increasing appreciation of the interconnectedness of human beings, regardless of the often-arbitrary lines drawn on political maps. Due to sophisticated technological systems like the internet and seemingly simple ones like containerization, individuals, cultures, and economies are more connected—globally—than ever before. In turn, these changes have resulted in historians and other scholars applying this new reality to their own fields of study. In my case, for instance, I thought about Fletcher, Local 8, and Philadelphia in a more international manner than I previously had. Another important shift is that many more people now appreciate the reality of racial capitalism in the United States, a country where the economic and racial systems are inextricably linked, dating back to the seventeenth century. As the perniciousness and persistence of racism becomes more apparent, more people understand that solely changing laws banning racial discrimination is insufficient to achieving racial equality. Further, as economic inequality grows ever vaster in the US and worldwide, more people question the inevitability and desirability of capitalism; hence, more of us are searching for alternatives, and some of us seek historical lessons in the past. Altogether, there exists far more interest in Ben Fletcher today than in the early 2000s.

Specifically, this edition includes more than double the number of historical documents on Fletcher, Local 8, and the IWW. It should go without saying that there must be other materials that remain to be found, so I never would make the claim that I have found every document written by Fletcher or about him. A few documents included here were written in languages other than English and have been translated for this collection. There also is more information about Fletcher's personal history, albeit still far less than desired. To make use of these new documents, as well as other information gleaned about Fletcher and Local 8 since creating the first edition, the introduction has been revised and expanded, too.

Thank you for reading this second edition of *Ben Fletcher*. Solidarity forever!

Introduction

Benjamin Harrison Fletcher surely ranks among the greatest African Americans of his generation and top echelon of black unionists and radicals in all of US history. In the early twentieth century, Fletcher helped lead a pathbreaking union that likely was the most diverse and integrated organization (not simply union) despite the era's rampant racism, antiunionism, and xenophobia. Fletcher and thousands of his fellow Philadelphia dockworkers belonged to Local 8, affiliated with the Industrial Workers of the World (IWW), perhaps the most radical unions in all of US history. IWW members were, and still are, affectionately known as Wobblies. If one has heard of A. Philip Randolph, Hubert Harrison, and Harry Haywood—black working-class radicals who lived in the same time—one should know about Fletcher, the greatest black Wobbly. If one has heard of militant black organizers of the 1960s, like Fred Hampton, Ella Baker, or Stokely Carmichael, one should know about Fletcher. Yet today Fletcher is unknown save for aficionados of black labor and radical history.

Fletcher was born in 1890 in Philadelphia and raised there, his parents having separately escaped the racist horrors of the South in the late 1880s—not long after the overturning of Reconstruction in what should be understood as a counterrevolution to preserve white supremacy. In a sense, one might think of the migration of Fletcher's parents to Philadelphia as similar to the desperately poor Sicilian immigrants and Russian Jews fleeing the murderous, anti-Semitic pogroms in Russia. In the working-class slums of South Philadelphia, African Americans like the Fletchers lived on the same streets as East European Jews and Italians as well as poor and working-class Poles and Lithuanians, Irish and Irish Americans, and more. Fletcher was one of the countless thousands of young men who walked to the Delaware River waterfront looking for a day's work to support themselves and their families. These sons of peasants (no daughters, then) loaded and unloaded ship cargo and submitted themselves to the "shape-up," an oppressive hiring system, in order to get hired to work in one of the country's busiest ports. Philadelphia boasted of itself as "the workshop of the world" and, alongside Chicago and other industrial cities, had made the United States into the world's mightiest industrial powerhouse. The unloading of vast amounts of coal, iron, cotton, and other raw materials and loading of all sorts of manufactured goods—everything from buttonhooks to locomotive engines—meant thousands of backbreaking, dangerous, low-paying jobs for desperate men with strong backs.

Fletcher, who always went by "Ben," started working along the shore *and* joined the IWW in 1910 or 1911, when he was about twenty years old. He quickly developed into an accomplished street speaker—nicknamed a soapboxer for the wooden boxes that speakers stood atop to be seen and heard above the crowds that jostled together on the bustling streets of south Philly. In 1913, at the age of twenty-three, he became a leader in the newly created Local 8, born out of a victorious two-week strike that had shut down the port. At that time, the IWW was among only a tiny handful of unions in the country (and the world) actively seeking to organize workers regardless of race, sex, color, or nationality. Even fewer sought to overthrow the capitalist wage system and usher in a new society from the ashes of the old.

The importance of Local 8 dominating the Philadelphia waterfront for nearly a decade—a symbol of what was possible—cannot be overstated. The last major port workforce in the country to be represented by a labor union, instead of joining the more mainstream dock union that belonged to the American Federation of Labor (AFL), Philadelphia's longshoremen signed up with the revolutionary industrial union, the IWW—the Wobblies! Even their nickname demands that one sit up and take notice. Never before or since has there been a labor union like the IWW. Upon formation, Local 8 was roughly one-third African American, one-third Irish and Irish American, and one-third immigrant from other European countries. This incredible diversity was not uncommon in American workplaces. Unionizing such a workforce in an era when most unions (generally affiliated with the AFL) were racist or xenophobic was rare to the say the least. Thus, in the decade that marked the start of the African American Great Migration (out of the South) and the end of thirty years of massive European immigration, Fletcher helped lead the most diverse and integrated working-class organization in the land.

In his time, Fletcher was celebrated by the most prominent, radical black intellectuals. A. Philip Randolph and Chandler Owen, coeditors of the *Messenger*, an openly socialist monthly which billed itself as the "only radical Negro magazine in America," regularly praised Fletcher and

Ben Fletcher, linocut by Carlos Cortez. Courtesy of Charles H. Kerr Publishing Co.

Local 8. In 1923, they labeled Fletcher "the most prominent Negro Labor Leader in America." Claude McKay, the Jamaican-born writer, Harlem Renaissance celebrity, and committed anticapitalist, told of the story of Local 8, and thus Fletcher, in the legendary novel *Home to Harlem* (1928). W.E.B. Du Bois, a cofounder of the NAACP and editor of its influential monthly, wrote, "We respect [the IWW] as one of the social and political movements in modern times that draws no color line." Of course, it was Local 8, led by Fletcher, that turned the Wobblies' antiracist vision into that reality. In short, Fletcher and a bunch of so-called unskilled working-class black and white folks, native-born and immigrant, managed to do what most American institutions *still* have not achieved in 2020: equality and integration.

Sadly, Ben Fletcher typified non-elites in that he did not leave nearly enough of a paper trail behind, especially for the liking of historians. He did not have children to pass along his stories and memories to, and all of his friends passed away long ago. More than seventy years after his death and an entire century since he made history, a complete biography of Fletcher seems impossible. Fortunately, he was important and respected enough that some of his writings have been preserved and numerous others documented his exploits. Ironically, another useful source of information comes from the federal government's spies and prison wardens who documented Fletcher's activities.

Since a biography of Fletcher is intertwined with the union he championed, this introductory essay will not try to extricate one from the other. This introduction will describe the biographical details of Fletcher combined with the history of Local 8, highlighting Fletcher's role when possible. After the introduction, this book will reproduce magazine and newspaper articles, correspondence, interviews, memoirs, and other writings either by Fletcher or about him with introductory remarks intended to provide needed context.

Fletcher's Early Years

Almost nothing is known about Ben Fletcher's childhood, family, or personal life. He left behind no diary, memoir, journals, or extensive correspondence—at least that is known. Granted, this problem is commonplace among historians researching non-elite people in most societies and eras. Yet his example illuminates how, even among the leadership cadre of a vital international organization, such is the case.

Benjamin Harrison Fletcher was born on Sunday, April 13, 1890, hence his given names, after the sitting president of the time, Benjamin

Harrison. Overwhelmingly, African Americans of that generation strongly identified with the Republicans as "the party that freed the slaves," and apparently Fletcher's parents were no different. His parents were born in the Upper South—Dennis on the "Eastern Shore" of Virginia and Esther in Virginia or Maryland—in the 1850s. Though not definite, given that the great majority of African Americans in those states (and the country) were enslaved, most likely his mother and father were born enslaved and, thus, likely only freed with the Thirteenth Amendment in 1865. Fletcher never made mention of family stories about enslavement. Some reported that Fletcher possessed American Indian ancestry, which is not uncommon among African Americans. Though no evidence exists to confirm or deny that claim, some African Americans in Virginia did mix with local American Indian peoples.

Foreshadowing the much larger wave of southern blacks who later moved north of the Mason-Dixon line, called the Great Migration, Fletcher's parents moved to Philadelphia sometime before 1890. They married in Philadelphia in 1899 and had their first child, Ben, the following year. His first sister died as an infant, a sad if all-too-common reality for African Americans and the working poor. His parents had four more children, two daughters (Helen and Laura) and two sons (Clarence and Edward). According to the 1900 census, his father was a laborer, and, in 1910, his occupation was "hod carrier," someone who carried bricks and other items on construction sites. No occupation was listed for his mother but the most common paid work for a black woman in a city was domestic help. Though Fletcher made no mention of it, either, his mother passed away sometime between 1900 and 1905, in other words before he was fifteen. During his childhood, his family moved at least several times including to the east side of the Delaware River—to Camden, New Jersey—just a short ferry ride away from Philadelphia; the first bridge to span the river, the Delaware River Bridge (now the Benjamin Franklin Bridge), did not open until 1926. Like Philadelphia, Camden was a heavily industrial city that included a black working class alongside many European immigrants.

By all accounts, Ben Fletcher was quite intelligent but, like many working-class Americans in that era, never graduated from high school. According to records from his stint at the federal prison in Leavenworth, Kansas, he completed several years of high school. Rumors have circulated that he attended Wilberforce University, the first black school of higher education in the nation, affiliated with the African Methodist Episcopal church, and based in Ohio. Yet historian William Seraile, the first person to deeply investigate Fletcher's life, uncovered no such evidence when he corresponded with Wilberforce's registrar in the 1970s. Based upon his writings and speeches, Fletcher clearly was both intelligent and quite knowledgeable. There was plenty of time between shifts of heavy labor on the docks, and between jobs, to read, especially in the winter months. Fletcher belongs to a long line of highly intelligent, well-read, self-taught maritime workers (sailors and dockworkers) who often had time to read and think when work dried up. Similarly, there is a very long history of African Americans in Philadelphia, the name of which derived from the ancient Greek, meant City of Brotherly Love.

Black Philadelphia

Before joining the Wobblies, Fletcher already belonged to Philadelphia's large, well-established African American community. Even before William Penn and other English Quakers established Pennsylvania, Dutch and Swedish people brought enslaved Africans to the Delaware River valley. As Quakers started to build the city of Philadelphia, founded in 1682, they imported more enslaved Africans, though not as many as neighboring New Jersey and New York. Penn himself enslaved Africans, and other Quakers bought and sold Africans, as happened in every other port in British North America. Either immediately after the notorious Middle Passage from Africa or by way of the British West Indies, enslaved Africans were auctioned off at the city's London Coffee House. But a small antislavery movement, also called abolitionism, already existed. In 1780, soon after the United States declared itself independent, the state of Pennsylvania passed a law that gradually and slowly abolished slavery.

Due to the relatively liberal racial politics of the white Quaker community in and around Philadelphia, many "free blacks" made the City of Brotherly Love their home. By the 1830s, the city was a hotbed of abolitionist activity. One of the most important black "conductors" of the Underground Railroad, William Still, lived in Philadelphia and headed the militant Vigilance Committee of the Pennsylvania Anti-Slavery Society. Still and his wife, Letitia, worked with the legendary Harriet Tubman and others in the 1850s to aid hundreds of black people escape slavery, including sheltering them in their South Philadelphia home. In one story reported around the nation in 1855, five black dockworkers coordinated with Still to assist Jane Johnson, an enslaved woman, and her two sons escape from their enslaver while boarding a Delaware River ferry.

There is a long history of black people working in the maritime economy of Philadelphia, the largest city in the new nation, because it was deeply connected to the economy of the larger Atlantic world that tied together North America, Western Europe, West Africa, and the Caribbean (or West Indies). Starting in the colonial era, African American men, both enslaved and free, worked on the Delaware and (smaller) Schuylkill Rivers, which converged in Philadelphia and explain why William Penn selected the site for Pennsylvania's first capital city. No black mariner became more successful or wealthy than James Forten, whose grandparents had been enslaved. After working as a sailor, Forten owned and operated his own sail-making business for the first forty years of the nineteenth century. He also was heavily involved in the abolitionist movement.

That is not to say, however, that the city was free of antiblack racism, far from it. White supremacy was the norm as in every other place in the United States. For instance, early streetcars were racially segregated, and many white employers refused to hire black men and women. Worse, on at least three occasions before the Civil War—in 1834, 1842, and 1849—large white mobs rampaged through black neighborhoods, beating and killing innocent black residents as well as targeting white abolitionists. The 1842 riot spilled over to the docks along the Schuylkill River, where recent Irish immigrants viciously attacked African Americans, a clear indication that job rivalries factored into at least some white people's hatred of black people.

Nevertheless, Philadelphia was a far better place for black people than the South, so a steady stream of black migrants continued into Philadelphia throughout the nineteenth century and first half of the twentieth century. Like Fletcher's parents, most of the city's black residents hailed from the Upper South states Maryland, Delaware, and Virginia. In addition to the birthplace of the African Methodist Episcopal faith, Philadelphia headquartered the Odd Fellows, a historically important black fraternal organization. The city's black population suffered from intense prejudice in housing, jobs, and more but was not residentially segregated yet. Most blacks lived in the southern half of the city, nestled within the three miles between the Delaware and Schuylkill Rivers (east to west) that William Penn had platted for the city. While blacks congregated together on specific streets, a great many Anglo Americans, Irish immigrants, and Irish Americans also lived in South Philadelphia in the mid-nineteenth century. Later, in the 1890s and early 1900s, huge numbers of southern Italians, East European Jews, and other "new" immigrants came to make "South Philly" and other parts of the city their home. Fletcher was born into what was, by 1900, the largest black community in any US city outside of the South. He also grew up in a city where he regularly came into contact with people of many other ethnic groups.

Working in the Workshop of the World

The first documentation of Fletcher as an adult, then aged twenty, was in the 1910 census. At that time, he boarded at 1802 Wilder Street, in the Point Breeze neighborhood in South Philadelphia, along with several other young black men. Interestingly, the census records confirm that—before the World War I–induced Great Migration—the area was racially diverse, with white folks living literally next door. According to this same census form, Fletcher worked as a "laborer." Both of these facts were typical for a young African American man. Possibly, Fletcher already worked on the city's docks, but he may not have worked exclusively on the waterfront; otherwise, he would have identified himself to the census taker as a "longshoreman" or "stevedore" though the latter term long has fallen out of use. In his pioneering study *The Philadelphia Negro* (1899), W.E.B. Du Bois described the opportunities of black men and women in Philadelphia as defined by racism. In terms of job opportunities, that meant racism restricted black people to an extremely limited range of occupations. Even black men with skills or formal education found themselves entirely shut out of whole sectors of Philadelphia's job market, even though black people had formed the backbone of the southern working class so had sufficient skills for many occupations. But Philadelphia's employers, nearly all white, consistently hired native-born white Americans and European immigrants over African Americans. Almost the only jobs open to black men were unskilled, casual manual labor and domestic service, thus Fletcher's occupation as "laborer." The opportunities for black women were even more circumscribed.

Philadelphia, the third-largest city in population and manufacturing in the early twentieth century, operated somewhat peculiarly for a large industrial city. Specifically, the city had far fewer of the gargantuan mass production factories, for instance steel mills, where thousands of unskilled European immigrants toiled. Rather, the city housed a great many small- and mid-sized industrial companies that required a much greater percentage of skilled laborers who disproportionately were native-born white men of English, Irish, and German descent. The one important exception was the massive garment and textile factories, the city's largest industry, which accounted for most of the work performed by Italian and East European Jewish immigrants. But as mentioned, black workers, even if they had the requisite skills, simply were not hired

Municipal Pier 78 South, Philadelphia, Department of Wharves, Docks and Ferries, Municipal Pier Construction Photographs, 1917–21.

in that industry in that time, which also was the case in the southern textile industry. Generally, unions willingly collaborated with employers in maintaining "lily-white" workplaces. Nevertheless, southern blacks continued moving into Philadelphia due to the city's proximity to the South, partially deserved liberal racial heritage, and large economy, and away from horrors that defined the Jim Crow South.

Philadelphia dockworkers came from an interesting mix of ethnic and racial groups. During the colonial and early republic eras, black workers made up a significant number of the waterfront workforce. However, the Irish literally fought to take over the docks in the 1840s and 1850s. The Irish and, subsequently, Irish Americans dominated the longshore workforce for the rest of the century if not entirely. Moreover, the presence of thousands of desperate African Americans and East European immigrants, particularly Polish and Lithuanian Catholics and Jews, who proved willing to work for lower wages, exerted an inevitable pressure on employers to hire them. In this case, employers' "natural" instincts—that is, to find the cheapest possible labor and create a diverse (and, they hoped, divided) workforce—ultimately laid the groundwork for the rise of Local 8. Similarly, the inability of Philadelphia's Irish to form a lasting union also benefited black and "new" immigrant job seekers. For in northern ports such as New York and Boston, once dock unions formed that were dominated by Irish Americans, black men found their job prospects virtually disappear. Such was not the case in Philadelphia. Thus, prior to the rise of Local 8, the 1910 census reported Philadelphia's 3,063 longshoremen consisted of 410 native-born of native parentage, 440 native-born of foreign-born parents, 844 immigrants, and 1,369 African Americans.

Wobblies Rising in Philadelphia

Like much of his biography, it is uncertain when Fletcher became a radical, though one cannot help but wonder if it happened while walking the streets of his neighborhood. So many of the early records of the IWW were never saved, destroyed by the federal government, or lost along the way. Unfortunately, Fletcher left little accounting of his motivations and personal history though he seems to have joined in 1910. As a young, working-class African American he had plenty of reasons to reject mainstream politics and unions. White supremacy was the norm in both. The Republican Party, which dominated politics in Philadelphia, in Pennsylvania, and across the nation in that era, had long abandoned its commitment to racial equality. Unions, mostly, were job trusts for white men of certain ethnic backgrounds. Moreover, the near total absence of regulation of corporations—and corresponding lack of worker rights—had turned the United States into a country with a thin layer of fabulously wealthy industrialists and a vast sea of working-class urban residents struggling to make ends meet. Given such a society, and on top of pervasive racism, it might not take much to convince a young black man that the system was broken and in need of revolutionary changes.

Indeed, in a society that one IWW poster aptly named the "Pyramid of Capitalist System" (1911), radical recruiters found fertile terrain as many thousands were drawn to the Wobblies, including a young Ben Fletcher. All he would have had to do was walk the streets of his neighborhood with his eyes and ears open. When heading to a job or looking for one, while going to buy some food or other necessity, while heading to meet a friend, Fletcher would have heard street speakers commanding corners, wherever people congregated, to spread their messages. Religious organizations like the Salvation Army competed for the attention of passersby with Wobbly organizers and all sorts of peddlers. In a time before radio, television, mobile phones, or the internet, literally the most efficient way to reach people was to stand on a soapbox and shout. It is easy to imagine Fletcher stopping, once and again, to listen to a particularly compelling Wobbly soapboxer. Perhaps after a few listening sessions

Fletcher purchased a copy of an IWW newspaper such as *Solidarity* (then published in Cleveland) or the *Industrial Worker* (then published in Spokane). Pamphlets appealing specifically to African Americans had not yet been published ("Colored Workers of America: Why You Should Join the IWW" and "Justice for the Negro: How He Can Get It" are included in the appendix). But Fletcher easily could have picked up any number of other Wobbly pamphlets that explained to working people, in common sense language, why they should join what the Wobblies called their One Big Union—literally any worker could join regardless of race, sex, or nationality. He joined in 1910, according to a letter he wrote to scholar Abram Harris, and quickly became active in the IWW.

Though details are minimal, Fletcher also belonged to the Socialist Party of America (SP). Most likely, he joined the SP around the same time he first signed up for the IWW, 1910–12, while developing his political worldview in his early twenties. At that moment, numerous people belonged to both the IWW and SP. Eugene V. Debs, the legendary SP leader and an important unionist before that, helped found the IWW though never was active and withdrew from the IWW around 1912. The most prominent Wobbly also in the SP was William "Big Bill" Haywood, a cofounder of the IWW. Haywood, born and raised in Utah and a hard-rock miner across the Rocky Mountains, was known to declare, "I'm a two-gun man from the Wild West" and proceed to pull out his red IWW card and blue SP card. Though the SP was relatively progressive on race matters, few African Americans belonged to the Socialist Party in that era; W.E.B. Du Bois was a member from 1910 to 1912 but dropped out because of the racism of some leaders and members. To Haywood, Debs, and quite possibly Fletcher, the IWW sometimes was described as "socialism with its working clothes on" because some Socialists hailed from middle- or even upper-class backgrounds. Haywood sat on the SP executive committee for a few years until 1913, when a major rift occurred between the SP and the IWW over the tactic of "sabotage," which the SP rejected but Haywood and IWW were known to embrace, at least rhetorically. Moreover, the SP increasingly focused its attention on electoral politics, while the IWW increasingly rejected "electoralism" as a waste of time. Instead, the IWW concentrated its energy at "the point of production" since that was where workers had their most power. As Fletcher wrote a Socialist friend in 1920, "While I do not countenance against the working class striking at the ballot box, I am firmly convinced that foremost and historical mission of Labor is to organize as a class, Industrially." Essentially, Fletcher did not mind if workers voted, but he had no faith that the radical changes that needed to happen would come from voting. Instead, Fletcher was resolute that the path away from capitalism to socialism was via worker power, on the job, in industrial unions that eventually would pull off a mammoth general strike to seize power from capitalists.

Active in Left circles in Philadelphia, Fletcher would have met everyone in the city's Wobbly scene as well as those passing through, including, possibly, Joe Hill and John "Jack" Reed. The Wobblies' most famous songwriter, Joe Hill, very possibly traveled through Philadelphia before heading out west and becoming a legendary troubadour. His songs like "There Is Power in a Union" and "Preacher and the Slave" as well as songs about him, such as "(I Dreamed I Saw) Joe Hill," are sung to this day. Reed, meanwhile, graduated from Harvard in 1910 and spent the rest of the decade working as a radical journalist in the States, Mexico, and Europe. His dramatic account of the start of the Russian Revolution, *Ten Days That Shook the World*, resonates to this day. Whenever the likes of a Hill or Reed found themselves in Philadelphia, they surely stopped into or spoke at the local IWW hall, as did ordinary Wobs and fellow travelers. In the age before technology brought entertainment into one's home, many workers passed their nonwork hours at their union hall. Since Reed later corresponded with Fletcher, while imprisoned at Leavenworth, perhaps their friendship began nearly a decade earlier, in Philadelphia.

No later than 1912 Fletcher was an IWW activist. It is not clear what sort of work Fletcher did to survive but, quite possibly, he already worked as a longshoreman at least occasionally. The 1910 census reported that more than a thousand African Americans worked the docks. Almost certainly, the census undercounted the number of black longshoremen because of the transient nature of the work and consistent underreporting of minorities by census takers. Fletcher first showed up in the pages of the IWW weekly newspaper, *Solidarity*, in 1912, a year before Local 8's birth. He spoke at rallies in both Philadelphia and nearby Chester (just downriver on the Delaware), served as secretary of Local 57, and even attended the IWW's national convention in Chicago in 1912. Fletcher's presence there, as well as that of D.B. Gordon, a black man representing the IWW's Brotherhood of Timber Workers in Louisiana, were cited in *Solidarity* as "proof that we have surmounted all barriers of race and color" in the struggle for the One Big Union—a debatable claim considering the (then) paltry number of black Wobblies. Prior to the chartering of Local 8, IWWs who worked as longshoremen likely belonged to Local 57, a "mixed local," meaning that it served as the union for all workers in a city without industry-specific locals. Fletcher wrote numerous articles about organizing in Philadelphia for *Solidarity* in 1912 and 1913. Even at that early date, other correspondents commended his brilliant oratory skills. Howard Marston reported, at one meeting in Chester, Fletcher "certainly knows how to deliver the goods. . . . The crowd was very attentive, taking to everything the speaker had to say regarding the class struggle." Fletcher soon took his skills to the waterfront.

At the same time the IWW celebrated its black convention attendees, the union made a nationwide call for "Negro Workers" to unite with their fellow workers of European descent. One article in *Solidarity* noted, "YOUR RACE [African Americans] know better than any about injustice, off and on the job." The open letter pointed out that (white) employers intentionally kept black and white workers fighting each other by convincing white workers that the "social equality" of blacks was the true threat to white workers—as opposed to employers. As a result of this divisive and cynical use of race and racism, the IWW asserted, both white and black workers were hurt. This article fit well with the socialist preamble of the IWW, the union's statement of principles, which boldly declared in 1905, "The working class and the employing class have nothing in common!" In short, racial and ethnic differences never should deter workers from uniting against their shared and primary foe. Further, workers needed to remain ever mindful that employers used race to confuse, divide, and weaken workers. The circular challenged black workers to unite with white workers in the IWW. Little did the author of that article know that, while the Brotherhood of Timber Workers would soon collapse under the weight of massive repression, another interracial union would soon rise.

The Birth of Local 8

On May 14, 1913, Philadelphia longshoremen walked out and "re-entered the Labor Movement after an absence of 15 years," as Fletcher described this historic event in the pages of the IWW's *Solidarity*. Fletcher's mention of returning to unionism indicated that he, and at least some other dockworkers, knew about earlier organizing campaigns. Of the approximately four thousand workers who struck in 1913, a little over half were African American. The remaining were mostly Polish and Lithuanian immigrants and Irish Americans. Representatives of the IWW and the American Federation of Labor's International Longshoremen's Association (ILA) quickly appeared, hoping to convince the strikers to join their respective unions. At a meeting shortly after putting down their cargo hooks, strikers voted to affiliate with the IWW despite Fletcher's assertion of the presence of "lots of good AF of L booze . . . [and ILA officials] offering salaries to branch officers," both common tactics to undermine worker democracy.

Although no other mention of this meeting exists, it is crucial to understand why the strikers chose to join the IWW. After all, the long-shoremen could have joined the ILA, which was ready to line up African Americans, admittedly as second-class unionists and quite possibly in segregated locals, rather than the IWW—a far more radical union with an awful reputation in the mainstream culture. While the IWW had no prior history on the Philadelphia waterfront, it already included maritime workers along all four US coasts (Atlantic, Great Lakes, Gulf, and Pacific). Further, the union had been active in Philadelphia for at least six years and, that same spring, undertook a mammoth strike among silk workers in nearby Paterson, New Jersey. Ultimately, though, the most reasonable explanation is also the most basic: there simply were too many black workers to ignore and the IWW's ideology of inclusivity resonated far stronger with this group than the AFL's, whose racial policies of exclusivity were understood. In fact, Booker T. Washington, the country's most well-known African American, wrote an article for the *Atlantic Monthly* that same year castigating the AFL for racism and even encouraged black workers to act as strikebreakers. As black longshore-man and Local 8 member James Fair much later recalled, in a 1978 interview, "To my knowing at that time the IWW was the only thing that was accepting negro or black workers . . . I mean freely. They would accept them and they did advocate just this thing, solidarity."

Ben Fletcher's role in this vote, and the strike more generally, is conspicuously absent from the documentary record, but he surely was central. It seems obvious that Fletcher, already a local leader in the IWW and working as a longshoreman, must have played a decisive role in the strike and subsequent decision to affiliate with the IWW. Further, his widely noted brilliant oratorical skills could have convinced wavering longshoremen on which union to support. The ILA did not appear to have a local black organizer. Nevertheless, Fletcher's name only appeared briefly in contemporary reports aside from his own article. Perhaps Fletcher's omission from the record speaks to his modesty, giving credit to other organizers while keeping his own name absent. Perhaps the IWW did not want to highlight that he was the only prominent black longshoreman. Most definitely, he was the most prominent African American in a workforce more than a third of African descent. Thus, it seems reasonable that Fletcher played an important, if invisible role, in the chartering of Local 8.

The other strikers, Irish Americans and Eastern European immigrants, also toiled in the underpaid, dangerous marine transport industry and stood on the margins of society. A fighting union that addressed the concerns of a heterogeneous and unskilled workforce must have sounded quite appealing to them, as well. For the Lithuanian and Polish immigrants, who still were learning from American society that they were "white," black workers on the waterfront did not represent an existential threat. From their perspective, African Americans did not necessarily see such immigrants as "white" either, so might more easily unite with immigrants than native-born white Americans. As for the Irish Americans, perhaps they simply followed the able leadership of the Irish American IWW organizer John J. McKelvey and local Irish longshoreman George McKenna, who had participated in the failed 1898 union drive. McKenna and some others also remembered the ILA's previous botched efforts and did not want to return to that organization. Moreover, numerous Irish Americans already were or soon became leaders in the IWW, Elizabeth Gurley Flynn being the most famous. Similarly, Irish labor leaders and revolutionaries, namely James Connolly and Jim Larkin, were drawn to the IWW when they lived and traveled in the States. In other words, a long history of Irish and Irish American radicalism existed alongside the more conservative, racist traditions of other Irish Americans.

No matter how the IWW managed to unite the city's diverse longshoremen, their newly founded union faced the combined opposition of the business community and local government. Employers brought in many strikebreakers, mostly black men recruited from neighboring Chester along with some from as far as Baltimore and Norfolk. There is no evidence that the replacement workers' race played a role in the strike. Pitched battles, however, were fought among strikers, strike sympathizers—including hundreds of women, most likely family members—and the police, who protected strikebreakers. John McKelvey, an IWW strike leader, was beaten unconscious by the police and thrown in jail without charges. Despite the employer-government coalition, between twenty and thirty ships were tied up at any one time during the two-week strike.

From the start, the IWW sought to promote democratic and inclusive policies. Customarily, workers in Philadelphia labored in segregated groups based upon ethnicity, race, and gender. Employers used this time-tested strategy to keep employees divided and wages down in the proverbial "race to the bottom." But during this strike, an elected committee of fifteen longshoremen—with at least one member of each nationality on strike—represented the workers' interests. As described in *Solidarity,* "The Polish, Jewish, Negro and English speaking fellow workers were solidly lined up. . . . These boys realize what the one big union can do." Although the IWW paper clearly had an interest in championing Local 8, that the paper celebrated—rather than ignored or downplayed—the union's diversity is noteworthy and testifies to the importance the IWW placed upon racial and ethnic equality. In addition, Philadelphia's longshoremen no doubt had learned the value of solidarity from their own work experiences, as their occupation's gang labor system inculcated in workers that they belonged to one class and their employers to another one.

The strikers also displayed their commitment to industrial unionism by attempting to take the strike to other Atlantic ports. Wobbly longshoremen in Baltimore and New York City received telegrams informing them not to handle cargo of ships coming from Philadelphia, nicknamed "hot cargo" for goods handled by strikebreakers or management. During the strike, Fletcher traveled to Baltimore to convince longshoremen to respect Local 8's "beef," or grievance, and not to touch hot cargo. On May 15, representatives of all of the steamship companies and employing stevedores formed a committee, with P.F. Young as chair, to defeat the strike. Young, who managed stevedore operations for multiple shipping lines, maintained that steamship companies would fight the IWW as long as it took and threatened to abandon Philadelphia altogether if the companies could not maintain wages at the present level. When possible, shipping companies diverted their vessels to other ports, most commonly Baltimore, hence the reason for Fletcher's trip.

After two weeks in which dozens of ships remained anchored and idle, the bosses accepted defeat, and Local 8 secured its place on the waterfront. On May 28 a committee of three longshoremen met with Fred Taylor, who ran Charles M. Taylor & Sons, one of the largest stevedoring companies in Philadelphia. The strikers were represented by one Irish American, one Polish immigrant, and one African American—possibly Fletcher. The two parties agreed to end the strike based on a wage of thirty cents an hour, time and a half for overtime, and double time for Sundays and holidays, where previously no overtime rates applied. Overtime pay was particularly helpful in an industry where longshoremen customarily worked shifts that lasted twenty-four or even thirty-six hours. The bosses also agreed not to discriminate against strikers and to recognize a workers' committee. It must be highlighted that the IWW never signed contracts with employers so that workers retained their greatest weapon, the strike. Instead, Local 8's agreements were oral and generally lasted a year.

Again, it is almost eerie how Fletcher was conspicuously absent from the IWW reporting on Local 8's initial strike. He already was an active Wobbly, frequently praised for his speaking abilities, and labored as a longshoreman. But he was rarely mentioned during the strike. IWW historian Fred Thompson speculated in 1982 that Fletcher purposefully maintained a low profile during the strike, "with the full knowledge of the [other] IWW organizers [hence, he] avoided giving the impression he was their [the longshoremen's] lone contact [to the Wobblies]." Thompson was correct that other IWW strike leaders, mentioned by name, were not longshoremen; instead, they were local or national organizers dispatched once the strike began. The IWW must have had an inside man to convince the thousands of strikers to join this radical outfit. Quite likely Fletcher was that person.

Building Local 8

With this stunning success, which brought in thousands of new members to the IWW, Local 8 could not afford to rest. Waterfront employers, who formed a unified front during the strike, continued assailing the IWW and tried to refused to deal with the union. Nevertheless, even Fred Taylor acknowledged the IWW's growing presence. In a letter to P.A.S. Franklin, vice president of International Mercantile Marine Co., Taylor wrote of "a great increase since that time [the strike] in the number of longshoremen wearing the IWW buttons." He added, "Two or three incipient efforts were made through the IWW influences to threaten strikes on our boats unless certain men working on them without an IWW button were knocked off," proving that Local 8 members quickly adapted Wobbly direct-action tactics (constantly threatening to strike if a demand was unmet) in addition to the organization's egalitarian precepts.

The use of buttons to ascertain current membership remains fascinating and instructive. After its victorious strike, Local 8 proved sufficiently powerful to force employers to stop using the oppressive hiring system known as the shape-up, truly one of the union's great victories. Workers despised the old system, which also existed in every other port in the US and many others worldwide, for they understood that, when hundreds showed up for the boss to picked, workers were forced into competition that weakened their solidarity, thereby resulting in lower wages, longer hours, and more dangerous workplaces. In place of the shape-up, Local 8 instituted a system in which employers called the union hall and requested workers for dispatch; for instance, Monday morning at eight, send 120 workers to Pier 5 to unload general cargo. With some exceptions, until late 1922 most longshore employers followed this procedure if only grudgingly. After a member paid his monthly dues, he received a new button, entitling him to work on any IWW-controlled dock for that month. These buttons were emblazoned with the month and year as well as various terms such as: IWW, Local 8, MTW, or some variation. (The practice of an employer withholding a portion of one's wages to be sent to the union, "dues checkoff," did not yet exist, though, when it did, the IWW refused to utilize it.) The monthly button was essential to indicate to employers and fellow workers who was a member of Local 8 in good standing. Simply put, if a person was not wearing his button, he was not supposed to be hired. Unsurprisingly, employers hated hiring Wobblies and periodically tested the workers' commitment to their union by hiring workers outside of Local 8. Ultimately, Wobblies—as opposed to bosses, who never could be trusted—were supposed to enforce this rule.

Countless conflicts, often of short duration and rarely documented, illuminate how what may seem like a minor issue, a monthly dues button, was a crucial aspect of class consciousness and struggle as Local 8 built its power. In the summer of 1913, for example, the International Mercantile Marine Company tested the newly established Local 8. As the *Philadelphia Inquirer* reported, five hundred longshoremen put down their hooks and walked off their ships "in sympathy with five men who were discharged . . . because they declined to take off union buttons which they were wearing." The strike quickly tied up three ships, as "armed detectives and several squads of uniformed policemen" along with "scores of private detectives" protected strikebreakers. The longshoremen had walked off the job, as the *Public Ledger* commented, "at an inopportune moment, as two [other] vessels . . . just arrived with large general cargoes." Of course, it was no coincidence. In solidarity, sailors from one ship "threw garbage and bottles at non-union longshoremen." The company reverted to hiring Local 8 members exclusively. Such experiences, on the job and in the fire, educated workers about working-class power through solidarity activism.

Dockworkers in Philadelphia—and worldwide—well understood the "logic" of capitalism, aptly summarized in the phrase "the ship must sail on time," gave them incredible power if they withheld their labor at the proper moment. Local 8 members, like dockworkers in other ports (organized, if not always in formal unions) engaged in countless "quickie strikes." Abraham Moses, an African American in Local 8, much later recalled one instance, "If you told one of them [a Wobbly] something, and they didn't like it, you know what they'd do? They'd run the [cargo] load about half way up, cut the steve hold [nautical term describing part of cargo-moving process] and walk off the ship . . . everybody walked off the ship and out the pier and went home." That sort of militancy and solidarity resulted in tremendous power.

Beyond winning raises and improving conditions, Local 8 used its power on behalf of racial equality—setting a standard that few US workplaces met for more than fifty years; in many instances, a standard still unmet. Before Local 8, gangs (of ten, twenty, upward of forty workers) were ethnically and racially segregated, for instance all-Irish, all-Italian, or all–African American gangs that employers created and intentionally pitted against each other, simultaneously increasing productivity while fomenting further ethnic and racial divisions. After winning its founding strike, Local 8 integrated work gangs, period, and they remained integrated for the entire period that the IWW dominated the Philadelphia waterfront. The Wobblies' actions were unprecedented in nearly every other Philadelphia and US workplace; it was not until the Civil Rights Act of 1964 that workplaces and unions had to end racial segregation, though resistance persisted well beyond that. To attack racism and its legacy, Local 8 also instituted a system whereby the chair and other leaders at its meetings alternated between black and white members; this approach existed for all of Local 8's history, as described in the *Messenger* in the early 1920s, and continued, at the local level, when the ILA took over in 1927. Such racially inclusive and egalitarian policies extended to parades, picnics, and other social events.

While educating its new members in IWW tactics and ideology, Local 8 quickly started lining up other port workers. Fletcher and others understood that the key to worker power was organizing all laborers, industry by industry, into the One Big Union. Within a few months of Local 8's creation, workers on the barges and small boats up and down the Delaware River had organized a branch within Local 8 and struck for wage hikes. Wobblies also attempted to organize longshoremen in the coastal and banana trades, railroad pier workers, dockside sugar refinery workers, and teamsters. Local 8 targeted every worker with a role in the (marine) transport industry, quite aware of the need to organize what now is called the supply chain. Local 8 proved so successful that even its rival acknowledged IWW power. In June 1913 ILA secretary-treasurer for the Atlantic District, William F. Dempsey, wrote his superiors that "the city" (i.e., the port) was "in absolute control of the IWW."

That same month, Fletcher returned to Baltimore to organize there and periodically visited to do so. He and other Philadelphia Wobblies understood that their hold was never secure until other Atlantic ports also were within the IWW fold because in their initial strike and subsequent job actions, employers diverted ships to other ports of call. Baltimore was Philadelphia's main mid-Atlantic rival, and the ILA had failed to establish a strong local there, at least in part because its diverse workforce mirrored Philadelphia's: African Americans, Polish immigrants, and Irish Americans. On multiple occasions in the 1910s, Fletcher traveled to Baltimore as well as Norfolk, Providence, Boston, and other ports to build the Marine Transport Workers Industrial Union (MTW). Ultimately unsuccessful in dislodging the ILA from other ports, Fletcher and other Wobblies never stopped trying.

1913 Convention

Competition from the ILA was just one of the issues confronting Local 8 discussed at the IWW's eighth annual national convention in September 1913, as always in Chicago. Continuing the tradition of a strong Irish American presence among the city's longshoremen, James H. Murphy represented Local 8 at the convention. Curiously, Ben Fletcher still represented Philadelphia's mixed branch, Local 57, perhaps so the longshoremen could double their representation. Meanwhile, a debate ensued over the seating of Murphy that shed light on an otherwise invisible, complex matter, the National Industrial Union of Marine Transport Workers (NIUMTW), and foreshadowed years of disagreement over the relationship of Local 8 to the IWW. The Credentials Committee asked why Local 8 sent a delegate when the NIUMTW, which later and more simply became known as the MTW, did not. Should not Local 8 be represented by the industrial union it belonged to rather than independently? C.L. Filigno, NIUMTW acting general secretary-treasurer, steadfastly defended Local 8's representation. He recently had attended a Local 8 meeting and gave quite a favorable report: "In Philadelphia I had to do business nearly every day with them getting supplies and due stamps and that is the only local in the organization that is practically in good standing." The local purchased more than two thousand dues stamps each month. Moreover, the NIUMTW had not yet held a convention or a referendum since its formation earlier that year. As a result, while in Philadelphia Filigno decided to turn over one of his two credentials, for the upcoming national convention, to Local 8. Filigno argued that, as the only local in good standing in the NIUMTW—and among the largest in the IWW—Local 8 certainly was entitled. George Speed, an IWW organizer who also helped during the May 1913 strike, added his respected voice, "My understanding is that there were three of Local [8] Philadelphia running for delegates and this one was the one elected," thereby confirming the democratic nature of Local 8.

Ben Fletcher spoke numerous times, and impressively, at the convention. The most interesting of his speeches involved a lengthy debate over whether or not the General Executive Board (GEB) should be abolished. Fletcher opposed abolition and spoke poignantly on the subject. It must be highlighted that Fletcher, here, essentially opposed decentralization, but during the Philadelphia Controversy, in 1920, took the opposite view and resisted the overarching power of the national organization. Elsewhere, he addressed the issue of why workers joined the IWW, particularly interesting in relation to Local 8. Fletcher contended that workers took out an IWW card because of short-term, "bread-and-butter" issues, not necessarily because they already believed in revolutionary class struggle. On this matter, Local 8 later would be taken to task, as well—for not being revolutionary enough and too concerned with "mundane" matters like better wages and fewer work hours. After the convention, Fletcher and the rest of Local 8 continued with the vital, if sometimes mundane, task of consolidating power on the waterfront.

Local 8's First Anniversary and Beyond

To celebrate their first anniversary and "make this a L-e-g-a-l holiday under our jurisdiction," Local 8 members decided that, instead of working, they preferred to throw themselves a party! Such plans defied their employers, who threatened to fire anyone who did not show up that chosen Saturday morning. (Remember that a six-day workweek was the norm before the Fair Labor Standards Act of 1938.) To the surprise and consternation of the bosses, on the appointed Saturday close to 2,500 longshoremen, virtually the entire deep-sea workforce, took the day off to celebrate themselves and their union. The Wobblies marched through South Philadelphia, first alongside the Delaware River, and then downtown with three bands in tow. According to an IWW newspaper, "Workers representing most European countries, many who could not speak the English language, together with natives, both colored and white, marched as they worked." The article demonstrated the IWW's conscious commitment to equality, a goal few other unions aspired to, let alone had achieved, in 1914. The statement reconfirmed the integration of longshore gangs. Fifteen years prior, scholar W.E.B. Du Bois had noted the pervasive reality of segregated work in Philadelphia; where it had the power, the IWW ended segregation—without a legal contract, without an electoral campaign, and with zero influence among local or national politicians.

After the parade, a picnic occurred with a round of obligatory speeches in English and Polish. Several black men, including Fletcher, addressed the interracial crowd in English. Fletcher, recently elected secretary of Philadelphia's IWW District Council, encouraged "having his [black] friends write 'down home' about the IWW" in order to increase the union's visibility among African Americans in the South. After speeches, the members danced, played baseball and other sports, and listened to music. Perhaps nothing better demonstrates the power of Local 8 than their annual birthday strike, which shipowners and stevedoring agents were forced to accept because the IWW had won the loyalty of the workforce.

Local 8 continued to organize, but a war-induced recession in the maritime economy hurt the port and union activity on the docks declined. When it sparked again, in a January 1915 strike against some of the most notoriously anti-union piers, Fletcher was among the leaders. Ever the organizer, Fletcher helped convince nonunion men at the Independent Piers Company and Southern Steamship Line to join the strike. Once more, several thousand longshoremen struck their employers and, again, though this time more quickly, most employers agreed to the strikers' demands. Other major strike actions occurred in 1916 and countless unrecorded "quickie" strikes also occurred. Such direct-action tactics, "at the point of production," possess an especially long history in the shipping industry where "the ship must sail on time." Few know it, but the very word "strike" has maritime origins! In 1768 in London, then the world's busiest port, sailors stopped work until receiving a raise by taking down their ship's sails; the nautical term for that action is to strike the sails. That the English word for work stoppages is a maritime one confirms the centrality of this industry to capitalism. The power of (dock)workers at a choke point of global trade was well understood by both bosses and workers. Wobblies and countless other militant workers exploited this inherent weakness in the supply chain to their advantage whenever they could.

On the Road

In addition to helping lead Local 8, Ben Fletcher regularly traveled to organize, particularly to port cities where the ILA excluded or segregated black dockworkers. Fletcher was personally known as far south as Norfolk and as far north as Boston. Truly, he himself was the best argument that the IWW could make to black workers. While the IWW Constitution declared that any worker, regardless of color or creed, could join the organization, at least some AFL unions, notably the ILA, included black workers albeit as distinctly second-class. To counter them, the IWW could—and did—point to Fletcher and Local 8 as proof that the Wobblies organized all workers, regardless of race, equally. When Fletcher arrived in a city like Norfolk and declared to black workers that the IWW desired their membership, they could see with their own eyes the truth of such a claim.

His most concerted efforts outside of Philadelphia focused on his home port's rival, Baltimore. In that city, a hundred miles closer to the Atlantic, European Americans dominated a small ILA local that generally excluded African Americans. Multiple times, from 1913 to 1920, Fletcher traveled to Baltimore, occasionally accompanied by the Irish American John J. "Jack" Walsh, a national IWW organizer who came to work with Local 8 in 1914 and became an integral part of the union. In Baltimore, Fletcher and Walsh worked with a Russian-born machinist and IWW organizer known as Jack Lever. In 1916–17, hundreds of black longshoremen held the red card of the IWW in their pockets but drifted in and out of the fold, perhaps because no local black leadership emerged. That said, joining and dropping out of the IWW was typical for the IWW, which signed up perhaps ten times as many workers as those it kept for any significant length of time. The generally transient nature of IWW membership contrasted sharply with Local 8, which remained a large, interracial, and *durable* outpost in a radical union far better known for fluctuating membership and spectacular failures.

In the winter of 1916–17, having just been appointed a national organizer by the General Executive Board, Fletcher headed to Providence, Rhode Island where a strike was brewing. Fletcher was dispatched, in part, because many dockworkers there were of African descent, especially from the island of Brava, in the Cape Verde archipelago; centuries prior, the Portuguese had colonized Cape Verde and brought many thousands of enslaved Africans to that Atlantic island chain. Sure enough, a strike erupted though the outcome is unknown. Fletcher attempted "breaking in some delegates," that is, local organizers. Meanwhile, Fletcher headed to Baltimore where a strike also seemed possible. In fact, nationwide there was a surge of labor activism among Wobblies and other unionists.

Fletcher, along with Walsh and Lever had organized in Baltimore, off and on, since 1913. Interestingly, the number of black longshoremen had grown dramatically after a failed 1916 strike, in part broken due to black dockers brought up from nearby Norfolk. Lever and Walsh started with these nonunion black longshoremen. Due to the history of racism practiced by Baltimore's white longshoremen in a white-only ILA local, along with the IWW's firm stance on racial equality, Lever and Walsh signed up nearly 1,500 black longshoremen. Then, Walsh wrote to Walter Nef, in Philadelphia, to bring Fletcher down from Providence. Not long after arriving in Baltimore, in early 1917, he learned of growing agitation in Norfolk, among the largest ports in the South and where African American longshoremen predominated. As Fletcher recalled in 1931, "I was preparing the longshoremen of Baltimore for a strike in 1917 for higher wages, shorter hours and better working conditions when I received instructions from headquarters to proceed to Norfolk where the dock workers were becoming restless and asking that an organizer be sent them." Although an organizer for revolutionary industrial union-ism, Fletcher still was a black man in a white supremacist society. Not long after he crossed into the heart of the old Confederacy—the state in which his father was born and raised—Fletcher narrowly escaped being lynched!

The IWW already had a presence in Norfolk among both dockwork-ers and sailors, like in many other port cities in the US and across the seven seas. Fletcher recounted what happened next: "I found the men responsive and eager for a union. But I had not been in town long before word was circulated that I represented a dangerous element set on the destruction of property and the overthrow of the Government. Then I began receiving messages of a threatening character. I would be lynched if I spread that doctrine around Norfolk, I was told." His Left radicalism cohered with his blackness to enrage some local white folks. Later in life, Fletcher recounted his experiences to friends including the anarchist couple, Esther and Sam Dolgoff. In his memoir, Sam Dolgoff described what happened next:

> Fletcher, undoubtedly the most eloquent, humorous speaker I ever heard (his ringing voice needed no microphone), was address-ing an open-air street meeting attended by white racists out to make trouble. They flung the sure-fire embarrassing question: "Do you approve of intermarriage or sexual intercourse between whites and blacks . . . have a nigger marry a white woman?" To show that the racist troublemakers were hypocrites when it was common knowledge that intercourse between white men and

black women produced racially mixed, lighter skinned children, Fletcher remarked: "I don't see anyone as black as I am. But we all damn well know the reason." The meeting proceeded without further interruption. [ellipses in original]

Fletcher's bold response predicted a far more widely known, yet similar, remark made by the writer and activist James Baldwin, who once quipped to a white man, "You don't want us to marry your *wives'* daughters—we've been marrying *your* daughters [due to white men raping enslaved black women] since the days of slavery." In that moment, when Fletcher rhetorically disemboweled a white supremacist questioner, some white folks likely bristled at this "uppity" black man so perhaps planned to murder him. Fletcher soon learned, "I would be lynched if I spread that doctrine around Norfolk, I was told. One night, friends, fearing that my life was in danger, smuggled me aboard a northbound ship to Boston." That was how, sometime in early 1917, Fletcher ended up in Massachusetts.

Ironically—given the Norfolk question about miscegenation—just a few months later, Fletcher ended up marrying a white woman in Boston. Based on his occasional reports published in *Solidarity*, no later than March 1917 (quite possibly a month earlier), Fletcher had relocated to Boston. Typical of organizers, he apparently settled into the city for a few months to more effectively agitate and educate. He took a job at a soap factory in Cambridge, just across the Charles River from Boston, and lived in an apartment in the South End, not too far from work. At that same time, tensions between Germany and the United States heated up, and, in April 1917, the US declared war. A few months later, in June, Congress passed the Espionage Act to silence the emerging antiwar movement. Even before its passage, though, various government agencies including the US Department of Justice and Naval Intelligence already were spying on the IWW, instantly perceived of as the single greatest domestic threat to the war efforts.

In fact, the first indication of Fletcher's marriage to Carrie Danno Bartlett, a white woman originally from New York City, came in a June report of an agent in the Department of Justice's Bureau of Investigation investigating—spying—on Fletcher *prior* to the passage of the Espionage Act. According to Boston marriage records, however, they married in August. Already in June, they lived in a sparse apartment in the North End, a working-class, immigrant neighborhood where ancient finger piers snaked out into Boston harbor; Fletcher apparently moved in late

May and it is uncertain if they lived together in Fletcher's first place. It was in their new apartment where agents interrogated him on at least two occasions in June. It is quite possible that Fletcher and Bartlett lived together, with her daughter, before getting around to legally marrying. In the Boston Marriage Register, Fletcher was listed as "Col[ored]" and a "building laborer," so perhaps had changed jobs. Bartlett was listed as white, widowed, and without an occupation. Unfortunately, few other details of this relationship exist. How they met, when they met, where they met? These questions and many more remain unanswered.

Their interracial marriage is worth further consideration. Although the great majority of states banned interracial marriages, at one time or another, Massachusetts repealed its antimiscegenation law in 1843, one of the first states to do so. About half the states in the US still had laws banning interracial marriage in the 1910s. Even in states that allowed for such couplings, it is hard to overstate how unusual they were in 1917. Again, almost nothing is known about Bartlett, but Fletcher's radicalism already was well established. His interracial relationship and marriage only added further evidence of his willingness to tear down social norms. Another interesting aspect of this tantalizing, much-too-brief record was that the justice of the peace who married them, quite likely, was Jewish, though neither Fletcher nor Bartlett were. Ben Fletcher's first marriage legally commenced just a month before being indicted, along with 165 other Wobblies, for espionage.

World War I and the IWW

Although the nation actively assisted Britain and France from the war's beginning, it was not until April 1917 that the US formally entered World War I, which presented new opportunities and, particularly, new dangers for the IWW. The war greatly increased the pressure on anyone in the United States critical of US society, including Wobblies, to cease their critiques and rally around the flag. The IWW, along with other leftist organizations and individuals, well understood they were at great risk of persecution, legal and extralegal, from zealous "super-patriots" inside and outside of the government. However, the crisis that war brought to the country also resulted in openings for the IWW as capitalism's contradictions became more apparent. The war sharply reduced the labor surplus that traditionally weakened workers, and working-class people questioned what they had to gain from a war in which they were asked to kill or be killed for the profit of others when the country had not been attacked.

Prior to the US declaration, the IWW in the United States condemned the war as deflecting attention from the union's primary goal of a working-class, socialist revolution. Wobblies (and many like-minded people) understood that World War I, like other wars, enriched powerful businesses and individuals at the expense of working people told to sacrifice their lives for nations that exploited them. Yet, as critical as it was, the IWW in the United States never took an official stance against the war. Notably, the IWW in Australia did officially oppose the war and conscription, resulting in some of its members being jailed and the organization banned; in Canada, too, the IWW was banned for fear of its opposition and power. In the United States, though a great many Wobblies opposed the war on principle and in public, the organization let members decide for themselves whether to support or oppose the war. Many members of Local 8 registered for the draft (nationwide, most IWWs likely did as the law demanded), hundreds served in the armed forces, and members bought "liberty bonds." As most Local 8 members were black, whether they volunteered or were drafted, they found themselves in a segregated military. Due to this racism, many black longshoremen shipped to Europe worked not as soldiers but, rather, longshoremen—just like their fellow workers back home, who loaded countless tons of ammunition and other war materiel. In other words, Local 8 members loaded war materials in Philadelphia, some of which was unloaded by Wobblies in Europe.

Perhaps the most extraordinary example of Local 8's support of the war was a meeting organized by Fletcher, Jack Lever, and Paul "Polly" Baker (a Lithuanian Jewish immigrant and leader in Local 8) sometime in early 1917. At the behest of Colonel Freely, commander of the Schuylkill Arsenal, an Army supply depot in Philadelphia, the Wobblies set up a meeting at Local 8's hall in South Philadelphia. The building was filled to capacity, six hundred strong, to hear Fletcher, Walter Nef (a German-Swiss immigrant who was fiercely anti-Kaiser), and Jack Walsh address the members on the need to support the Allied war effort by working efficiently at their jobs. Lever later commented that Fletcher's "high standing with his race, who formed about 60% of the port workers, was invaluable." (Quite possibly, Fletcher took the train from Boston to Philadelphia and back again.) Ironically, given the governmental repression soon to rain down on the IWW, Local 8's membership voted not to strike for the duration of the war with one exception. Fletcher's younger brother, Clarence, ended up in the US Army, a private in the all-black 813th Pioneer Infantry, that spent time in France during the war. It is unknown whether he volunteered or was drafted. It also is unknown if he saw combat, but, due to pervasive racism in the military, few black units did; instead, the 813th often dug trenches and graves. Because he shipped over to France in mid-September 1918, and the armistice happened just two months later, he would have been more likely to dig graves than trenches. He safely returned from France in July 1919.

Local 8's promise to not interfere with the war effort was noteworthy because Philadelphia was deeply important during the war. Out of the port of Philadelphia shipped many of the soldiers as well as much of the food, munitions, oil, steel, and more on its way to Europe. In 1917 more than 75 percent of the cargo that left Philadelphia went to help fight the war. A report in 1919 by the recently created US Shipping Board indicated that the longshoremen of Local 8 "loaded a large part of the munitions sent to Europe."

Local 8 conducted only one work stoppage during the war, in May 1917, to celebrate the fourth anniversary of its founding strike. The membership notified employers that, despite US entry into the war, longshoremen would perform no work on Saturday, May 15. That morning all Wobbly waterfront workers met at their union hall and, led by three bands, proceeded to march down Delaware Avenue, the major thoroughfare paralleling the Delaware River. Then they boarded street cars for Point Breeze Park in Southwest Philadelphia. As IWW organizer C.L. Lambert wrote, "you could see in the lines of men walking five abreast, American, Polish, Lithuanian, Belgian and colored in the same line" chanting, "No creed, no color can bar you from membership" and the official IWW motto, "An injury to one is an injury to all." That must have been a rousing scene as thousands marched through their working-class neighborhoods in South Philly. The success of Local 8's annual strike celebration, demonstrating once more their commitment to racial and ethnic solidarity, continued to disprove the notion that the IWW could not organize a radical yet stable union.

Some Wobblies and other leftists, at that time and since, have criticized Local 8, and Fletcher, for aiding the war effort instead of opposing it. This critique aligned with the principles laid out by the IWW, albeit unofficially, that wars by nation-states violated the internationalist principles of socialism and the "real" war was the "class war." In 1917, debates about the war raged within the IWW and like-minded organizations in the United States and many other countries. As is widely known, nearly all the self-declared socialists in European countries fighting in World War I ultimately sided with their political elites and national identities, taking up arms against fellow workers in other countries. To put it crudely, most British, French, German, Hungarian, and other peoples who claimed to be socialists donned the uniforms of their respective militaries and killed workers wearing the uniforms of other armies. So, too, in the United States, where Wobblies, SP members, anarchists, and others on the left debated this matter, as did those who believed in isolationism and pacifism. Ultimately, Fletcher and others in Local 8 chose to not defy the federal government. No doubt, mindful of the swift passage of the Espionage Act in early June 1917, they knew full well the IWW was the likely target of governmental repression.

Sure enough, starting on September 5, US Department of Justice agents, with support from local police forces, raided Local 8's and the other IWW hall in Philadelphia as well as IWW offices in dozens of other cities including the Chicago headquarters. Federal agents confiscated literally tons of records including membership records, correspondence, dues books, meeting minutes, publications (from the IWW and other groups), stickers, rubber stamps, bank books and checks, office furniture and supplies, printing equipment, portions of Joe Hill's ashes still in envelopes, and more.

That same month, a federal grand jury in Chicago indicted scores of IWWs on multiple counts for conspiring to hinder various acts of Congress and presidential decrees. Specifically, the Department of Justice issued warrants for the arrest of Fletcher and 165 other Wobblies on charges of interfering with the Selective Service Act, violating the Espionage Act of 1917, conspiring to strike, violating the constitutional right of employers executing government contracts, and using the mail to conspire to defraud employers. Five other Philadelphia Wobblies were among the indicted. One might say that the US government had declared war on the IWW.

Fletcher was the only black Wobbly indicted but, curiously, it took more than four months until he was actually arrested. Fletcher had been married for just two weeks when the warrant for his arrest was issued. Most of those indicted had been arrested quickly and imprisoned, though many were released on bail in advance of the trial scheduled for Chicago, but such was not the case for Fletcher. Instead, Fletcher, his wife, and his stepdaughter relocated to Philadelphia in September or October. They rented an apartment in the South Philadelphia neighborhood of Grays Ferry, and Fletcher found work as a laborer in the mammoth railyards of the Pennsylvania Railroad that commanded a large swath of the Grays Ferry's western section, abutting the eastern side of the Schuylkill River. Then, for the next four months, while agents in Boston, Chicago, Philadelphia, and elsewhere searched for Fletcher, he "hid in plain sight." No doubt, Fletcher knew he was being looked for and chose not to voluntarily surrender. In mid-February 1918, agents found Fletcher and his family in their apartment. He was arrested and imprisoned for two weeks at the jail in City Hall before Local 8 pulled together the money to bail him out.

Fletcher's pretrial story has one final component, recounted in his 1931 interview. In late March, when finally headed for the trial in Chicago, his train got into an accident. Apparently he was fine, but that incident further delayed his arrival. When he finally made it to the federal court building—on his own recognizance—the local police neither knew who he was nor let him into the courtroom. Fletcher insisted that he was one of the hundred Wobblies on trial, produced identification (perhaps his IWW card), was allowed in, and took up a seat beside his fellow Wobblies, two hours late for their trial on charges of espionage and sedition.

The Persecution of Fletcher and the IWW

Despite their belief in the inherent unfairness of the US criminal justice system, the IWW worked hard to exonerate its members. Out on bond prior to the trial, Local 8 leaders E.F. Doree and Walter Nef volunteered for the IWW's General Defense Committee (GDC), formed shortly after the first wave of raids. In Doree's words, the GDC worked "to raise funds, secure legal counsel, locate witnesses, and generally assist in the defense of the various members of the IWW." In Philadelphia, Local 8 sold GDC "liberty bonds," appropriating the name used by federal bonds, to raise money for the defense fund and defendants' families. The Office of Naval Intelligence reported Local 8 had "contributed liberally to the Defense Fund." Fletcher's wife received ten dollars a week to help care for herself and her daughter.

The purpose of the raids and arrests were abundantly clear: destroy the IWW. The "100% Americanism," a toxic combination of jingoism, white supremacy, and nativism, greatly heightened pressure to support the war and practically guaranteed trouble for the IWW. These forces added to the already existing ways the US government aided employers to prevent unionism, break strikes, and weaken workers. In his book *Aliens and Dissenters*, William Preston noted that the US entry into World War I allowed President Woodrow Wilson's administration to equate the threat of IWW strikes with "seditious interference in war production." Predictably, federal investigators sought to depict the IWW as "a vicious, treasonable, and criminal conspiracy," which intended on calling a general strike in crucial industries across the nation in order to undermine the war. It is undeniable that the IWW wielded real power in numerous industries particularly strategic for the war effort, including marine transport, copper mining, agriculture, and wood products. At the federal trial in Chicago, which started on April 1, 1918, April Fool's Day, the prosecution tried to equate the IWW's anticapitalism with pro-German sentiment and, by extension, treason.

The inclusion of Local 8 leaders in the arrests lent further credence to the idea that the government was more interested in wrecking the IWW than protecting the nation from traitors, considering that Local 8 members worked diligently during the war. As discussed, Philadelphia's longshoremen loaded thousands of ships with but one short work stoppage and not one major mishap. Hundreds of members of the local were in the military, and others bought liberty bonds. Nevertheless, Local 8 was undeniably an IWW outfit, proudly wearing their buttons to work—even at the US Navy Yard where Wobblies, exclusively, were hired. During the trial, the prosecution offered no specific evidence against any of the Philadelphians aside from their IWW membership. The Philadelphia branch of the Department of Justice was not even consulted in advance about the September raids. Nevertheless, many government officials and the Wilson administration believed the IWW to be a major threat that had to be eliminated. Since the IWW was powerful on the Philadelphia waterfront, itself so important to the war effort, it should come as no surprise that Local 8's leaders were slated for arrest.

The federal trial against the IWW became the longest in US history up until that time. During those months, they were held at the Cook County jail, the same one where the Haymarket martyrs had been held thirty years earlier before four were executed, including Albert Parsons, the husband of IWW cofounder Lucy Parsons. When asked, while being checked into the jail, their religious affiliation, supposedly the most typical response was "IWW." During the trial, when called to the stand, Local 8 leader Jack Walsh "kept the courtroom in an undignified state of continual laughter with his references to 'Fellow Worker Nebeker' [the prosecuting attorney] and other Irish pleasantries." Fletcher also kept his fellow defendants in stitches with the typical gallows humor for which the IWW was famous. In his autobiography, Big Bill Haywood repeated one such comment: "If it wasn't for me," Fletcher joked, "there'd be no color in this trial at all." Fletcher, curiously, did not testify at the trial, perhaps because he knew the proceedings to be a farce. In a letter to the editor published in *The Crisis* in 1919, F.H.M. Murray wrote of running into Fletcher during the trial and asking him for his thoughts; according to

Murray, Fletcher "smiled broadly" and replied that Judge Landis was "a fakir. Wait until he gets a chance; then he'll plaster it on thick."

Sure enough, after four months of testimony—in which the entire government case was based upon letters, newspaper articles, and other materials produced *prior* to the US declaration of war—the jury delivered a verdict in less than forty-five minutes: every defendant guilty on every count. The jury barely had had time to take their seats and read the charges before making their decision, surely without considering any of the individuals as such. The members of Local 8 were sentenced as severely as others on trial even though their branch never interrupted cargo shipments. On August 30, 1918 Judge Kenesaw Mountain Landis, who became the first commissioner of Major League Baseball after the "Black Sox" scandal in the 1919 World Series, sentenced Fletcher to ten years and fined him $30,000 and court costs. As the sentences were announced, Haywood reported: "Ben Fletcher sidled over to me and said: 'The Judge has been using very ungrammatical language.' I looked at his smiling black face and asked: 'How's that, Ben? He said: 'His sentences are much too long'." Fletcher's joke spread far and wide, repeated many times in various sources.

To the membership of Local 8, the loss of their leaders, Fletcher particularly, was devastating. Black longshoreman James Fair recalled, decades later, "Some of us were very hurt over it, because we knew what he was doing was something for us to earn a livelihood to support ourselves and families and it was just like well, I would say it was to ones who was interested in organized labor and improving our standards of life it was something near like Martin Luther King [being sent to jail]." The ninety-three Wobblies waiting to be sent to Kansas did so in the Cook County Jail, where B.B. King recorded a legendary live album fifty-two years later. After boarding a special train for Leavenworth, Fletcher again sought to make light of the situation while simultaneously calling into question the legitimacy of the proceedings. Years later in Moscow, Haywood still recalled Fletcher holding this mock court aboard the train. Imitating Judge Landis, "looking solemn and spitting tobacco juice," Fletcher "swore in the prisoners as a jury; calling the guards and detectives up to him he sentenced them without further ado to be hanged and shot and imprisoned for life."

Ben Fletcher was just twenty-seven years old when arrested, and twenty-eight when sentenced to ten years in a federal penitentiary. What might he have accomplished if he had another ten, twenty, forty years as a black revolutionary unionist?

Local 8 without Fletcher

Ben Fletcher had been a key organizer and widely respected member of Local 8 since its founding as well as the most important African American organizer in the IWW, so his arrest and imprisonment were tremendous blows. Nevertheless, Local 8 had no choice but to carry on without him and its other imprisoned leaders. Fortunately for the union, the democratic and inclusive ideology had fostered an environment that produced many leaders, rather than just one or two. At all Local 8 meetings, black members held at least half the leadership positions—generally, an African American held the chair, while a member of European descent or European immigrant served as secretary. When an issue threatened to divide the members along racial lines, the union discussed the matter openly at meetings and attempted to counteract the problem with education. Quickly, a second cadre of leaders, black and white, stepped into the void. Black members such as Charles Carter, William "Dan" Jones, Glenn Perrymore, Alonzo Richards, Ernest Varlack, Joseph Weitzen, and Amos White held leadership positions. Still, they had to learn on the job, in a time when there was little margin for error. After the bitter wartime repression that the IWW suffered, the Delaware River piers in Philadelphia still were, very likely, the strongest link in a much-weakened Wobbly chain. Despite immense difficulties, Local 8 continued to forge a heterogeneous workforce into a unified, powerful union.

Nevertheless, racial equality *always* was a contentious issue within the union—particularly as hundreds of, perhaps as many as a thousand, southern blacks entered Local 8's ranks during the World War I era. The combination of the Great Migration, almost total cessation of European immigration due to the war, and the power of Local 8 meant that, as the port's workforce grew, African Americans were the primary beneficiaries. According to the 1920 census, 4,036 longshoremen worked in Philadelphia: 2,388 "Negroes," 397 native-born of native-born parents, 436 native-born of foreign parentage, and 814 immigrants. The reported workforce, thus, had risen by a thousand since 1910 and, essentially, blacks accounted for the entire increase. But these new members did not possess the same experiences with unionism or with white workers as the original black members of Local 8 did. The challenge for (the few) unions that strove for an interracial membership, such as Local 8, was to convince black migrants that a union with many white and European immigrant members could protect black workers' jobs, improve their conditions, and perhaps be a revolutionary force for both racial and economic justice. Decades later, in response to historian Herbert Hill's question about whether blacks were "amenable" to joining the IWW, organizer Jack Lever replied, "No, but we had as much success in organizing Negroes as whites; all in spite of the many Negroes from the South who could not read or write." Without the support of these migrants, the union would have been weakened severely. A second problem that Local 8 confronted, also not unique, was the very real possibility of competition between and among black and white longshoremen for work, due to a postwar maritime recession that resulted in a major decrease in jobs. Thus, the loss of the leading black "old-timer," Ben Fletcher, was doubly troubling since it came at such an inopportune moment.

Another potential source of disorder that Local 8 confronted was that the local black population, of course, was hardly monolithic. That is, as southern blacks started to increase, vis-à-vis the established black community, tensions among black people increased, further complicating the union's efforts. As Robert Gregg insightfully wrote, significant differences among blacks existed in class, gender, regional background, and religion. Further, historian Charles Hardy documented noticeable conflicts between African Americans native to the city, who labeled themselves "Old Philadelphians," and those who recently migrated from the South and quickly outnumbered the "OPs," but who felt distinctly second class. Similarly, class divisions within the black community persisted, perhaps most clearly revealed by the fact that the local black newspaper, *Philadelphia Tribune*, never reported on the fact that several thousand African Americans belonged to Local 8 or that Ben Fletcher was sent to Leavenworth. Without Fletcher, himself an "OP," it was that much harder for Local 8 to keep the dockworkers united.

Fletcher in the Big House

Shortly after sentencing in Chicago in August 1918, Fletcher and ninety-three other convicted Wobblies were sent, via a dedicated train, to the notorious US penitentiary in Leavenworth, Kansas. For most of this journey, they had been handcuffed in pairs but, as Harrison George later recounted, they started to sing in grand Wobbly style: "After the train had crossed the Missouri river [into Kansas], it stood on a switching track between rows of factories. Merrily we piped up, 'Hold the fort, for we are coming, union men be strong,' and the workers began hanging out of shop windows to listen."

Fletcher and the rest of the Wobblies arrived on September 7 and spent most of the next four years in the largest, most notorious federal prison in the country. Upon processing, a number of details were recorded that, now, are publicly available. Fletcher stood at little more than five feet four and weighed around 150 pounds; he was tough enough to lift and load cargo even if he was not tall. Some might use the term "stocky" to describe him. He had attended two years of high school but did not graduate. He smoked tobacco and drank alcohol but did not use morphine or opium—standard questions on his intake form. Fletcher confirmed his marriage, listed as Mrs. Carrie Fletcher, who then lived in the same home as Ben's father, at 1613 S. Ninth Street in the heart of South Philadelphia.

Life in Leavenworth was hard. Opened around 1900, Leavenworth was the first federal prison and remained the largest as a few others were constructed. (Previously, federal prisoners were housed in state or even county prisons and jails, including Eugene Debs who served six months in Woodstock, Illinois.) Generally, prisons were overcrowded, dirty, hot in the summer, cold in the winter, and full of rats, roaches, and other creatures. Many prisoners, at that time, were "political," particularly for opposition to the war, but there also were "ordinary" criminals serving time for murder, counterfeiting, and so on; tensions between the two groups, with prison officials intentionally inciting conflicts, were neither uncommon nor ever-present. All inmates were assigned various jobs that often were physically hard, tedious, or boring. Beatings from guards or other inmates, times in solitary confinement, and other forms of punishment were normal. In his memoir, Ralph Chaplin recalled Leavenworth as "a feverish world of explosive repression and frustration." Fights and sexual exploitation, by prison guards or fellow inmates, did not prevent the tedium: "Life in prison [which] went on, day by day, relentlessly. We had to harden ourselves to avoid cracking up emotionally."

The imprisoned Wobblies, with centuries of union experience among them, started to organize their prison despite severe restrictions. Much of their focus, not surprisingly, was on their legal struggles, so a great deal of correspondence between inmates and the IWW General Defense Committee occurred. Wobblies received permission to publish a "News and Views from the Labor World" column in the prison newspaper, *Leavenworth New Era*. But as Doree wrote in one letter to his wife: "The matter of our freedom is out of our hands. We are not permitted to write for publications. We cannot conduct meetings. We are limited in the number of letters we may write. Our mail is subject to censoring. What we may do is not much." J. Edgar Hoover—who later headed the Federal Bureau of Investigation and, before that, ran the General Intelligence Division of the Department of Justice's Bureau of Investigation—had

Fletcher's correspondence monitored for "Negro agitation" though all of his fellow Wobblies also were surveilled.

The benefit of the fact that every single piece of mail Fletcher sent or received was logged opens up a window into his connections, on "the outside," with family, friends, and union. He corresponded with dozens of people including his wife, siblings, and quite possibly other family members who cannot always be identified with certainty. He received many packages including cans of tobacco, candy and cakes, apples, lemons and oranges, gum, clothing, and books. Doree's letters to his wife, that she preserved for decades and bequeathed to her daughter, reveal that he shared books with Fletcher and other Wobs—not just political tracts but also classic works of literature.

While in prison, Wobblies read a lot, taught each other, and actively corresponded with activists, organizers, and fellow unionists. Fletcher wrote and received letters from Wobblies and other radicals in Philadelphia, Chicago, New York City, and elsewhere. His correspondents included John Reed, author of the classic about the Russian Revolution *Ten Days That Shook the World*, and Oswald Villard, a cofounder of the NAACP and grandson of William Lloyd Garrison. Fletcher exchanged letters with Joe Ettor, the Italian Wobbly organizer.

As the most prominent African American Wobbly, it makes sense that Fletcher kept in touch with many other black socialists. He regularly corresponded with both Chandler Owen and A. Philip Randolph, coeditors of the New York City–based *Messenger*, who were nicknamed "Lenin and Trotsky" in Harlem due to their embrace of socialism. In one editorial in the *Messenger*, Owen and Randolph declared, "Our fellow worker, Ben Fletcher, who was sentenced for twenty years along with Haywood, has read with much satisfaction and enjoyment the *Messenger* during the last few months, and many of the Radical and IWW men in Leavenworth are subscribing for it." Fletcher also corresponded with R.T. Sims, a Wobbly who organized black janitors in Chicago, and Otto Huiswood, born in Surinam and the first black member of the Communist Party in the United States.

Evidence of Fletcher's continuing influence within the IWW, especially on matters concerning race, comes from Bill Haywood. Haywood accepted Fletcher's advice and instructed Charles Carter, a black leader in Local 8, to attend a meeting of the National Brotherhood of Workers of America. The Brotherhood's founder, the aforementioned Wobbly and a former Socialist Labor Party member, Sims, wished to establish a black version of New York's United Hebrew Trades. Three black longshoremen from Local 8 attended that convention, which refused to seat delegates from the segregationist AFL.

Fletcher exchanged letters with Joseph J. Jones and William Monroe Trotter, two African American militants in Boston. Trotter, the nationally prominent publisher of the black newspaper *Boston Guardian*, constantly assailed the accommodationist ideal of Booker T. Washington, instead taking a hard line on demanding full equality for African Americans. According to his latest biographer, Kerri K. Greenidge, Trotter met Fletcher when he lived there in 1917 and, subsequently, they regularly corresponded. Interestingly, Greenidge also suggests that, later in Philadelphia, Fletcher recruited African Americans to attend National Equal Rights League meetings, which Trotter led during World War I and could be seen as a more militant, black-only rival to the NAACP. Quite possibly, Fletcher introduced Trotter and Jones, who closely worked together during those years. Jones took up Fletcher's mantle and, according to Greenidge, "became the most visible colored Wobbly in Boston." Fletcher and Trotter also corresponded with A. Philip Randolph to rally support for Jones who was harassed and, in 1919, arrested in the Red Scare before meeting a tragic end. Meanwhile, in a letter to Jones, Fletcher demonstrated his ongoing commitment to revolutionary, multiracial unionism: "I hold that the IWW is all sufficient to get the 'goods'."

The head of the US Department of Justice's Bureau of Intelligence, J. Edgar Hoover, rightly feared Fletcher, other Wobblies, and political prisoners of various ideological persuasions in Leavenworth who discussed, read, wrote, organized, and dreamed in what historian Christina Heatherton and others named the "University of Radicalism." As Heatherton highlighted, "Bulgarian communists, Indian Ghadarites, Mexican anarcho-syndicalists, and African American socialists—made for an unusual convergence of radical traditions." Among the most noteworthy radicals in Leavenworth was Ricardo Flores Magón, a legendary Mexican anarchist who, along with his brother Enrique, led the Partido Liberal Mexicano (PLM), a group of border-crossing, anticapitalist revolutionaries of the American Southwest and northern Mexico. Quite likely, Fletcher felt right at home.

Fletcher did what he could to help other black inmates, quite possibly imprisoned due to racism as opposed to any crime. Scholar Sara Benson wrote about political prisoners in Leavenworth, including from the IWW and PLM, who rubbed shoulders and shared cell blocks with sixty-two members of the "Black Twenty-Fourth Infantry of the US Army." These black men had been imprisoned for life due to their militant resistance to racism in Houston, where they had been stationed, a complicated matter that resulted in several waves of mass hangings of black soldiers. According to Benson's research, Fletcher befriended some of these soldiers. When released from Leavenworth, Fletcher smuggled information about these inmates' mistreatment to NAACP officials in New York City and a contact at the *Baltimore Afro-American* in the hopes of securing their release from prison. Presumably, they all understood themselves as victims of a system—inside and out of prison—that oppressed black people.

Indeed, during and after his stint in prison, Fletcher was building networks of radical black activists. Fletcher's prison correspondence became the basis for numerous articles in Owen and Randolph's *Messenger*, which no doubt raised alarms among federal authorities. Similarly, in *Seeing Red: Federal Campaigns Against Black Militancy, 1919–1925*, historian Theodore Kornweibel noted that federal agents feared Fletcher was grooming other black Wobblies to be his protégé upon release, including the aforementioned, Joseph J. Jones. As Kornweibel wrote, "Fletcher and the other imprisoned IWWs, regarding themselves as political prisoners, lost no opportunity to organize political and educational activities, circulate books and pamphlets, deliver speeches, recite original poetry and stories, and convert other prisoners. The will to dominate their surroundings triumphed in an intellectual life and political activism that was not quenched even by solitary confinement."

Like other inmates, Fletcher worked a variety of menial jobs in prison and, like on the outside, refused to follow rules on the inside. On at least six occasions he was punished for "violations" including "loafing" while at work, leaving his workstation, disobeying orders, talking when he was not supposed to do so, and "creating a disturbance." For these infractions, he received formal reprimands, was placed in isolation, put on restricted diet, and had "amusement" and yard privileges suspended numerous times. It should be noted that the food offerings already were poor and that isolation is a notorious form of punishment in the "big house." Fletcher, of course, was hardly the only Wobbly who resisted prison authority and punished for doing so.

The Campaign to Free Fletcher and Out on Bail

The IWW and its allies began calling for pardons shortly after the sentences were announced. Once an armistice was declared, in November 1918, many Americans started to question the legality and legitimacy of the wartime measures and call for the release of those people imprisoned during the war. Many liberal Americans, including some churchgoers, were sympathetic to such efforts led by the newly created American Civil Liberties Union, cofounded by Roger Baldwin who briefly had belonged to the IWW. In 1920–21, most political prisoners, including socialists and those who had opposed World War I due to their religious beliefs, were released. On Christmas Day in 1921, the most famous federal prisoner and a cofounder of the IWW, Eugene Debs, walked out of a federal prison in Atlanta. By 1922, most of those not yet released were Wobblies, suggesting how they were seen by mainstream America and particularly political elites.

As the only African American among the imprisoned IWWs, Fletcher's case drew additional support. Local 8 raised money for all their imprisoned leaders, starting in 1918 and continuing until they all were released in late 1922. In addition, families, friends, and other sympathizers in Philadelphia wrote many letters to the US Pardon Attorney's office. Fletcher's case received extensive coverage in the *Messenger*; Fletcher's supporters also sold five-dollar "liberty bonds" advertised in its pages. Local 8 sent funds directly to their imprisoned members in Leavenworth. For instance, in late 1919 Fletcher received twenty-five dollars from the local, which also sent money to the national headquarters in Chicago to help all "class war prisoners." Funds also were raised to get them temporarily released on bonds.

When Fletcher was released on bail from Leavenworth, during an appeal in 1920, the IWW's *New Solidarity* loudly proclaimed: "Ben Fletcher Is Out." The article reminded readers that Fletcher was "the only colored Fellow Worker tried and convicted on the Chicago federal indictment . . . received a ten-year bit and, it will be remembered commented that Judge Landis' literary style was going on the blink [when] he was pronouncing such long sentences." The efforts to raise the money necessary to get Fletcher released on bond as well as to win a pardon had received nationwide attention, becoming a minor cause célèbre among African American radicals, thanks to Randolph and Owen's campaign in the *Messenger*. The magazine ran several articles on Fletcher's case, contending, "Ben Fletcher is in Leavenworth for principle—a principle which when adopted, will put all the Negro leaders out of their parasitical jobs. That principle is that to the workers belong the world." Dozens of individuals also wrote letters to President Harding on Fletcher's behalf. For instance, C.S. Golden, a Philadelphia representative of the International Association of Machinists, wrote that Fletcher believed "in promoting human progress and happiness." Peter Curtin, a foreman for the stevedore firm Murphy, Cook and Company, "saw him [Fletcher] at the meetings of the longshoremen. He always counseled the men to be tolerant and to work for their ends by peaceful means." Of course, the thousands of members of Local 8 petitioned the president to release Fletcher, too.

Immediately upon his release in February 1920, and despite potentially having his bail revoked, Ben Fletcher began speaking to promote the ideals of the IWW. Fletcher took up residence with his family, including his father and sister in the Grays Ferry section of Philadelphia. Why he did not move in with his wife and stepchild is unclear. Previously, Fletcher's wife had applied for assistance to the South West District of the Society for Organizing Charity; this application supplemented the ten dollars per week the GDC provided for his wife and stepchild. Nevertheless, one thing is certain, Fletcher remained committed to the IWW cause, writing in one letter shortly before his relief that "the first and most important duty is for all of us to prepare ourselves for the final chapter in the life of Capitalism."

Fletcher soon spoke at a newly created weekly forum, organized by the Philadelphia IWW, advertised to "increase your knowledge on current events, economics, Industrial Unionism," and more, held on Sunday afternoons, at a street corner in South Philadelphia. Fletcher was going back to his roots as a soapboxer. His lecture was entitled "The Price of Progress," something he knew quite well, having served several years in a federal penitentiary for his beliefs. Fletcher also continued to help raise bail money to get other IWWs still in Leavenworth; for instance, Fletcher addressed a meeting of "liberals" on behalf of Philadelphia resident, Wobbly sailor, fellow Leavenworth inmate, and Spaniard Manuel Rey. Fletcher also traveled to Baltimore to continue organizing longshoremen. His actions are noteworthy because, as historian Eric Thomas Chester wrote, some other Wobblies, after being released, were "demoralized and defeated, and did not return to active participation in radical politics or the IWW."

Fletcher proved helpful not just as a lecturer but also on the waterfront in Philadelphia, during Local 8's mammoth strike. That June, thousands of Philadelphia longshoremen struck, ultimately growing to almost ten thousand waterfront workers, far and away the largest strike in the history of the port. This strike was a part of a national and international wave of labor uprising and revolutions that occurred in the aftermath of World War I. Fletcher pointed out to the sailor and fellow Philadelphia organizer Rey, still languishing in the federal penitentiary in Leavenworth, the ongoing support that Local 8 received from seamen's unions, particularly those British sailors aligned with the syndicalist Shop Stewards Movement, and local railroad and machinist unions. That is, Fletcher was mindful of the internationalism of workers who espoused what Wobblies called the One Big Union and whose name clearly declared that the struggle was global. As part of the effort to win the Philadelphia strike and expand the IWW, Fletcher traveled once more to Baltimore to share news of the strike and discourage the unloading of "hot cargo" there. With the help of some ship firemen, who belonged to one of the more militant maritime unions (and that once had considered affiliating with the IWW), Fletcher convinced members of four vessels to strike in sympathy with Local 8. It must be repeated that Fletcher helped with this strike while out on bail, a risky proposition for his actions threatened to send him back to Leavenworth and forfeit the bail money.

Fletcher fondly recalled the working-class solidarity exhibited during this strike in a 1929 letter to the historian Abram Harris. "The IWW button was a passport every where's hereabout. The town was electrified. If you were operating a Restaurant, Saloon Club, or other whatnot, where Longshoremen and Marine Transport Workers and their allies frequented, you were outspoken in your support of the IWW." As in previous strikes, local businesses dependent on of their working-class neighbors for their livelihood also possessed many family, ethnic, and religious ties to the strikers and, thus, generally supported the strike.

Although the strikers began the summer with high hopes of reducing their standard shift to eight hours, getting a much-needed raise, and reasserting the primacy of the IWW as "lords of the docks," at best the strike can be called a draw. Local 8 did not achieve any of its goals, though it had convinced ten thousand workers to lay down their tools for a month and managed to call an end to the strike without collapsing, "taking the strike to the job." The experience of participating in a major strike surely was instructive even without achieving its goals. Alas, only a month later Local 8 experienced another threat.

The Philadelphia Controversy

The crisis that became known as the "Philadelphia Controversy" was not caused by hostile employers or a repressive government. Instead, powerful forces swirling around the Left in the United States and worldwide, specifically the rising tide of communism, almost destroyed Local 8. In the summer and fall of 1920 Local 8 was suspended twice—first for allegedly loading ammunition for anti-Soviet forces in the Russian

Civil War and then for violating the IWW constitution by charging high initiation fees. Local 8 did not fully return to the IWW fold for more than a year. This section cannot fully explore its complexities, but the Philadelphia Controversy exemplified the intensity of conflicts across the globe as anticapitalists were forced to decide where they stood on the newly created Soviet Union. The IWW—after much soul searching, heated debate, and "losing" many members to communism—chose to distance itself from the Soviet Union and its communist allies. So did most other anarchist and syndicalist organizations but not without great cost and consequence.

Ben Fletcher firmly agreed with the IWW's decision to remain committed to a socialist worldview while remaining anticommunist. While many Americans, then and now, may find these distinctions to be irrelevant, they most definitely were not and are not. Wobblies who consciously remained apart from communists still very much believed in the Marxist notion of class struggle, that "the working class and the employing class have nothing in common," but nevertheless recoiled from the top-down, antidemocratic, authoritarian approach championed by V.I. Lenin and then Josef Stalin. Fletcher was one such person. In correspondence with Abram Harris, he assailed communist "disrupters" for running roughshod over Local 8's (and the IWW's) democratic structures. He understood that the communists very much wanted to "turn" the IWW into the Bolshevik vanguard in the States: after all, the IWW was the largest, most influential revolutionary organization in the United States during and, despite massive state repression, immediately after World War I. Fletcher squarely blamed communists for the Philadelphia Controversy by fabricating a story about Local 8 members loading ammunition for antirevolutionary forces, the "Whites," in the Russian civil war. The communist motivation, according to Fletcher and the many others who shared this view, was to punish the IWW for refusing to embrace the "Party line" and avoid folding the entire IWW into the emerging communist movement. Historians do not have sufficient documentation, even a century later, to ascertain what precisely happened, but Fletcher's feelings are easy to discern. Despite being sent to federal prison for his beliefs, he still held true to the notion that an interracial industrial union movement was necessary to make society truly democratic and equitable, and that communism was not the path to reach such a destination.

When the IWW suspended Local 8, Fletcher and other Local 8 leaders out on bail, E.F. Doree and Walter Nef, along with others compiled

"A Complete and Detailed Statement of All That Has Occurred" that they entitled *The Philadelphia Controversy*. While true that members of Local 8 had loaded countless tons of war matériel during the war, Philadelphia's longshoremen denied loading ammunition to support anti-Soviet forces in Russia aboard the *Westmount*. As historian Fred Thompson later asked, quite thoughtfully: why would the United States send military supplies to the Whites in Siberia by way of Philadelphia? Instead, most of the weaponry that the US was known to have sent to counterrevolutionaries shipped from West Coast ports. By contrast, Local 8 knew of no such shipments from Philadelphia and rejected that they existed. The cover page of this booklet boldly declared: "The IWW must now decide whether it shall be an industrial union in name only or whether it shall be an industrial union in fact. The day of test is here. We have sacrificed much for the principle of industrial unionism, now let's have it."

Ben Fletcher was active in this issue from the start. When MTW Secretary-Treasurer James Scott came down from New York City to castigate Local 8, Fletcher was one of the first to meet him. Along with Fletcher, Local 8 leader Polly Baker and others protested to Scott about the suspension. When Scott demanded a meeting with the membership that same night, they insisted they could not arrange a representative meeting on such short notice. The local's bylaws specified that a meeting held at any time other than the regularly scheduled ones must be announced in handbills distributed all along the fifteen-mile waterfront. Typically, two days were required to notify the thousands of members, not all of whom worked on any given day. Fletcher was not cowed by Scott's brusque demands; after all, both Fletcher and Scott knew full well that Fletcher was one of the premier organizers in the entire IWW and out on bail for his commitment to the union. Fletcher also asked Scott why Local 8 had not yet received word from the full General Executive Board (GEB) in Chicago. Scott returned to New York without having convinced Local 8 of anything.

When the GEB dispatched longtime organizer George Speed to investigate the situation, again Fletcher was among the first to meet him. Speed and Fletcher knew each other at least as far back as May 1913, when Speed helped organize Local 8. Speed also was out on bail from Leavenworth. In the name of international worker solidarity, Speed convinced members of Local 8 to stop loading ammunition on *any* vessel. Speed wrote back to his colleagues in Chicago that the GEB had been too hasty, listening to hysterical charges from Scott and others in New York before even getting the Philadelphians' side of the story. Also relevant, it is quite possible that James Scott already was a communist; later, he did belong to the Communist Party. Eventually, the GEB lifted the first suspension. Another significant factor in doing so, quite possibly, was that the membership of the GEB changed that fall and became distinctly less procommunist than the previous board, but a new issue resulted in a second suspension.

The second phase of the Philadelphia Controversy dealt with other sticky issues, initiation fees and the level of central control in the national IWW. For its first seven years, Local 8's initiation fee was quite low, but in 1920 the union raised its initiation fee to twenty-five dollars even though the IWW Constitution established a two-dollar maximum. In so doing, Local 8 sought to limit the labor supply in a postwar era marked by a deep recession that inflated labor surpluses. Since the union had established a dominant presence over who could be hired (the "closed shop"), Local 8 wanted to limit the labor supply—especially important in an industry notorious for massive surpluses that regularly had been used as a bludgeon to decimate worker power. In so doing, Local 8 followed a practice more commonly used by the AFL. But the IWW was not just interested in short-term material gains, such as improving wages and hours (though those would be most welcome by most working-class people), but also fomenting revolution. That was why the IWW intentionally kept initiation fees and monthly dues low, to facilitate the admission of poor workers. Hence, Local 8 was in a logjam: limit entry to the union to help current members or throw open membership to all workers to (possibly) move that much closer to revolution while (definitely) flooding the labor market. Many non-Philadelphia/longshore Wobblies castigated Local 8 for putting its immediate economic interests over long-term goals. Neither Local 8 rank-and-filers nor leaders like Fletcher, Doree, and Nef— whom, it must be noted, were sent to prison for their commitment to the IWW—backed down. Doree wrote most forcefully, pointing out that Local 8 had far more members than all of the other IWW longshore locals, which had lower initiation fees, combined. Further, according to Doree, if Local 8 lowered its fees, then the union would be flooded with new arrivals who knew nothing about Wobbly ideals and simply wanted to get into the union that controlled some of the best jobs any Philadelphia worker could find.

Not surprisingly, given Local 8's intransigence, on December 4, 1920, Local 8 received notification of its suspension from MTW headquarters in New York, "On account of Philadelphia failing to live up to the Executive Boards [sic] instruction to live up to the Constitution of the IWW." Further,

Fletcher and Ernest Varlack, as members of the now-suspended Local 8, were denied their seats as secretary-treasurer of the MTW and member of the General Organizing Committee respectively, despite being "overwhelmingly elected" in recent MTW voting. Since Local 8 made up a large majority of the MTW's total membership, Fletcher's and Varlack's victories were givens. The second suspension conveniently kept Local 8 from taking control of the MTW, also meaning the procommunist James Scott remained in power. After the better part of another year, Local 8 agreed to lower its initiation fee but this suspension of what probably was the largest and definitely the most diverse IWW branch greatly weakened the Philadelphia dockworkers as well as the entire union.

These matters never have been fully understood, and documentation remains quite limited, but Fletcher always believed—as later did Fred Thompson, the IWW's "in-house" historian for decades—that it was this IWW-Communist Party (CP) conflict that lay at the heart of the Philadelphia Controversy. The ultimate IWW rejection of Bolshevik overtures, and Lenin's decision to focus on capturing the mainstream AFL, had resulted in a final and fierce split between two competing left-wing traditions. As a result, communists in the US sought to destroy the IWW, beginning with its most powerful branch, Local 8. While the communists failed to capture or destroy the IWW, the members of Local 8 found themselves caught in a vicious power struggle that greatly harmed the entire union.

1922 Lockout: Local 8 Torn Asunder

Despite Local 8's efforts, its days of dominating the Philadelphia waterfront were numbered. In October 1922 more than four thousand members of Local 8 again tried to achieve the eight-hour workday, by then a goal of working-class people for more than fifty years. In typical Wobbly fashion, they simply announced their intent to impose an eight-hour day by reporting to work an hour later than usual—and without consulting their bosses! Alas, 1922 was not 1913: US employers had been busy consolidating their power after defeating an unprecedented postwar strike wave that included Local 8's 1920 strike. The city's waterfront employers, feeling confident in an era that historian David Montgomery named as the one in which the "house of labor" fell, locked out dockworkers. The moment was not fortuitous since the union had recently initiated many new members (mostly southern blacks without union experience) and, in the wake of the Philadelphia Controversy, the rival ILA had signed up hundreds who likely would scab in the event of an IWW strike or employer lockout. Further, the US Shipping Board significantly aided employers by bringing replacement workers from the South aboard one of its vessels and paying the stevedoring companies of Philadelphia on a cost plus 10 percent profit basis for the strike's duration, thereby giving employers additional incentives to break the union. The Shipping Board further colluded with Philadelphia shipping corporations by participating in daily meetings and contributing federal resources, including Shipping Board and Department of Justice spies who infiltrated the strikers' ranks.

The best news during the lockout came on October 31, 1922, for, on that day, the sentences of Fletcher, Nef, and Walsh were commuted. Not surprisingly, the Department of Justice had opposed granting Fletcher clemency: "He was a negro who had great influence among the colored stevedores, dock workers, firemen, and sailors, and materially assisted in building up the Marine Transport Workers Union which at the time of the indictment [1917–18] had become so strong that it practically controlled all shipping on the Atlantic Coast." Yet the US pardon attorney who investigated the cases of Local 8's leaders wrote that he had "considerable difficulty" in "ascertaining just what" these longshoremen had done "that constitute[d] the offense of which they were convicted." As the federal agent who conducted the raids on Local 8 in 1917 later admitted, "I personally do not know of any crime that he [Nef] has committed against the country." The same could be said of Fletcher and the other imprisoned members of Local 8.

Although he spent time at Local 8's hall during the lockout, it does not seem that Fletcher was active. When Fletcher, under a conditional pardon, appeared at the hall, he declined an offer to address the members. Perhaps Fletcher did not participate because, as he later claimed, the IWW leaders were under Communist influence. Or perhaps Fletcher did not want to risk having his newly issued pardon rescinded though "his rebel persistence after coming out of jail," as Thompson later put it, and active participation in Local 8 after this lockout, suggest otherwise.

The employer lockout succeeded in no small part because Local 8's celebrated interracial solidarity broke apart. Race relations across the nation were deteriorating steadily—as evidenced by a wave of racist terrorism unleashed during the Red Summer of 1919 as well as the resurgence and massive expansion of the Ku Klux Klan. In Philadelphia, employers, after helping foment the difficulties in the first place, actively worked to split the longshoremen along racial lines by hiring black replacements, a practice that US employers regularly used with great effectiveness. The continued intransigence of employers combined with the persistence of the ILA (simultaneously supplying strikebreakers and courting Local 8's black members) proved too much for the union to combat. Local 8 began to split asunder along race lines, with the black majority losing faith in the union and wanting to return to work. Despite the ongoing commitment of some African Americans, notably leader Alonzo Richards, most of those dedicated to staying out were white. When the lockout succeeded, white members blamed the blacks for a lack of commitment. Given the already tense racial environment of the postwar era, more black longshoremen began leaving Local 8, some temporarily rushing into the ILA, and racial animosity returned to the Philadelphia waterfront after a nine-year hiatus.

While no other contemporary source did so, Fletcher later claimed that the situation had been forced upon the rank and file by a "Communist element" with orders from Moscow, who "were successful in stampeding the Phila[delphia] Longshoremen into another strike." According to him, when communists (their identities never have come to light) realized that they could not "capture the Port," that is, seize control of Local 8 for the CP, they engaged in a "Liquidating Program." While his assertion cannot be confirmed, various communist front organizations such as the Soldiers', Sailors' and Workmen's Council and the Communist Propaganda League did exist in Philadelphia during that era and some prominent local Wobblies did join the communists. Assuming Fletcher was correct—and he knew far more about the situation than later historians possibly could—communists in Local 8 and perhaps other branches of the MTW still resented the IWW's rejection of communist overtures so wished to destroy it. Historian Fred Thompson echoed Fletcher's view; namely, what communists had initiated with the Philadelphia Controversy succeeded two years later with the ending of Local 8's vaunted control along the Delaware.

Although Thompson did not mention it, quite possibly the absence of Fletcher from the action was another major reason for the fracturing of Local 8. In 1922 the undeniable leader of the union had become Polly Baker, a Lithuanian immigrant. Fletcher was not visible and took no major part. The African American leader Glenn Perrymore clearly wavered in his support of the IWW, having temporarily led a black exodus to the ILA during Local 8's suspension. While true that the black leaders Alonzo Richards and "Plug" Dickerson supported Baker, both made it quite clear that they disagreed with Baker's decision to strike in the first place. What is certain is that, after 1922, Local 8 no longer commanded the allegiance of most Philadelphia longshoremen; in particular, black dockworkers continued to stay away from the IWW, though Fletcher remained true to his union.

On the Philadelphia Waterfront after 1922

In 1923 William "Dan" Jones, an African American longshoreman, founding member of Local 8, and former secretary of the union, wrote in the *Messenger*, "It is an undeniable fact that the employers will use one race or one group of workers to defeat the other group." Jones, no doubt, was thinking about the disastrous events of 1922, when the city's shipping interests skillfully used race to divide Local 8. Yet it did not simply wither away. Instead, the ILA competed with the IWW—and a third, independent union led by Jones and Fletcher—for the allegiance of Philadelphia longshoremen.

In 1923 Fletcher and Jones led a group of Wobbly longshoremen out of the MTW to form the independent Philadelphia Longshoremen's Union (PLU). Fletcher, still the most respected leader on the waterfront, later wrote that the PLU "was organized in Jan. 1923, by those IWW members who refused to go along with the Communist stampeded IWW element, who seceded and opened another Hall etc. This schism and breach could and would have been averted and the IWW yet maintained" were it not for the communists to whom Fletcher constantly referred. Fletcher contended, in 1929, that he, Nef, and Doree had been expelled by "insincere local officials of the IWW who had come under the influence of the ILA and communist teaching . . . while [Fletcher, Nef, and Doree were] serving time in the US Penitentiary at Leavenworth, Kansas; on the grounds and false charge that they had made applications for pardons to the president of the US and agreed not to have anything else to do with the IWW." Although, as with other of Fletcher's statements, it is impossible to corroborate this one, it is true that Fletcher, Nef and Doree had submitted pardon requests and none of the three—whose combined experience in the IWW totaled more than thirty years—immediately resumed active participation. It is impossible to ascertain whether or not communists controlled the IWW in Philadelphia and unlikely that many communists were in the local ILA.

Shortly after the IWW-PLU split, Fletcher wrote an article for the *Messenger* that provided a second reason why he and some others chose to establish an independent union. Fletcher argued that they were "forced to sever their connections with that organization [IWW] in order to prevent the annihilation of their local autonomy by that unreasonable and inefficient Centralism." Fletcher went on to complain that the

General Executive Board was "unacquainted in a practical way with the problems arising from a job-controlling organization, numbering 3,000 members." Fletcher's argument paralleled those made by Doree and others during the Philadelphia Controversy and was at the heart of the "Emergency Program" split at the 1924 IWW Convention. At the most recent national convention, Local 8's Austin Morris had made the same point: in order to ensure that Local 8 maintained its power, they had to maintain local control over issues such as entry into the workforce. That way, if employers hired only paid-up Local 8 members, men looking for a quick day's work could not be able to take the job away from a union man and the organization could control the waterfront hiring process for the greater good.

Fletcher's complaints also attest to ongoing differences Local 8 had with the universal transfer system of the IWW, which allowed Wobblies from anywhere else to come to the Philadelphia waterfront and immediately be eligible for work without paying the "proper" assessments. In 1921, Local 8 had allowed some of these "footloose" Wobblies into the branch, in accordance with the constitution that they accepted unconditionally in order to return to the IWW. These Wobblies, many of whom came to Philadelphia after Seattle's waterfront employers blacklisted them, caused a great deal of tension in Local 8. In his *Messenger* article, Fletcher argued that members "acquire[d] a determining voice and vote on any question relating to Local job or Financial matters." Here is, perhaps, evidence of the communists whom Fletcher blamed for stampeding Local 8 into the lockout/strike debacle in 1922. Historian Fred Thompson later substantiated this charge by referring to a 1934 conversation he had with Polly Baker: "he [Baker] gave me the mental picture of '110 cats wintering in Philadelphia to lick up the cream off 510 struggles.'" These "110 cats" belonged to the Agricultural Workers Industrial Union of migratory harvest hands. Once harvests ended in the Pacific Northwest, such workers traditionally wintered in cities. But with Western ports turning increasingly hostile to the IWW—Seattle dominated by employers and Portland longshoremen locked in their own brutal strike in October 1922—Local 8's renowned power over the Philadelphia waterfront must have been quite a draw: just ride the rails across the continent, show one's red card, and get good paying work on the Delaware.

Similarly, IWW principles had proven so valuable to Philadelphia's longshoremen that, even though they abandoned the organization, they held fast to its ideals. That these longshoremen, led by Ben Fletcher and disillusioned with the IWW administration, chose to form an organization modeled after the IWW rather than signing up with the ILA revealed much about these (black) Philadelphia longshoremen's beliefs, for it would have been far easier simply to join the ILA. In September 1923 Dan Jones also wrote an article for the *Messenger* about the merits of interracial organizing and industrial unionism, suggesting the strength of his commitment to Wobbly principles. Jones noted, "The Negro is a large factor in American industry," but generally, "the Negro has not been admitted to membership in the trade unions." Jones pointed out the shortsightedness of white workers, saying, "Employers will use one race or one group of workers to defeat the other." Similarly, Jones declared, "There is no advantage to the Negro in being in a separate union" because employers exploited segregated black unionists—a critique of those influenced by Marcus Garvey and black nationalism. To combat these many challenges, "it is absolutely necessary that all workers, regardless of color, should join together in one solid union." As proof of the merits of such an ideology, Jones cited his "personal experience in a mixed [interracial] union for the past ten years." Through this union, Local 8, "the members succeeded in advancing their wages and bettering their working conditions to the point where they were the best paid of all unions that are in the same industry in this country." Jones believed the key to such success was "on account of solidarity." Two particular strategies Jones believed essential for overcoming white workers' racism were the use of integrated work gangs and the election of "mixed" (black and white) officials, both longtime Local 8 practices. Thus, Jones displayed his commitment to some core IWW principles learned in Local 8 while he and Fletcher formed a new union.

Nevertheless, it was not coincidental that the PLU (like ILA's Philadelphia branch, Local 1116) consisted almost entirely of African Americans. The PLU leaders, Fletcher and Jones, were two of the oldest and most respected black workers on the waterfront. By contrast, the leader of the IWW longshoremen was the Irish American Jack Walsh; Polly Baker had been blacklisted and worked at a dockside sugar refinery where most workers were Polish and Lithuanian immigrants like himself. The same reasons that convinced hundreds of black longshoremen to join the ILA in 1921 and 1922 applied to the PLU in 1923. Race relations in the city and nation were horrid and continued deteriorating. In the aftermath of 1922, racial tensions in the waterfront communities of South Philadelphia increased considerably. In the summer of 1923, a series of violent racial clashes occurred, including several South Philly street fights that pitted whites against blacks and an attempted lynching of two black men for allegedly insulting a white woman. Considering this white hostility, that some blacks thought they were better off in their own organization was unsurprising; that Jones spoke out against all-black unions indicated the existence of such sentiment. Fletcher did not comment specifically upon an all-black union in 1923, but he wrote about the vital need to organize black workers, indifference of existing unions to do so, and the possibility that a Negro Labor Federation as an answer. Hence, while both Jones and Fletcher preached interracial unionism, they were practicing segregated unionism or at least entertaining that possibility.

Even though many Philadelphia longshoremen remained true to the ideals of equality and industrial unionism, understandably the IWW organization wished to formally retain what had been its strongest MTW branch and possibly the mightiest IWW local in the United States. The GEB quickly dispatched one its own to Philadelphia to bring the defiant longshoremen back into the IWW fold. John Johnson organized a meeting at the Lithuanian Hall (a telling location), just a few days after the creation of the PLU. That night a second GEB member, Ted Fraser, spoke on "Industrial Unionism versus Craft Unionism and the Philadelphia Longshoremen's Situation." Fraser likely highlighted the differences between the industrial unionism of the IWW, which emphasized solidarity of all workers, and the craft unionism of the ILA, which was only loosely affiliated with other AFL unions. Fraser also, no doubt, disparaged the PLU. As industrial unionists, both IWW and PLU supporters could agree that having formal ties to other workers in the marine transport industry was not simply desirable but necessary. The MTW also sent three members of its General Organizing Committee, all with little success.

In the aftermath of Local 8's collapse, employers proved uninterested in negotiating with either the ILA or PLU. Further, the Shipping Board director of industrial relations J.C. Jenkins and Chairman T.V. O'Connor decided that the Shipping Board would not negotiate with the PLU. Since the longshoremen were divided into three different organizations, no doubt the employers realized their commanding position. Only when Local 8 had represented the entire riverfront workforce did employers concede any ground. The situation in 1923 was far different.

In this era, Philadelphia dockworkers were the big losers. While the PLU persevered through 1923, it did not possess much power; neither did the IWW or the ILA. The following year, the PLU voted to disband and at least some of its members, most notably Fletcher, returned to the IWW.

In spring 1925, the Philadelphia MTW organized their first mass meeting in some time. Veteran IWW national organizer George Speed spoke about the irreconcilable differences between employers and workers. Fletcher discussed the history of the IWW on the Philadelphia waterfront, noting that after every defeat the MTW had returned to fight; the longshoremen had to learn from their past mistakes, and; the longshoremen must rejoin the IWW in order to resist the awful conditions that existed. The following week a second large meeting was held with speakers Fletcher, Speed, and John Korbein (who spoke in Polish). Fletcher's talk "held the audience spell bound for over an hour." Fletcher claimed he would love to debate ILA president Anthony Chlopek. The Wobblies' renewed efforts excited many old-timers and led to the decision to strike the powerful Jarka Stevedoring Company, that had refused to hire any longshoremen who wore IWW buttons.

The 1925 Jarka strike revealed a grave difference between the past and the present, as the IWW no longer possessed many African American members. Although Fletcher, the most well-known African American Wobbly, and Ernest Varlack, a highly respected member born in St. Thomas, both played active roles, few other black longshoremen followed their lead. At the start of the strike, Jarka's white foremen walked off the job with the longshoremen, while the three African American foremen remained on the job. The IWW itself reported that the ILA's membership consisted almost exclusively of African Americans. Why blacks continued to shirk the IWW was unclear—no doubt the memory of the brutal divisions from 1922 played a major role. Even three years after the failed Jarka strike, in 1928, Thomas Dabney, an interviewer for the National Urban League, found the bitter legacy of 1922 still strong. Another likely factor was that the African Americans who worked the riverfront in 1925 were not the same ones who had in 1913. The IWW claimed that many followers of the ILA were "new to Philadelphia." Approximately seventy-five thousand African Americans moved into Philadelphia, from the South, between 1916 and 1930 including many in a spurt in 1923. As migrants to the industrial city from the rural South, these black men were unfamiliar with unionism let alone the radical IWW or its legacy along the Delaware River; perhaps that explained why Fletcher felt the need to lecture longshoremen about the history of Local 8. While the IWW continued to affirm that there was "no place for race prejudice in the IWW," few blacks were willing to join anymore.

By the end of 1926, the ILA had displaced the IWW by convincing most longshoremen that it could protect their interests better than the IWW. One of the ILA's major advantages was that it had a stable, albeit subservient, relationship with bosses. Joining the ILA meant that the employers would sign a contract making certain guarantees, most notably an eight-hour day. Employers only agreed to negotiate with the ILA, though, after the US Shipping Board's chief O'Connor pressured them to do so; not coincidentally, O'Connor was a past president of the ILA. Crucially, the ILA maintained an integrated branch with guarantees of equal representation among the local's officials and always possessing a black president—in contrast to other ILA locals, where blacks often were in "Jim Crow" branches and rarely held leadership positions.

Local 1116 was not quite firmly established, though. Polly Baker, the former Wobbly who had proven to be the key powerbroker in bringing black and white longshoremen together, reported that, after the contract had been in effect for a month, "the employers began to take advantage of our wage agreements. Internal dissension started among the Philadelphia Longshoremen." Into this gap, the IWW opened a new hall, arranged meetings, and made one final effort to reclaim the longshoremen, with longtime Local 8 leader Fletcher serving as district organizer, along with A.L. Nurse, a footloose and active Wobbly, as branch secretary, and another old Wobbly leader, Jack Walsh, rounding out the organizing team. Fletcher and the others championed the IWW as necessary to improve living standards, shorten hours, reduce the speed of work, and increase wages. Fletcher claimed that 1116's membership had plummeted because the ILA either could not or would not stand up to employers in a dispute over wage rates. Yet the ILA proved able to stave off growing dissatisfaction, again with the help of the Shipping Board, which ran interference with employers. Ultimately, the IWW's effort went nowhere, and the ILA managed to stabilize its situation.

Yet even though the ILA maintained a peaceful relationship with the waterfront employers and preserved the racial balance of the union, the workers suffered considerably. For the first time, the Philadelphia longshoremen had an ironclad legal agreement with their employers. This contract, unfortunately, ensured that workers earned lower wages than in the open shop era while sacrificing their right to strike at will, which the IWW considered essential to maintaining and expanding worker power. Further, their autonomy declined dramatically once the bureaucratic and hierarchical prerogatives of the ILA were substituted for the democratic traditions of Local 8. Within a few years, regular meetings and contested elections were distant memories. By 1930, New York–style ILA corruption was rampant.

Equally alarming, though ILA Local 1116 did include the black and white former members of Local 8, race relations worsened considerably. Work gangs remained segregated, as they had been since the employers had torn Local 8 asunder in 1922 and the ILA seemingly made no effort to resist. Relations off the job between black and white workers and their families were similarly poor—no more interracial picnics as during the Wobbly era. Thus, the transition from the IWW to the ILA was both difficult in the short term and disadvantageous in the long. Yet Philadelphia's longshoremen did manage to preserve their union and some semblance of racial accommodation in an era when many of their peers in other ports did not.

After Local 8: Ben Fletcher and the IWW

Despite his brief foray into independent unionism, Fletcher remained active in the IWW into the 1930s and committed to its ideals until his death at the young age of fifty-nine. While no longer an official IWW organizer, he spoke at numerous events in the 1920s and 1930s—and it is reasonable to assume that, for every documented talk, at least several more probably have been "lost." In 1925, for instance, Fletcher spoke to a Philadelphia forum of the American Negro Labor Congress, a Communist-dominated organization of black workers and unionists. In front of a group of people, mostly black and clearly sympathetic to communism, Fletcher "brought the audience to its feet, when he told them that industrial unionism, as expounded by the IWW, is the hope of the suffering and exploited Negro workers in his struggles for real freedom." He pointed to the IWW's commitment to organizing workers regardless of race, sex, or country of origin on an international level because employers were not constrained by national boundaries. According to Harry Haywood, a leading black Communist, Fletcher was not invited to a Negro Labor Congress convention only because he was considered too good a speaker so might upstage the former black Wobbly and current Communist, Lovett Fort-Whiteman.

In 1927, Fletcher undertook a speaking tour that included multiple events in Detroit ending on the northern side of the Great Lakes, in Ontario, Canada. The IWW publicized Fletcher's Detroit talks entitled, "Can and Shall Workers of All Races, Sexes, Colors, Creeds, and Nationalities Organize Together and Build One Big Union of the IWW?" In 1968, Nick DiGaetano, an immigrant from Palermo, Sicily who worked for Chrysler in the 1920s and belonged to the IWW, recalled Fletcher speaking in Detroit: "The hall was at capacity, perhaps five hundred. I don't remember seeing any Negroes in the audience, perhaps there were some. Ben Fletcher was a good speaker." In the 1930s and beyond, DiGaetano organized for the United Auto Workers (UAW), one of countless examples of how IWW members and ideals profoundly influenced the industrial unions formed in the 1930s, most of which belonged to the newly established Congress of Industrial Organizations that rejected the craft unionism, racism, and sexism of the AFL. Amazingly, his Ontario talks were documented in the Finnish-language IWW press.

While unclear precisely when or why, Fletcher moved to New York City around 1931. That year, he gave a lengthy interview with the *Amsterdam News*, a Harlem-based black newspaper, thereby confirming that he was running an IWW recruitment office out of a rented storefront, at 90 East 10th Street between Washington, Union, and Tompkins Square Parks in lower Manhattan.

That same year, 1931, an AFL functionary wrote to the IWW's *Industrial Solidarity* praising Fletcher's soapboxing abilities. This man had planned to watch an IWW street meeting, in New York City, for just a few minutes but ended up remaining for an hour because Fletcher was in the midst of one of his legendary speeches. "I have heard all the big shots of the labor movement over a period of twenty-five years, from coast to coast and it is no exaggeration when I state that this colored man, Ben Fletcher, is the only one I ever heard who cut right through to the bone of capitalist pretensions, to being an everlasting ruling class, with a concrete constructive working class union argument." Fletcher also spoke at a large meeting, at Irving Plaza Hall, in solidarity with coal miners in the midst of the mine war in Harlan County, Kentucky. That Fletcher stood alongside the likes of Roger Baldwin, Arturo Giovannitti, Reinhold Niebuhr, and Norman Thomas is further confirmation that he was respected and well known.

As late as 1933, Fletcher continued agitating for an IWW renaissance until waylaid by a major stroke that year, at the age of forty-two. What might Fletcher have done in the mid 1930s when, sparked by a Great Depression that seemed to prove the failures and contradictions of capitalism, a massive surge in unionism and antifascism occurred? Would he have, like DiGaetano and some other Wobs, jumped into the organizing drives of one of the new CIO unions? Many of those new unions, including the West Coast dockworkers who broke away from the ILA to form the International Longshoremen's and Warehousemen's Union, surely would have welcomed a crack organizer and renowned speaker like Fletcher. Alas, that did not come to pass. While he lived another sixteen years, by his and others' accounts he never was healthy again. In fact, his health steadily deteriorated. Hence, he could not take part in the massive wave of union and anticapitalist organizing that exploded in the United States and worldwide in the mid and late 1930s. Ironically, he and many of other Wobblies finally were pardoned by the newly elected president, Franklin Roosevelt, in 1933.

Fletcher's Life off the Waterfront

Evidence on Fletcher's activism is sparse, considering how important a figure he was, but far less is known about his personal life, especially his later years. For instance, after he left the docks, it is not clear what work Fletcher did—that is, how he earned a living. Wobblies organizers rarely got paid a salary and, after 1925, there is almost no evidence that Fletcher ever served as a professional organizer. Some said he hand-rolled cigars, a skill he seemed to have picked up somewhere along the way. He also smoked cigars. In 1930, Fletcher was single and lived in the same rented apartment as his elderly father, Dennis, in Philadelphia. Sometime around 1931, Fletcher moved to New York, but it is not sure which part. If not immediately, he spent most of his New York City years in Brooklyn's Bedford-Stuyvesant neighborhood.

As for his personal relationships, sometime in the 1920s, Fletcher and his first wife divorced, and sometime after 1930, he married a black woman named Clara. It is unknown why he and his first wife got divorced nor what happened to her. It is unclear when he married Clara, nor where—Philadelphia or New York City. According to the 1940 census, Clara was born in Maryland and just a year younger than Ben. Oddly, though, that census listed them as brother and sister and not husband and wife, as did his *Philadelphia Tribune* obituary in 1949. Ellen Doree Rosen was just a child but commented on this matter. The source of confusion might have been that she was younger, perhaps much younger despite the census, than him. She most definitely was his wife. They had no children though spent time with siblings, nieces, nephews, and other extended family. It seems that most of Ben's people lived and remained in the Philadelphia area. Some of their family, at least on Ben's side, also lived in Brooklyn in the 1940s, and by the late 1940s in the same building. Much later, in the early 2000s, at least one grandnephew was quite proud of Ben Fletcher's activism but, according to him, some others in the family were not. In the late 1960s, another of his grandnephews might have belonged to the Black Panthers in Philadelphia. Clara apparently remarried some years after Ben passed away.

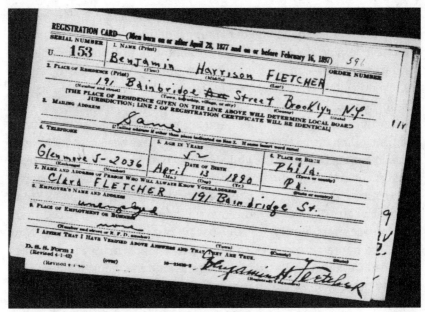

Ben Fletcher, World War II registration card, 1942.

Ben and Clara Fletcher were fortunate to have old friends and fellow
Wobblies living in their Brooklyn neighborhood. Walter Nef and his wife
Feige as well as Chiky Doree, the widow of E.F. Doree, and her two children already had moved to Bedford-Stuyvesant in the late 1920s. It even
is possible that the presence of the Nefs and Dorees explain why the
Fletchers moved there. Sam and Esther Dolgoff, along with their two
sons, also lived in the neighborhood in the 1950s. Decades later, Ellen
Doree Rosen, who was just three years old when her father died in 1927,
lovingly recalled spending time as a child with Ben and Clara. Various
accounts suggest he worked as a janitor or live-in building superintendent, a common occupation for a "handy" man in New York City's brown-
stones. Clara was a nurse and almost certainly the household's primary
breadwinner, quite possibly as early as his stroke in 1933. The last documentation about his work is from 1942, in the mandatory registration
card that he filled out for the US government. In that form for men too
old to serve in the military, he indicated that he was unemployed. Quite
possibly he had not had a steady job for years.

At a shockingly young age, Fletcher's health declined greatly and
permanently. In 1933, he suffered a stroke—at forty-two—and may have
experienced additional ones. Strokes far more commonly occur among
people sixty-five and older, not in their early forties. Fletcher also wrote
of having hypertension (high blood pressure), a malady that is both cause

and effect of having a stroke. These conditions are particularly prevalent among people of color and higher among working-class and poor people who have less access to medical treatment, healthy food, and the like, but rarely in people in their early forties. Apparently, he was never the same physically after his first stroke. Fletcher also wrote of suffering from sciatic rheumatism and painful feet. Possibly his list of maladies was even greater than those known about and some of the ailments he suffered from, including the last few listed, easily could have been caused by years of heavy manual labor on the Philadelphia waterfront. Like miners, dockworkers can die on the job in an instant or the work can kill them slowly.

Health woes aside, Fletcher seemed to have lived a good life in his later years. Clara and Ben remained happily married, based upon existing accounts, until he passed away. Throughout his time in New York, Fletcher remained in close touch with friends, many of whom also belonged to the IWW. Based upon letters and reflections, Fletcher kept up with other "old-timers" but became less active in the IWW—at least in the written record—after the early 1930s. E.F. Doree's and Walter Nef's families helped Fletcher out regularly. Sam Dolgoff (sometimes called Sam Weiner), who later became a noted anarchist, Wobbly, and writer, became good friends with him in the 1930s and 1940s. Dolgoff recalled that Fletcher was friends with noted Wobbly poet and writer T-Bone Slim, in the late 1930s and early 1940s; they often would hang out at the hall the MTW rented in lower Manhattan, just off South Street. Sam's son, Anatole, recalls visiting Ben's home while he listened to the Dodgers— the local baseball team—on the radio, which famously had "broken the color line" when Jackie Robinson joined the Dodgers in 1947. Fletcher regularly visited the MTW's hall in the 1940s, and one of Anatole's most touching recollections makes up the last document in this book. While frustrating that more is not known about Fletcher in his final decades, by all accounts, he was loved and deeply respected. What more can one wish for?

A Wobbly to the End

Exploring Fletcher's ideological beliefs, especially in his later years, is tricky because he did not leave behind a memoir, diaries, or any other personal records. In this way, Fletcher was like most working-class people. Similarly, while Wobblies were fiercely committed to industrial unionism, racial equality, anarcho-syndicalism, and socialism, few wrote long treatises on these topics. That just wasn't their way. Fletcher's politics seemed to mimic the stances of Local 8 or perhaps the reverse. No doubt, the clearest sense of his views came in a series of letters between Fletcher and Abram Lincoln Harris, the pioneering black historian and economist. In the late 1920s Harris collaborated with the more senior historian Sterling Spero on what remains a classic of African American and US labor history, *The Black Worker* (1931). Although Fletcher wrote in 1929—several years after Local 8 had lost control of the Philadelphia waterfront—his commitment to the principles of the One Big Union remained unflagging. Further, he continued to believe that what black and white workers shared in common was more important than their racial differences. Fletcher wrote to Harris that "the Negroes who join the IWW are no different in their motives for doing so than the whites." That is, his view of race, race relations, and racism seems very much informed by socialist thinking and it seems quite reasonable that such views explained why he joined the IWW in the first place, back in 1910. Namely, black and white workers share the same interests because they are workers; by the same token, employers had the same interests because of their economic power and class position. Race seems distinctly secondary. At the same time, Fletcher repeatedly pointed out that black workers suffered more because of their racial heritage and, no doubt, knew that from personal experience. He clearly understood racism on the job, in unions, and in society at large. Even in 1923, when he helped create an independent union, he remained committed to Wobbly ideals. It is clear that, until the end of his days, Fletcher firmly believed that the best way to help *black* workers was through interracial unionism—that is, a class-based solution to the very real racially linked problems of poverty, discrimination, and powerlessness.

He remained committed to the goal of abolishing the wage system, that is, capitalism, but also was pragmatic, which some so-called revolutionaries chastise. For a decade on the Philadelphia waterfront, he promoted Wobbly, direct action methods, meaning at the point of production. He repeatedly reminded workers that employers did not care about workers and only wanted to maximize profit. Generally, Fletcher did not talk about abstract ideals—less about industrial democracy and more about short-term, material issues such as reducing work hours or raising wages. Fletcher believed that promoting "bread-and-butter" issues was useful for workers in the present but also brought more workers into the movement where then they could become better educated on the longer-term goal of socialism. Moreover, he remained a tried-and-true Wobbly in his distaste for communists and communism. Fletcher blamed the Philadelphia Controversy and Local 8's disastrous 1922 lockout on communists, who he labeled "disrupters."

His beliefs in socialism, in class struggle, in organizing a society based upon use/need, not profit—all the concepts he first embraced in the 1910s—remained his touchstones throughout his life. Like other socialists, he believed that the wealth created by industrialization could be harnessed for the good of all and provide for everyone's basic needs. Under capitalism, he saw how many millions suffered from unemployment, hunger, and poverty while a precious few amassed tremendous fortunes, and this system had to be overthrown—all the more so for black people. In Wobbly terminology, Fletcher very much believed that a new society needed to be built from within the shell of the old. But, first and foremost, he believed in working class solidarity. As James Fair recalled, "Ben Fletcher would tell us that we had to live together, we must work together. And his pet word was, all for one and one for all, solidarity was the main thing. And it sank in with a lot of us."

Fletcher died in 1949. The passing of such a noteworthy man did not go un-mourned or unnoticed. Obituaries in the Wobbly newspaper *Solidarity*, in the *Philadelphia Tribune*, and even the *New York Times* recorded his last gasp on earth. A hundred people showed up to pay their respects at his funeral. Though unheralded in the twenty-first century, Fletcher was a powerful force for economic and racial justice in the early twentieth. He was the greatest black union leader of the 1910s and early 1920s. The union that he led was the most successful interracial local of its time.

What he helped achieve on the Philadelphia waterfront in the 1910s rarely has been replicated. Indeed, one hundred years on, the achievements of Fletcher and Local 8 in forming an interracial, multiethnic union whose power resulted in virulently antiunion employers agreeing to oral contracts with the IWW seems unthinkable today. An avowedly revolutionary union led by a black man forced corporations in America's third-biggest city and fifth-largest port to deal with a union in which the great majority of members were African Americans and European immigrants. And they did it without ever signing a contract, instead enforcing their demands based upon the ever-present threat of a strike. Fletcher's name and the union he helped lead definitely have been forgotten—perhaps more accurately "disappeared" by those who cannot imagine or oppose the vision espoused by Fletcher and other Wobblies. No doubt, Ben Fletcher deserves far more recognition than he has received.

Widely regarded as a brilliant speaker, Fletcher was bold enough to tackle racist bosses head-on, smart enough to analyze the intricacies of racial capitalism, wise enough to see the inherent unjustness of the system, clever enough to use humor to point to the flaws and crimes of those who defended the status quo.

Hopefully, this book can help increase awareness of Fletcher's life and beliefs. He deserves to be included in the ranks of the greatest African Americans on the left including W.E.B. Du Bois, A. Philip Randolph, Claude McKay, Ella Baker, Paul Robeson, Pauli Murray, Martin Luther King Jr., Angela Davis, and others.

As the most important black Wobbly ever and among the greatest African American labor leaders and socialists in US history, Fletcher demands remembering—but not simply to set the record straight. Instead, as he wrote in the *Messenger*, "No genuine attempt by Organized Labor to wrest any worthwhile and lasting concessions from the Employing Class can succeed as long as Organized Labor for the most part is indifferent and in opposition to the fate of Negro Labor." In 2020, a hundred years on, the working class has yet to catch up to Fletcher and his union. For those who wish for a socialist world or, as the Wobblies proclaimed more than a century ago, "to build a new society from within the ashes of the old," antiracist revolutionary unions still offer a path not yet taken.

The Book's Organization

This introduction has served as a biography of Ben Fletcher or as close as possible given what is known about him. Sadly, Fletcher never wrote a memoir nor did any historian or activist conduct a life history with him. Similarly, no "Ben Fletcher Papers" ever were deposited in any library or archives, nor are there any official collection of materials on Local 8. What the US government confiscated in its 1917 raid of Local 8 disappeared long ago, quite possibly destroyed; so, too, with many IWW records. Instead, this introduction has drawn from my twenty-five years of research on Fletcher, Local 8, and the IWW.

This introduction was intentionally crafted without notes to make it more readable, but most of the quotations and evidence, in this section, are drawn from this book's documents portion. The Bibliography near the end of the book lists all the documents cited in this introduction and the documents section. I also have included a handful of scholarly works that I find useful and recommend.

The majority of this book consists of a series of documents—some quite short, none more than a few pages—that, together, chronicle Fletcher's life, especially his public life in the IWW. Every known letter or essay written by Fletcher is included as is nearly every mention of Fletcher by someone else. Historians call such documents "primary sources" for they serve as the building blocks that people interested in the past use. Primary documents are what historians examine—first and foremost—to learn the details of what happened in order to analyze them. When historians write articles and books, such as my book *Wobblies on the Waterfront*, these are labeled "secondary sources." This book is a hybrid, with the introduction written by a historian and the documents section providing a wealth of primary sources for readers to assess for themselves. To assist readers, every primary source document is introduced with a few sentences or paragraphs to provide historical context and fill in gaps. Although some annotations suggest my viewpoint, by reading primary documents for oneself, readers are able to draw their own conclusions. Part of the beauty of history is that reasonable people examining the same evidence might develop different interpretations. In crafting this book in this manner, readers can be their own historians, engaged in the detective work necessary to unearth the past in order to learn from it. In addition to the desire to give Ben Fletcher his due, this volume also was created to let readers decide for themselves what to think about Fletcher, the IWW, and the history of radical unionism.

One of the Wobblies' many great mantras is "agitate, educate, organize." Hopefully, this book will help educate readers. By providing a deeper understanding of the past, they can engage in more agitation and organizing because the struggle continues to make the world we want to live in. Solidarity forever!

WRITINGS AND SPEECHES BY AND ABOUT BEN FLETCHER

1

Soapboxer

This brief report is the first-ever mention of Fletcher in the public record (aside from his entries in the 1900 and 1910 US census). It is not certain when he joined the IWW though quite possibly in 1910. In 1912, at twenty-two years of age, Fletcher already was an activist.

The IWW had been organizing in Philadelphia for years, chartering its first local—of Hungarian metalworkers—in 1907. Like Philadelphia, Chester lies along the banks of the Delaware River, about fifteen miles south (downriver).

The magazine *Solidarity* was one of the IWW's two main English-language publications in that era. That the IWW already sought to organize African American workers is noteworthy since few other unions in the United States then did so due to pervasive racism.

We are pushing the work of propaganda around the [town]. Held a meeting at the corner of Third and Edgemont streets. Chester. On Saturday, July 20, with Benjamin H. Fletcher as the main speaker. Fellow Worker Fletcher is the only colored speaker we have here, and certainly knows how to deliver the goods. The crowd was very attentive, taking to everything the speaker had to say regarding the class struggle. We sold a bunch of *Solidarity* and a lot of literature. The negro workers are greatly interested in the IWW, and I believe we shall get a local started in Chester in the near future, as there is a bunch of colored workers anxious for the One Big Union.

H. Marston, job hustler

■ *Solidarity*, July 22, 1912, 4.

2

On the Importance of the IWW Press

These are the first two articles known to have been written by Ben Fletcher. Before helping found and lead Local 8 (longshore workers), Fletcher belonged to and was a leader in Local 57, which the IWW called a "mixed local." These were established in many cities where membership numbers did not yet justify industry-specific locals. Almost certainly, the majority—perhaps the great majority—of Local 57 members were European immigrants or of European descent, so it is noteworthy that Fletcher was elected to an office, an early example of the antiracism of the IWW in Philadelphia.

FOR THE CONVENTION.
To All Locals and Members of the IWW
Fellow Workers:
Philadelphia, Pa., July 2.

The Local 57, IWW, in regular meeting have passed the following motion, and are forwarding same to General Secretary-Treasurer Vincent St. John for him to send to *Industrial Worker* and *Solidarity*, for your seconding, with comments.

Motion: That the seventh annual convention of the Industrial Workers of the World devise ways and means of furnishing all members of the Industrial Workers of the World with the *Industrial Worker* and *Solidarity*, as an OFFICIAL ORGAN composed of the two papers, free of charge. The cost of same to be met by increasing the per capita tax to General Headquarters, or by re-apportionment of same.

BENJAMIN H. FLETCHER,
Corresponding Secretary

The time is here when the IWW must put their press beyond the pale of want and uncertainty. We would have you understand that without a press (properly established) the IWW is minus the most potent power of the age.

If we organized every textile worker in the IWW within the next six months unless the influence and circulation of our press increased correspondingly we would have builded [built] on the "Shining Sands" of ignorance.

If this motion is adopted it means the success of the IWW press will be assured, its power will develop, and the spirit of industrial freedom will soon triumph through the agitation and educational work of a well established press of the Industrial Workers of the World. Therefore, we hereby call for seconds to the motion.

(Signed)

BENJAMIN H. FLETCHER,
Cor. Sec. No. 57

■ *Solidarity*, August 8, 1912, 3.

3

The Seventh Convention of the IWW

One of numerous examples throughout the IWW literature where Fletcher, among other African Americans, was highlighted as proof of the union's inclusive nature. Aside from Local 8, the Brotherhood of Timber Workers (BTW) was the most successful IWW effort at recruiting black workers; from 1910 to 1913, many thousands of black and white timber and mill workers in Louisiana and Texas joined the BTW only to suffer ferocious repression from employers, police, and government officials. Although the IWW encouraged every worker to become a member, regardless of race or ethnicity, relatively few African Americans did so.

Chicago, Sept. 22 [1912]

The fighting Brotherhood of Timber Workers is represented by seven delegates who come with instructions from the membership of that organization to amalgamate with the IWW. One of the most encouraging developments in the American labor movement is the splendid band of rebels that has sprung up in the Southland within the past two years. Their delegates are able and aggressive upon the floor of the convention and, if the membership of the BTW is permeated with the same spirit of revolt which they manifest, there is no doubt that much will be gained for the IWW by the affiliation.

Proof that we have surmounted all barriers of race and color is here in the presence of delegates of many nationalities as well as that of two colored delegates, B.H. Fletcher from Philadelphia and D.B. Gordon of the BTW. Both of the latter are taking active part in the convention and show a clear understanding of the great idea of One Big Union of the whole working class.

■ *Solidarity*, September 28, 1912, 1.

4

Philadelphia Organizing

An excerpt from IWW organizer James Thompson's annual report indicating that the IWW was active in a variety of industries in Philadelphia, especially textiles, which employed more workers than any other in the city. Thompson also highlighted the important role that Fletcher played—prior to the chartering of Local 8. Notably, few textile workers were African American, meaning that Fletcher was organizing among European immigrants and European Americans.

In the better part of April in answer to telegram from Fellow Worker Fletcher, I went to Philadelphia. A joint meeting of two independent unions of carpet weavers had been arranged and I was sent for to address them.

These two unions, with a total membership of 1,800, joined the IWW. This gave us a good foothold among the textile workers in Philadelphia. They now have shop control in 11 different shops in that city.

Philadelphia is a good field for organizing work.

Fellow Worker St. John having written to me that he would route me West, I remained in Philadelphia all during the month of May.

I spoke before the different organizations of the IWW, held open-air meetings, and so on, expecting each day to receive word from St. John to start West.

James P. Thompson's Report:
As General Organizer, to the Seventh IWW Convention

■ *Solidarity*, October 26, 1912, 3.

5

The Strike at Little Falls

Published just two months before Local 8 was founded, Fletcher wrote about a lengthy, victorious IWW strike of textile workers in Little Falls, New York. Matilda Rabinowitz (anglicized to Robbins) was a Ukrainian-born Jewish woman long active in the IWW. The largest employer of workers in Philadelphia also was in textiles, and the IWW's largest textile strike occurred in nearby Paterson, New Jersey, in the spring of 1913. The previous year's "Bread and Roses" strike by textile workers in Lawrence, Massachusetts, remains among the IWW's most well-known. Despite never having graduated high school, Fletcher demonstrated great sophistication in his writing.

PHILADELPHIA WORKERS: Listen to Matilda Rabinowitz's Eloquent Appeal in Behalf of Little Falls Victims
Philadelphia, Pa., Feb. 24

In a manner that was convincing, with an eloquence that charmed, Fellow Worker Matilda Rabinowitz for an hour and a half drove home fact after fact that left no doubt in the minds of her audience that a damnable conspiracy has been entered into by the textile barons of America and their corrupt, servile courts of New York, to railroad to the penitentiary Bochino, Legere, Vaughan and other fellow workers now awaiting trial in Herkimer county jail. Their only "crime" is that they aided the striking "ignorant foreign" textile workers of Little Falls to triumph over their brutal, slave driving textile barons who, in their mad race for profits, had made conditions of their slaves so unbearable that they were forced to revolt or starve.

Owing to a misunderstanding by the proprietor of the hall hired for the occasion, a meeting of garment workers was scheduled for the same hour, which resulted in a small attendance for our meeting. This, however, had no effect upon the spirit or ardor of those present, as enthusiasm and applause were both prominent throughout Fellow Worker Rabinowitz's address, in which she portrayed in a masterly manner the conditions imposed upon Little Falls workers by the textile bosses: unsanitary conditions, increased speed of machines, low wages and strikebreaking policemen, some of them members of the AF of L.

In the evening, Miss Rabinowitz made a five minutes' appeal before the Revolutionary Laborers' Club, and was given $8.75, making a total of $23.50 as Philadelphia's contribution to the defense fund for the day. At the Lyric Hall meeting, ringing protest resolutions were adopted and forwarded to Governor Sulzer. Preparations are being made in revolutionary circles for a united protest demonstration in behalf of militants everywhere. Philadelphia is on the move.

BEN FLETCHER

■ *Solidarity*, March 1, 1913.

6

The Eighth Convention of the IWW

At the IWW's Eighth Convention, in Chicago in 1913, Ben Fletcher attended as a delegate from Local 8, the longshoremen's union recently born out of its victorious, two-week strike. He proved quite active, demonstrating intimate knowledge of the inner-workings of the IWW. Curiously, Fletcher's name never was mentioned in reports of that strike despite being the most prominent, perhaps only, black IWW activist in Philadelphia and despite the fact that one-third of Philadelphia longshoremen were African American. During one of his convention speeches, Fletcher discussed traveling to Norfolk and Baltimore; what he did not mention was that he undertook a previous trip, during Local 8's strike, to persuade black dockworkers to refuse to work as strikebreakers in Philadelphia.

Another of Fletcher's speeches joined a lengthy debate on charges leveled by the General Executive Board (GEB) against a member. Fletcher spoke at length and provided some details about Local 8 as well as his views on the issue of centralization which proved increasingly divisive and, in 1924, culminated in a deadly schism over the "Emergency Program." He also offered thoughts as to why workers join the IWW and, more broadly, how the union organizes for both short- and long-term goals while making clear his commitment to class struggle, industrial unionism, and being a "fighting" union.

FLETCHER: Fellow Worker Chairman and Fellow Workers, on the question of the abolition of the General Executive Board, I wish to state this, that the discussion, as the General Secretary and Treasurer stated Saturday, every one up to now has wandered away from the subject matter. I think that it would behoove us to come right back to that subject, which is, as the motion now stands before the house, that General Executive Board shall not be abolished?

Now the reasons that have been presented here as to why the General Executive Board should be abolished, have not appealed to me for many reasons. First, so far as I am concerned, I have been convinced by the arguments presented on the other side that they are not at the present time at least aware, they do not possess the knowledge of the structure, aims and hopes of the IWW and that, to my mind, is essential and necessary if the question of the abolition of the General Executive Board is to carry in this convention. Now, let us consider some of the arguments that have been introduced or given as to why the General Executive Board shall be abolished.

Fellow Worker Nilsson says that one reason why the General Executive Board should be abolished is this, that it can do great harm to the organization. On that I agree. I find that they can do great harm to the organization provided the General Executive Board fails to function in the capacity for which they were elected. If the General Executive Board fails to perform their function, not only the General Executive Board, but any other of this organization, whether it be a local Trustee, whether it be a local Secretary, whether it be a President or a Vice-President of the organization, why necessarily the organization will be harmed: for it is understood when we elect representatives of this organization they are to perform certain functions and each and every time they fail to do that by embezzlement of funds or by laying down on the job or in any other manner whatsoever, why it is a fact that the organization is harmed to just the extent they fail to function.

Now then there was another argument presented here why the General Executive Board should be abolished. Fellow Worker Van Fleet stated, for instance, on Saturday that the General Executive Board should be abolished—that is understood he was talking to the question—stated that the reason why workers joined the IWW was because of the fact that they have the principle of the organization at heart, which is the abolition of wage slavery, upon that basis—that is to organize the working class upon the basis of the class struggle, organizing industrially. Now I hold that is not the prime reason why the working class joins the IWW: that the prime reason why the working class joins the IWW is first because of the fact that they are seeking more wages and shorter hours. See! Now then they are not necessarily revolutionary because of the fact that they join the IWW upon those grounds and if they fail to join the IWW because of the fact they do not accept the principles of the IWW is, in my mind, no fault of the General Executive Board.

Now then there has been presented by Fellow Worker McEvoy, which is not pro to the subject of the abolition of the General Executive Board and wandering away from the subject, and I might as well speak on it, that the rank and file is not satisfied with the functioning of the General Executive Board, relative to the Smith-Heselwood controversy and when asked who is the rank and file he mentioned that seventeen locals went on record against the decision of the General Executive Board and I advance this argument that out of seventeen locals—I venture to say this that we have one local in Philadelphia made up of rank and file [Local 8, established in May 1913] that has more members than his entire seventeen locals today and so far as that is concerned if it was submitted to them the decision of the General Executive Board on the Smith-Heslewood proposition would carry.

If it was submitted to them, for instance, whether the General Executive Board should be affirmed, why they would vote without any question a majority in favor of the General Executive Board. For instance Local 8, Philadelphia has two thousand members paid up to date: has about thirty-five hundred members within three months that are the rank and file of the IWW as well as the 17 locals who have gone on record against the General Executive Board and I say that they haven't had anything to say on this question.

And again it has been stated that the General Executive Board has never functioned. Now I refer to the Constitution. First, the Constitution says: "Section 1, Article 111. The General Executive Board shall be composed of the General Secretary-Treasurer, the General Organizer, and one member from each National Industrial Department"—and then further on in Section 2, it states: "The General Executive Board shall have general supervision of the entire affairs of the organization between Conventions and watch vigilantly over the interests throughout its jurisdiction."

Now just stopping there, I want to state this. Now a situation arose in Philadelphia that has a direct bearing upon this particular clause in the Constitution. When I came back from the South, I had gone as far as Norfolk, Virginia. I found the organization of the IWW in a chaotic state. In fact, it was on the point of being disrupted entirely by men who were opposed to having a General Executive Board in the IWW, by men who held that the rank and file should run their own business without any interference from any central headquarters or General Headquarters whatsoever, and this, as I have stated, brought about a chaotic state of affairs because it developed later that the only reason that these men did not want the General Executive Board or the representative from the General Headquarters to interfere was because of the fact that they did not want any interference in their getting next to the workers' money.

For instance, they met, held a meeting, a mass meeting of the restaurant workers, who voted $115.00 to organize themselves into the IWW, and $10.00 was to come to the General Headquarters, but even the $10.00

charter fee did not come to the General Headquarters, but they kept it themselves. That was brought forth by representatives from the General Headquarters, and this peculiar state of affairs went further than that. The situation was worse than that.

CHAIRMAN: Two minutes, Fellow Worker.

FLETCHER: Two minutes! I might have to have a little extension of time on this proposition. Now, the matter of fact is this, they shout about the rank and file, and there in Philadelphia despite these conditions the rank and file is hardly ever considered. It is a fact that the Italian Workers, for instance, the building workers, got together and wanted Fellow Workers Ettor and Giovannitti to come over there to speak to them and I have the evidence right here on the floor of the Convention that when the motion was made in the Central Committee, it was called a district council, when the motion was made the Fellow Worker Ettor be asked to come over and organize amongst the Italian Workers—the Italian delegates themselves will state that the motion was not put on the floor because someone representing the other side, the so-called decentralizers, were not in favor of the proposition, and when the Italian Workers learned that they, the rank and file, had been ignored in this matter, they, in a business meeting, regularly assembled took account of the state of affairs in the Philadelphia District Council and practically decided to confine their efforts of promoting the IWW to their own local.

Afterwards they got in touch with me, that is, their Secretary [Local 57], and after going over the situation at length advised me to communicate with Fellow Worker Ettor and have him come to Philadelphia just as soon as possible. I did so.

The IWW to begin with is an organization that has got to fight and regardless of the sectionalism that has been prevalent here, I am satisfied that all the delegates, East and West, and North and South, are agreed upon that proposition that it is an organization that has got to fight and I hold this that if it has got to fight that the least disturbance, and the less trimmings, or the things that will tie its hands, the things that tie the organization or the hands of its representatives and prevents them from acting, that the less of this nonsense we have the better fight we will be able to put up against the employing class.

In the Board of Directors' meeting of the steel trust about a year ago a proposition was presented by a stockholder carrying something like twenty-seven votes . . .

CHAIRMAN: Time, Fellow Worker Fletcher.

MCDERMOTT: I move he be granted ten minutes. (Seconded.)

CHAIRMAN: It is moved and seconded that Fellow Worker Fletcher be . . .

O'BRIEN (interrupting): I object to this.

CHAIRMAN: Fellow Worker O'Brien. Delegate Flynn's time and other was extended. It is moved and seconded that Fellow Worker Fletcher's time be extended. How much time do you want to give him?

MCDERMOTT: Ten minutes.

KOETTGEN: I second it.

CHAIRMAN: All in favor raise your right hand. (Vote occurs.) The ayes have it.

FLETCHER: I was stating that the steel trust had a meeting. Now my object in stating this is only to show you how the ruling class, just what little regard they have for the philosophy or technical reasons advanced here on the floor of this Convention on the question of power—they had a meeting, and one fellow there, who puts me in mind of the Fellow Workers here who are deducing and presenting the argument for the abolition of the General Executive Board, was a reformer. Now I refer to you, Fellow Workers, as reformers. Now, then, this reformist element of the steel trust presented a motion to the effect that in view of the fact that the working class who were paying them dividends and high salaries and so forth were being worked, overworked in their mills and foundries to the extent of eleven or twelve or fourteen hours a day in some instances that an investigation should be held.

See that an investigation should be held, and if those conditions existed that immediately steps should be taken to reduce the hours to eight hours or bring about conditions in the mills that would make them more humanitarian, more satisfactory to humanity, so Mr. Gary, I believe that is his name, Judge Gary, he carried a million votes. Now he carried over ninety per cent of the number of votes. Each share of stock counts a vote, and he carried over ninety per cent of the voters of steel trust, by proxy. He voted that an investigation be held. Now I just go that far to show you just what absolute disregard they had for the idea of power, selfishness or any other thing that the reformers were squealing about.

The result was simply this, that the steel trust reported that in the year 1912 its dividends were bigger, saying it was successful as an institution of industry, business was growing—see! And I hold that the same thing out to apply to the IWW.

The General Executive Board, it has further been slated upon the floor, has never functioned. Now I am going to present to you a fact that has not been disputed: there are instances in the beginnings where the General Executive Board did function. I hold that it has functioned a thousand and one times, and I will present to you this argument, that the General Executive Board did function in the Great Falls controversy where a local had signed a contract with the employing class, where a member of the General Executive Board did go up there and the charter revoked through his action.

Now, if that is a fact, and you agree on that, I ask you this, in what other way could the IWW have saved itself of dishonor, disgrace, and so forth, that would necessarily have occurred had this local remained in the IWW with a contract with the employing class? What would you have substituted? You say you would have substituted in a referendum, a proposition that I have lost sight of years ago. But you say a referendum, then I am going to ask you if it is not a fact that if you had had a referendum in vogue on that particular and that referendum would have been initiated if it would have not have taken at least three months to have gotten the proposition throughout the country and it would also have taken at least two or three months to have gotten it initiated.

Now, then, if this referendum can get the local to withdraw from the IWW wouldn't it have been in line for them and their colleagues to have initiated another referendum counteracting the referendum just sent out? Now then, your answer is yes, because there is no other answer. I state this, that it is a fact that we have a GEB, and it is a fact that the GEB in that particular case did act, and they acted in the interests of the organization.

Now, it has been stated here that the GEB has caused some sort of chaotic state of the organization, has caused the organization to lose economic power; now I hold this, that any influence on the IWW that is harmful causes us to lose economic power. Now, it is a fact that the organization in 1911 reported $28,000 in receipts; that in 1912, with the GEB, with all its "autocratic" power, the organization increased in receipts

100% to $56,220.25—that this Executive Board, with all its "autocratic power, with all its despotic despotism," the local membership increased in the IWW from 154 locals, organized in 1911, to 262 locals, organized in 1912, a clear gain of 108 locals in good standing; that this organization with its "autocratic and despotic" GEB, had in 1911 organized 132 locals, and in 1912 had organized 236, see!

Now, Fellow Workers, in conclusion I want to state this, that if the IWW is to function, it first must be an organization that is based upon the class struggle; that is, organizing the workers industrially, and while this might be second, it is just as necessary that the IWW be a fighting organization; third, that it must have no shields; and when I say this, I mean that it must not have anything in the organization to which the workers can look to, rely upon to save them possibly from some power or from some "autocracy" that might occur in the organization. For instance, I refer in this particular instance to the referendum. Now, it has been my experience, and as well observation before joining the IWW, that the working class in general are given to looking for something to save them in any organization of the working class; for instance, in the Socialist Party they have a referendum, the "rumdum," as I call it. This rumdum is supposed to save them from the [Morris] Hillquits or the John Spargos and, as a matter of fact, it does not, and with all of that I claim that the Socialist Party is functioning as it was intended to function. It was intended to function that way; that is, that the rumdum act as a shield, and it is making good regardless of opinions to the contrary.

The fact that the AFL has a GEB and has built up a machine that no other machine on the inside of that organization is competent to successfully compete with and exist, is only an argument in favor of a GEB, and I am surprised that members come here representing the brains of the organization—deduce that argument as to why a GEB should be abolished in the IWW when as a matter of fact, the AFL, with its GEB and with its coterie of officers under the control of that GEB, are successful as a craft union and function just as it is intended to function and no more, and if that argument is deduced here against the GEB in the IWW, then I have this to say on the question, that we ought to go to work and build up just such a proposition in confirming with the IWW.

At the 1913 Convention, a battle erupted between, on one side, New York and Philadelphia delegates wanting local control in citywide District Councils as opposed to the Chicago-based GEB, wanting more control. Considering that, in 1920, the IWW suspended Local 8 for not following the rules established in the Constitution, it is interesting to see Fletcher's position here—and how he seemed to be a central player.

FLETCHER: I am speaking offhand and will state this, if my memory serves me right on this matter, it is like this: I returned from Norfolk, Va., about the 15th of July, and arrived in Philadelphia about a week later, about the 20th or 21st. There was a meeting held of the District Council, and subsequently there was a meeting held by members who were electioneering to be elected as delegates to the Eighth Annual Convention of the IWW. They had a little caucus and after this caucus they had a joint meeting of Locals 56 and 57.

At this joint meeting a motion was passed that J.F. Miller, now secretary of District Council, Philadelphia, be elected to go to New York to interview Fellow Worker [Thomas] Flynn on the question of whether or not he would accept the nomination of Philadelphia in the Convention as General Secretary-Treasurer. Now that in itself would not mean much, that is that Fellow Worker Miller be elected as a representative of the local from Philadelphia to go to New York to interview Fellow Worker Flynn as to his candidacy for the position of General Secretary-Treasurer of the IWW, but it seems there was a communication received from New York in which there was some reference made to this subject, because I know this much, that there was a letter received from New York, in the possession of [Joseph] Weitzen, Philadelphia, in which the matter of Flynn, as a possible candidate in this coming Convention was mentioned—of course you couldn't possibly get anything definite on the matter, because if you were to ask for the records now why they wouldn't have them—see!

But it was a common saying around the IWW headquarters and the IWW circles, in fact, that Flynn was going to be the nominee in the Eighth Convention, and [Simon] Kneble [actually Knebel, head of Philadelphia District Council], at one time they had two candidates, that is, [Peter] Warwick and Flynn, and two candidates for the General Organizer, Ed. Lewis [active in Local 8's initial strike] and Simon Kneble [who also was]; that is, they had two candidates, two sets of candidates, and after this explosion and the plans went up in smoke, why then, it was reduced to Fellow Worker Flynn.

Fletcher spoke many times on the abusive power of the GEB in Philadelphia and on conflicts between the IWW and Socialist Party then reaching a crescendo nationwide:

FLETCHER: I can say this, that it was a General Executive Board member, requested by the National Industrial Union of Marine Transport Workers' Secretary, after he himself, this particular National Secretary, had gone to Philadelphia and aroused such antagonism against the General Executive Board and machine in the IWW, with autocratic and despotic powers: it was that same Secretary that appealed to the Holy GEB to this end, through his coterie of followers, to save the IWW in Philadelphia so far as the Marine Transport Workers are concerned.

SAUTTER: I would like to ask, through the chair, is the IWW organized to educate the working class, or is it organized to organize dollars?

FLETCHER: In the IWW? Well, I can answer that, too. Just to suit him. The IWW is organized both ways; to get both things. (Applause.)

CHAIRMAN: Order! One at a time. Fellow Worker Fletcher, are you willing to answer those questions?

FLETCHER: Yes.

NILSSON: How many copies of the *Industrial Worker* does that Philadelphia Local take per week?

FLETCHER: I can answer you. They don't get one, because of this fact, see, that officials not of that Local Union, see but of that national body, who had more influence in the union than the local officers, were not catering to the IWW Press, but more or less were busy with the Social Wag.

O'BRIEN: May I ask two questions through the floor? (Laughter.) How many Socialist Party papers is this local getting at the present time and have got?

FLETCHER: What local?

O'BRIEN: That you speak of.

FLETCHER: Not any that I know of.

O'BRIEN: Is he aware that it is the referendum that ratifies all our actions here?

FLETCHER: Yes. Now he wants to know if I am aware that it is the rumdum that will ratify our actions here, and I will say yes, and that so far as I am concerned personally I am not in favor of that proposition because that is only another myth, a shield, a proposition—like that which the membership in general is being educated to . . . that we installed as representatives of this organization—and I am in favor of something like this, that the IWW hold a convention, of an industry that the locals in that industry have representation that shall stand upon the membership they have in contract, that those representatives of that industry meet, and when they meet, that they shall not be hampered or anything like that as regards instructions and all that bull-com, but they shall meet, free and equal, upon the floor of the Convention and decide things pertaining to that industry, and pass laws, rules and regulations, guiding themselves for the incoming year, see, subject to no referendum; subject to the majority vote of that Convention. Now that is my idea of how the IWW should be run.

VAN FLEET: I would like to ask him a question. If these Philadelphia locals know anything about the Heslewood affair, how does he know that they would answer one way or another?

FLETCHER: I will just tell you. When I came back from the South, the proposition that I met and the condition I met in the IWW was practically chaotic. The organization was all disbanded and disrupted. A committee of the rank and file, elected at a regular meeting, came to me and said: "Now look here, Fletcher, we are fair and honest," and before asking me my opinion they said: "God Damn! If this thing keeps on very much longer we are going to quit; it is nothing but a pie-card organization," and they would refer to the individuals leading the so-called conflict against the IWW.

Why, they had gotten so far as to arrange a slate of officers who were going to be nominated on this floor and these men were going to be here and all they were going to do were to be seated around the wall and just wave their finger and move their lips as to how motions were go to. They had gone so far as to hold a caucus meeting where members not holding to those views were not allowed to enter the hall when it was going on.

SAUTTER: Fellow Worker Fletcher stated only a moment ago that they did not take one *Industrial Worker* into the local union.

FLETCHER: I didn't say that; so far as Local 8 was concerned they didn't take one.

SAUTTER: Then he stated that those locals had a larger membership than the seventeen locals of the West.

FLETCHER: Yes.

SAUTTER: Now I have a letter in my pocket from the Editor of *Solidarity*, stating this, that the local unions of California take more bundle orders of *Solidarity* than the whole East combined, and I would like to ask this question, if they do not take the *Industrial Worker* and *Solidarity*, what papers do they take in the East?

KOETTGEN: Objection.

FLETCHER: I will answer it.

CHAIRMAN: Delegate Webert has the floor.

FLETCHER: Fellow Worker Chairman, won't you allow me to . . .

CHAIRMAN: This is not a contest, but a Convention of the IWW. Do you want to answer that question?

FLETCHER: The talk that I made answered the question that had you been paying attention, because I told you, in so many words, that the IWW was in control of an aggregation there in Philadelphia that was not in the control of the IWW, to advance the IWW and, therefore, since they were not in control of the organization to advance the IWW but their particular selfish interests; therefore, the IWW Press and the IWW as a whole suffered to that extent.

CHAIRMAN: Delegate Webert has the floor.

ETTOR: Fellow Worker Chairman, I would like to ask Fellow Worker Fletcher if it isn't a fact that the element in Philadelphia in favor of doing away with the General Executive Board and decentralizing this organization, that the one who was on the slate for National Organizer [Knebel] has in his possession seventy-five dollars, in his possession, without the knowledge of the local union, which gave it to him to send in to the General Headquarters with the knowledge of General headquarters who was supposed to receive it?

FLETCHER: I will state yes, and further state that it is a fact that the local union paid to the man slated for General Organizer of the IWW, paid in seventy-five dollars per capita tax, and we have here the documents and receipts to go before the Grievance Committee and the Convention will have to make disposition of that or else the local will have to go out of the IWW.

The debate over decentralization, specifically through the abolition of the General Executive Board continued on; ultimately, the GEB was retained. However, the issue of how much power the central administration should have in the IWW remained a festering conflict that erupted in the 1920 Philadelphia Controversy and 1924 Emergency Program.

7

War on the Waterfront

After the city's deep-sea longshoremen lined up under the IWW banner in May 1913, in Local 8, they proceeded to organize other waterfront workers on the Delaware River, including on tugboats and drays (horse-drawn carts used for moving cargo short distances). In so doing, they followed the industrial union-ism ideal: all workers in a given industry had to be organized together, other-wise those in unions were vulnerable to being undercut by nonunion workers, and one union could be on strike while members of another union continued working, "union scabs" in Wobbly parlance. Not surprisingly, Wobbly organizers were harassed, beaten, and jailed by local police and unfairly sentenced by local judges. This report in *Solidarity* also reveals Fletcher's ongoing activism on and off the waterfront.

Break This Conspiracy of the Shipping Trust
Philadelphia, Pa., Feb. 23.

Fellow Worker John J. McKelvey, organizer of Branch 4 [Local 8], Marine Transport Workers [MTW], IWW, with two other fellow workers, is in jail. Although convicted by a jury of their "peers" Dec. 17th, and committed on the 18th pending the hearing of their appeal, they have not yet been sentenced.

If this case is to have a proper presentation, it will be necessary to relate a little history. A battle was waged in this city last summer between the Marine Transport Workers and their employers, the shipping trust, for more control of industry.

After many unsuccessful attempts to use scabs, police, gunmen, bribery, race prejudice, etc., to break their ranks, the shipping trust was forced to surrender to the solidarity of labor.

Realizing the power wrought up in an organization of workers so trained and fitted, they proceeded to make those of the Industrial Workers of the World, who had paved the way for this organization in the port of Philadelphia, victims of their vengeance.

Being aware that for diverse reasons McKelvey had contributed no little part to the victory of the transport workers, they selected him for the first victim. So one evening while walking the public highway he was arrested by Sergeant Peoples, who, in keeping with his instructions, began beating him up with a blackjack, next with his revolver, after he had thrown his bulky form across him.

McKelvey was jailed, convicted at his trial, and sentenced to 60 days, which he served. Not being a "quitter," McKelvey upon being released, got active immediately and played his part in lining up the Boatmen—Branch 4, MTW, IWW, who won hands down in their struggle for better conditions, shorter hours and more wages.

All but two lines—Tucker and Oliver—surrendered. It was while they were proceeding to organize the workers of those lines that McKelvey, Loux and Wilmot were arrested. It was charged that these fellow workers conspired to beat up scabs—Loux charged with being the principal; McKelvey and Wilmot the accessories. This being based on the testimony of a detective.

Judge Kinsey overdid himself at their trial in impressing the jury that a conviction was desired. He stated in his charge: "If you gentlemen *suspect* that these defendants had either a MENTAL or ORAL understanding, they are guilty."

They were convicted Dec. 12th, and to date have not been sentenced. The shipping trust and their henchmen do not want McKelvey to be at liberty; neither does Judge Kinsey, who, since McKelvey has been in jail, has asked him very inferentially what he would do when released.

These are the facts in the case, and alone are sufficient evidence of a damnable conspiracy. To you, members of the IWW in Philadelphia and all other workers, is dedicated the duty of forcing the release of our outraged fellow workers.

You must get together. Act quickly and resolve that you are going to make this attempt on the part of a fossilized judicial lickspittle and the shipping interests to railroad to the penitentiary these working men, so costly that they'll forever remember with regret the price they paid if they dare to consummate their damnable conspiracy.

Hold meetings of your organization and send delegates to the McKelvey, Loux and Wilmot Defense Conference which meets every Wednesday evening at 128 South 8th St., Philadelphia.

Hold meetings and demand the release of McKelvey, Loux and Wilmot. Serve notice on the master class that we are not going to permit our fellow workers to be sacrificed.

On and off the job make the power of a class conscious protest heard everywhere.

This is the time to act! Do it today. Get busy immediately.

A protest meeting will be held Sunday, March 1, at 2 P.M, at Lyric hall, 928 S. 6th St. Speakers—General Organizer Wm. D. Haywood, in English, and others in Polish, Italian and Lithuanian languages.

BENJ. H. FLETCHER,
Chairman Press Committee

■ *Solidarity,* February 28, 1914.

Ralph Chaplin, "What Time Is It?"

8

Solidarity Wins in Philadelphia

Fletcher discussed the release of three imprisoned local activists, suggesting that the power of working-class organization scared the courts into releasing the Wobblies. That there was no solid evidence of the three's guilt also may have played a role.

McKelvey, Loux and Wilmot Released from Jail on Suspended Sentence

Another victory was scored by the IWW last week in Philadelphia. McKelvey, Loux and Wilmot were liberated from the capitalist hellhole, Moyamensing prison, February 19. Although sentenced to one year on probation, we are more than confident that the subservient lickspittles of the shipping trust will not dare lay their hands again on these fellow workers for that account.

McKelvey, Loux and Wilmont were convicted December 13, 1913, on a charge of mentally conspiring to beat scabs and "get Tucker." Tucker is one of the shipowners that refused to grant the demands of the workers during the boatmen's strike last fall.

A defense conference was organized shortly after their imprisonment. For obvious reasons the conference at first pursued the method of "watchful waiting." The judge, a faithful lieutenant of the parasites, took advantage of the conference's policy. He kept McKelvey and the other two fellow workers in jail for nine weeks, while making up his mind as to what sentence should be pronounced upon them, without arriving at any conclusion.

The up till now, somewhat slumbering rebels began to feel aggravated. The conference changed its tactics. The IWW began to manifest itself. A local newspaper, sympathizing with the working class, gave publicity to the case, arousing public sentiment. The different labor organizations readily answered the call for support. But the most essential factor that contributed to the release of the three fellow workers is the mighty weapon possessed by the waterfront slaves—the Marine

Transport Workers' Union of the IWW. The judge before sentencing the prisoners questioned Tucker as to his feelings toward McKelvey, Loux and Wilmont, to which he replied that he no longer held any grievance against them. The reason for it is as follows: As it reached the ear of the shipping trust that Bill Haywood was coming to Philadelphia March 1st, to have a consultation with the Marine Transport Workers relative to the imprisonment of the three fellow workers, Tucker's heart suddenly expanded to make room for a "Christian magnanimity" that was traveling with lightning speed towards his auricles and ventricles. This is what labor can do everywhere if organized. Make the bosses become "magnanimous."

BENJ. H. FLETCHER,
JAS. A. LEVINE

■ *Solidarity*, Philadelphia, March 3, 1914.

9

Free Ford and Suhr!

Philadelphia Wobblies regularly organized meetings to recognize the efforts of and protest repression against fellow workers in other locales. The Ford and Suhr case became one such cause after two Wobblies, working in California, were arrested for murder, a crime they had not committed. What had been happening was an IWW initiative to rally thousands of oppressed farm workers, from dozens of ethnic groups, to demand better wages and conditions.

Philadelphia, April 1.

Last Sunday afternoon a rousing protest meeting, well attended, was held at Grandese Theatre, in behalf of Ford and Suhr, who were recently sentenced to life imprisonment in California. The speakers were Joseph J. Ettor, J. J. McKelvey, himself recently spared from the penitentiary because of Labor's solidarity, and Edmondo Rossoni, associate editor of "Il Proletario." All three speakers covered the subject thoroughly and made stirring addresses.

A good-sized collection was taken up for the appeal now being sought for Ford and Suhr, also resolutions of protest demanding that the governor of California take action in behalf of our fellow workers were adopted unanimously. The meeting adjourned with more than one spirit resolved that Ford and Suhr shall not rot within the walls of the California penitentiary, if the solidarity of labor prevails.

BEN FLETCHER

■ *Solidarity*, April 11, 1914, 4.

10

Transport Workers Strike in Philadelphia

In May 1913, F.W. Taylor of Charles M. Taylor's Sons, a grain brokerage firm, had negotiated the original employer agreement with Local 8. Subsequently, Taylor was castigated by his fellow employers, which might explain his intransigence in this victorious Local 8 strike in early 1915.

Fletcher's article also discussed James Larkin, a leading trade unionist and Irish Republican, who cofounded Chicago's famous Dill Pickle Club with Jack Jones. Like his fellow Irish radical James Conolly, who also lived in the States for several years and belonged to the IWW, Larkin was a "syndicalist," a believer in militant industrial unionism, and fiercely committed to working-class solidarity. In 1915, Larkin spoke to the thousands who gathered, in Chicago, to memorialize Joe Hill after his execution in the state of Utah.

Philadelphia, Pa. Feb. 7

On January 27th, following a mass meeting of the grain trimmers in the port of Philadelphia, a strike was begun for an increase from 20 cents to 60 cents an hour, 90 cents an hour for overtime work, $1.20 an hour for all Sunday and holiday work.

The strike was settled with all boss stevedores, with the exception of Chas. M. Taylor, at the following scale: 40 cents an hour for a working day of ten hours, 60 cents an hour for overtime work, 80 cents an hour for all Sunday and holiday work.

52635—IWW

Chas. M. Taylor decided not to grant the increase and has locked out the union from his ships and docks. He has joined hands with Steve Shell, the chief mogul of the Hamburg-American line scab docks and by using Mr. Shell's scabs and whatever riffraff he can secure through other sources he hopes to be able to put the IWW down and out.

The IWW has not been sleeping, it generally being recognized that this move of Mr. Taylor's is nothing less than an attempt to break the union and establish former wages—20 and 25 cents an hour and complete domination by the boss.

The IWW is maintaining a militant picket line, and besides are receiving assistance from the scabs, who are beginning to use sabotage freely.

On Feb. 2, General Organizer J. J. Ettor stopped over while en route to New York and after a conference with the strike's executive committee it was agreed that James Larkin, General Secretary Treasurer of the Irish Transport Workers' Federation should be called to address the marine transport workers. He arrived on the following Tuesday and spoke that evening. In an able and eloquent manner he portrayed the conditions of the workers generally and clearly showed how by industrial organization on the job it was possible for workers to gain control of industry. His recital of how the marine transport workers of Dublin after striking for twenty odd weeks were forced to give up the struggle and go back to work apparently defeated—yet won the strike in a few hours when they got back to work again by practicing "ca canny" that is going easy [i.e., sabotage]—brought round after round of applause which bodes no good for Chas. M. Taylor if the strikers go back to the docks defeated.

Fellow Worker Larkin pledged the support of the Irish Transport Workers if necessary and promised to present the situation in this port of dockers across the sea with a request that they hold themselves in readiness and refuse to discharge any grain or cargo from ships loaded by scab labor.

At this writing the IWW has the strike or rather lockout well in hand and will succeed in breaking the lockout and wringing their demands from Mr. Taylor if they stick together and continue to maintain a militant picket line.

BENJ. H. FLETCHER

■ *Solidarity*, February 13, 1915.

11

Philadelphia Strike Ends

This second article in as many weeks on a Local 8 strike showed both the limits of the union's power as well as its ability to persevere. The US was in the midst of a recession at that time, so unemployment was particularly high, and the waterfront was a routine destination for men out of work looking for a day's labor.

Philadelphia, Pa. Feb. 11

The strike of the Marine Transport Workers has been declared off, the men returning to work with the organization intact. Owing to a combination of influences, coupled with much unemployment, it was deemed best to return to work at the former wage and renew the fight at some more favorable time. The Chas. M. Taylor Co., against whom the strike was waged, agreed to take back all men on strike, scabs being discharged and leaving voluntarily just as fast as the IWW men return.

Benj. H. Fletcher

■ *Solidarity*, February 20, 1915.

12

The Struggle in Baltimore

Wobblies and non-Wobblies alike understood that organizing single ports was useless because the marine transport industry, by definition, was capital on the move. Thus, once Local 8 became an IWW stronghold, the organization dispatched organizers—often Fletcher—to neighboring Atlantic ports to spread the gospel. Baltimore's African American longshoremen traditionally were excluded from the AFL's waterfront union, so sending Fletcher made great sense.

"Come to Baltimore" Baltimore, Md., December 7

All you foot-loose rebels who have a hunch that you want to help organize in the east have the best chance open for you at the present time in Baltimore where we are trying to get the Marine Transport Workers and where we are glad to state we are making good progress.

The only thing this village needs is some more "organizers on the job," and knowing who the best organizers are we extend to you a hearty welcome into our busy midst.

With the aid of a few rebels on the job in the port of Baltimore we know we can line up the slaves in this port as strong as we have them in Philadelphia, where we have job control. If you rebels will come here and put in a month or two we are sure to have this port before spring and that will us the necessary strength to line up the whole Atlantic seaboard. Don't you think this is worth fighting for? If you do grab the first Pullman [train] and come.

The General Office has Fellow Worker Ben H. Fletcher here, a longshoreman who knows the industry, as well as Fellow Worker E.F. Doree and there is lots of work, so come along. Wages at present 27 to 30 cents an hour, not quite as good as at Philadelphia, with its 40, 50, and 80 cents (IWW scale) but we are here to make it as good if you rebels come.

The hall is at No. 424 W. Baltimore Street.

—Jack Lever

■ *Solidarity*, December 16, 1916, 1.

13

IWW Growing in Baltimore

Officially designated an organizer, sometime in the winter of 1916–17, Fletcher traveled on behalf of the IWW, visiting Norfolk, Baltimore, New York City, Providence, and Boston—all of which had some Wobblies on the waterfront—though he did not solely focus on dockworkers. The demographics and industries in Baltimore were similar to Philadelphia so Fletcher already had experience with southern and eastern European workers.

In spite of the last Strauss Bros. strike lost by the IWW on last September, 1916, because of a base scabbism work accomplished by the Amalgamated Clothing Workers of America—the growth of our industrial revolutionary movement in this old city goes on more and more satisfactorily. The IWW hall is in the heart of the city, 424 Baltimore St., and there workers of every nationality meet: Negroes, Polish, Italians, Lithuanians. It is interesting to relate the history of our Industrial Union No. 192 and its Italian Branch, which were the cradle of the present IWW movement in Baltimore.

BEN FLETCHER

■ *Solidarity,* February 10, 1917.

14

Providence MTW

In the same issue of *Solidarity* as the preceding piece, Fletcher reported about his organizing efforts in Providence. Fletcher might have been particularly useful there because a large number of maritime workers in this southern New England port were of African/Portuguese descent (discussed further in Document 21). Local 8 belonged to the IWW's union for the shipping industry, the Marine Transport Workers Industrial Union, sometimes called the MTW or MTWIU. Later, the MTWIU was renumbered as 510.

In the port of Providence, Rhode Island, the Marine Transport Workers are getting ready to lock out the scabs and riffraff hereabouts in their second attempt to unionize the port in the IWW. They are determined to win for themselves a better life, working conditions and more job control, regardless of whether the costs be great or small.

Being a branch of Industrial Union No. 100 of the Marine Transport Workers of the Atlantic and Gulf coasts, it will have all the support necessary—for instance, the M & M line will not find a haven of security in Boston because that port has swung into the procession also.

The members here are solidly behind the Everett [Washington] fellow workers [where a massacre of IWW members had occurred in November 1916]. We are breaking in some delegates and expect great results from this source of activity.

With every port branch in good shape, the coming convention of MTWIU 100 should be a grand success. If you are an MTW and are on the Great Lakes, stay there and help build up a powerful union; do likewise on the Pacific and Atlantic coasts. Let us workers of the docks and ships draw an iron chain of Marine Transport Workers' solidarity around the USA. We shall then be in a strategic position to force the employing class to come to the workers' terms.

BEN FLETCHER

■ *Solidarity,* February 10, 1917.

15

Boston Organizing

This article is Fletcher's first written from Boston. He commented on the ferocious rivalry between the IWW's Marine Transport Workers and AFL's International Longshoremen's Association (ILA), which controlled many American ports. Fletcher's critique of the ILA, for dividing up workers by craft and destination of cargo even in the same port, is classic IWW. Despite Fletcher's bragging, the IWW never secured a real foothold in Boston, as the ILA remained both "lily-white" and the dominant force.

    While unclear when, and the details are sparse, Fletcher married his first wife, a white woman, in Boston that summer. Carrie Danno Bartlett was born in New York City, widowed with a daughter, and lived in Boston's North End when Fletcher married her.

MARINE TRANSPORT WORKERS LINE-UP IN BOSTON
Slaves Getting Wise to ILA Tricks

The One Big Union of Marine Transport Workers has been registering so many victories over the opposition in the past few months that it is safe to state that their endeavors to extend the organization among the longshoremen of the port will be crowned with certain victory. For the time being it will be necessary to concentrate our energies on the coastwise longshoremen and coal trimmers, in view of the fact that the International Longshoremen's assassinators have entrenched them-selves among the deep-water men.

The same labor pirates have fooled quite a number of coastwise men who are wiser now than they were before. They have learned by experi-ence that a paid-up card in the ILA will not permit them to work deep-water ships, even though these ships are being discharged by other ILA members. As a longshoreman mentioned to me the other day, the "ILA is a funny union." Live wires should take notice and get on the ground here just as soon as possible. Work is brisk and there never was a better field in which so much results will accrue if those who "savvy" get on the job. The One Big Union controls forty ships out of this port and are sailing twice that many besides. It just requires a little more effort to prove to the other marine transport workers that the IWW is the ship and that all else is the deep blue sea.

BEN H. FLETCHER

■ *Solidarity*, April 14, 1917.

16

Federal Investigation of Fletcher Begins

The federal government's massive and concerted persecution of the IWW began within days of the formal US declaration of war against Germany in April 1917. Congress wasted little time, either, passing the Espionage Act of 1917, in June. This and subsequent laws were used as bludgeons to imprison thousands of Americans on shockingly flimsy grounds that many believe violated Constitutional protections. Among other elements of the war against the IWW, the US Postal Service received the authority to ban newspapers and magazines from the mails and the US Department of Justice's Bureau of Investigation (later spun off as the Federal Bureau of Investigation) looked for individuals opposed to the war and draft. Congress also passed the Sedition Act of 1918, making it a federal crime to use "disloyal, profane, scurrilous, or abusive language" toward the US Constitution, government, American uniform, or flag. These laws were interpreted quite broadly, with the IWW suffering the first and most extensive persecution.

Quite possibly sooner but no later than May 31, 1917—*before* the passage of the Espionage Act—Ben Fletcher was being surveilled by federal agents and Boston police; no doubt, such was the case for other Wobblies around the country. In September 1917, more than 150 Wobbly leaders, including Fletcher, were indicted and many arrested. As seen in this and subsequent documents, the Bureau of Investigation collaborated with many other federal agencies including military "intelligence" in the US Departments of Navy and War.

This report confirmed that Fletcher was living, not simply visiting, in Boston. His address was just north of Roxbury, which was and remains the heart of black Boston, similar to Harlem in New York City.

Agent: Henry M. Bowen
Place report made: Boston, Mass.
Date report made: June 11, 1917
Period report made about: June 7, 1917

"In re: B.H. Fletcher: European Neutrality Matter"

At Boston, Mass.:

Pursuant to instructions from Special Agent in Charge Schmid to investigate one *B.H. Fletcher* (colored) who was reported to this office by Police Officer Allen of Station 5, as under suspicion of passing out Non-Enlistment literature, and being connected with the IWW. Agent went to 542 Shawmut Avenue, Boston, where Fletcher had moved from on June 1st, to #5 Medford Court, Boston.

At #542 Shawmut Avenue I examined all the refuse and scrap papers on and around the vacated premises but could not find anything to incriminate anyone.

Agent then went to #5 Medford Court and under representation of being a Health Inspector was able to gain admittance to the one attic room occupied by *B.H. Fletcher* and his white wife and white stepdaughter, 10 years of age. The room contained one bed, one couch, one table, and three chairs, two trunks and one suitcase, and one satchel.

Office Allen reported that he found the attached circular in a suitcase when he searched Fletcher's rooms at #532 [542] Shawmut Avenue, on May 31st. He also reported that the suitcase contained letters from the IWW headquarters indicating that *Fletcher* has been receiving checks for service from that source, and that Fletcher has been operating as an organizer of the IWW.

Agent engaged *Fletcher* in general conversation about labor conditions which brought out Statements from Fletcher that he is disgusted with Labor Unions and is now very "hard up" because of labor conditions. In the meantime Agent was mentally locating the above mentioned suitcase which he saw piled up behind the only door in the room with the trunks. I also learned that Fletcher is working nights at a soap factory in Cambridge, Mass.

This matter will be followed up closely and something definite learned.

■ Ben H. Fletcher, Case Number 29434, Investigative Case Files of the Bureau of Investigation.

17

A Bad Man or Gun Fighter

Although this report stated that Fletcher already was married, Boston's Marriage Registry indicated that he did not legally marry for another six weeks. One only can speculate on Fletcher's future (personal) life had he not been indicted, arrested, found guilty, and imprisoned.

Also of interest were the rumors and racist stereotypes this report attributed to Fletcher and how he responded to the officers' queries. It seems reasonable to hypothesize that Fletcher was intentionally dishonest with the agent, for instance about no longer being an active Wobbly when he clearly was. Quite possibly, at this soap factory job, he was "salting," a term used when union organizers take a job for the express purpose to unionize the workers. Oddly, Fletcher's height and weight were quite exaggerated in this report, compared to his measurements upon arrival at Leavenworth, the following year: 5 feet 4 and 158 lb.

Agent: Henry M. Bowen
Place report made: Boston, Mass.
Date report made: July 4, 1917
Period report made about: July 3, 1917

"In re: Ben Fletcher (Colored). European Neutrality Matter"

At Boston, Mass.:
Pursuant to instructions of Special Agent Keller to further pursue the investigation of Ben Fletcher, organizer of the IWW who it was alleged by Patrolman Allen of Police Station 5 had been passing out IWW literature, and when Patrolman Allen searched the room of Fletcher he stated he saw some IWW literature in a suitcase.

Agent today made a second visit to the room of *Ben Fletcher* and his white wife and white daughter, about ten years of age, and plainly stated the allegations to *Fletcher*, and asked him if he was willing to show me the contents of his suitcase, etc. He willingly submitted to a search of all of his effects on the premises. Upon leading *Fletcher* into conversation he stated he had been organizer of IWW longshoremen, but has discovered the folly of this as he has been unable to secure or keep any kind of a job, since his connection as organizer of the IWW.

He is now employed in a soap factory in Cambridge, working nights. Fletcher did admit that he formerly kept some IWW literature at his home but when he moved recently from 542 Shawmut Ave., to 5 Medford Court he threw out all of this literature he then had.

Fletcher is the real type of "Southern Nigger agitator" with no education, poor grammar. He is about 5 ft. 9 in. in height, weighs 185 lbs.; and is reputed by the police as a bad man or gun fighter. He did not display any of that to agent.

In reference to other matters about articles purported to be written by a "Colored Citizen" in which the Draft Act is criticised does not think Fletcher capable of expressing himself in the same manner as these matters have been expressed.

Agent feels that *Fletcher* is not very harmful to the United States government.

■ Ben H. Fletcher, Case Number 29434, Investigative Case Files of the Bureau of Investigation.

18

The Rebel Girl Remembers

Elizabeth Gurley Flynn, nicknamed the "rebel girl" in a celebrated song of the same name by Joe Hill, knew Fletcher well; they even corresponded while Fletcher was in Leavenworth. Before the war, Flynn regularly traveled through Philadelphia to speak at events hosted by the IWW and other militant groups. Later, Flynn helped found the American Civil Liberties Union, a leader in the efforts to protect those persecuted in the first Red Scare, was a women's rights activist, promoted suffrage, and more. In 1936, she joined the Communist Party, continued speaking and traveling widely, and was named chairwoman of the party in 1961. Along with Ella "Mother" Bloor, Flynn was the most well-known female Communist in the US.

On September 29, 1917, Carlo [Tresca] and I were arrested on the Chicago indictment of 168 persons. I was the only woman named. Ben Fletcher of Philadelphia was the only Negro.

■ *The Rebel Girl: An Autobiography, My First Life (1906–1926).*

19

Fletcher Indicted

Here is the official indictment against Ben Fletcher. Note the specific dates that Fletcher (and other Wobblies) were accused of beginning to violate the Espionage Act: April 6, 1917, the date that the United States declared war against Germany, meaning the IWW was accused of undermining the war effort starting on the exact day Congress declared war. Also note that Congress passed the Espionage Act of 1917 on June 15, meaning the US security state moved very quickly to squash the IWW. By contrast, significant numbers of US troops did not arrive in Europe until spring 1918.

As the federal court case later made clear, the government based its claims almost exclusively on IWW statements about the war in its publications—the great majority published *prior* to the US declaration of war. No specific evidence ever was introduced against Fletcher. Rather, as a leader in an important branch of the IWW, Fletcher (and others in Local 8) were deemed a tremendous threat to the state.

To the Marshal of the Northern District of Illinois,

Greeting:

You are hereby commanded that you take Ben Fletcher if he shall be found in your district and him safely keep, so that you have his body forthwith before the Judge of the District Court of the said United States for the Northern District of Illinois, at Chicago, in the Eastern Division of the said District, to answer unto THE SAID UNITED STATES in an indictment pending in the said Court against him charging that he together with William D. Haywood and others, during the period from April 6, 1917, to September 28, 1917, at Chicago, in the Eastern Division of the Northern District of Illinois, unlawfully and feloniously did conspire by force to prevent, hinder and delay the execution of the laws of the United States pertaining to the carrying on of the war with the Imperial German Government; to injure, oppress, threaten, and intimidate citizens in the free exercise and enjoyment of the right and privilege of supplying the United States with war munitions, supplies and transportation; to commit divers offenses consisting of procuring persons to fail to comply with the registration and draft laws of the United States, and of causing disloyalty in the military and naval service; to obstruct the recruiting and enlistment service; and to commit divers offenses consisting of placing in the post office at Chicago of mail matter for the purpose of executing a scheme to defraud employers of labor; contrary to the form of the statutes of the United States in such case made and provided; viz.: Sections 6, 19 and 37 of the Criminal Code of the United States, and Section 4 of the "Espionage Act" of June 15, 1917.

And have you then and there this writ, with your return hereon.

Witness, the Hon. Kenesaw M. Landis, Judge of the District Court of the United States of America, for the Northern District of Illinois, at Chicago, aforesaid, this 28th day of September in the year of our Lord, nineteen hundred and seventeen, and in the 142nd year of the Independence of the said United States.

T.C. MacMillan, Clerk
United States of America
Northern District of Illinois, Eastern Division

■ Miscellaneous Political Records, Political Prisoners, US Department of Justice Files, National Archives, in Philip S. Foner and Ronald L. Lewis, *The Black Worker*, Vol. 5: *The Black Worker from 1900 to 1919.*

"Parting of the Ways," *One Big Union Monthly*, May 1919.

20

Fletcher Investigation Continues

Clearly, Fletcher still was living in Boston, having moved there perhaps as far back as February. His indictment was one of scores of Wobblies who, the following year, were tried in federal court in Chicago. Shortly after this report, Fletcher moved back to Philadelphia, with his wife and stepdaughter, unbeknown to the Bureau of Investigation.

Agent: Henry M. Bowen.
Place report made: Boston, Mass.
Date report made: October 8, 1917
Period report made about: October 3, 1917

"In re: Ben Fletcher: IWW Matter"

At Boston, Mass.:
Pursuant to instructions of Special Agent in Charge Schmid to assist in apprehending *Ben Fletcher* (colored), recently indicted in Chicago with other IWW leaders, Agent located Fletcher at his room at #5 Melrose Court, Boston, and notified the office of US Marshal Mitchell, of the location of *Fletcher*, and advised fully of this man's character.

■ Ben H. Fletcher, Case Number 29434, Investigative Case Files of the Bureau of Investigation.

—

21

Fletcher and Cape Verdeans

The government's desperate attempt to drum up evidence, after the indict-ments and with the trial only two months away, brought to light a fascinat-ing bit of Fletcher's history: the significant inroads Fletcher had made among Providence dockworkers, who were of African descent and part of a wave of Portuguese immigrants to that city. As seen in this report, "Portuguese Negroes" also were referred to by their home place, the island of Brava in the Cape Verde archipelago. Colonized by the Portuguese in the fifteenth century, Cape Verde was deeply embedded in the transatlantic trade in enslaved Africans. Fast forward to the late nineteenth century, an era of enormous European immi-gration to the United States. The largest concentration of Portuguese, both of African and European descent, ended up in southern New England including Providence.

Agent: Robert Evans
Place report made: Providence, R.I.
Date report made: Jan. 30, 1918
Period report made about: Jan. 28, 1918

"In re: Ben Fletcher and John Avila: Possible IWW Activities in Providence"

At Providence:
Pursuant to instructions from Special Agent Nowick made investiga-tion of the above mentioned subjects relative to a request from *Division Superintendent Clabaugh* of the *Chicago Office* asking that this office inves-tigate the possible activities of the above subjects in this city.

Ascertained that about *14 months* ago the *IWWs* were active in the Longshoremens [sic] Strike here. Investigation fails to disclose that Fletcher or Avila were the instigators. For some there was considerable activity among the Bravas working on the docks and on one occasion a bomb was exploded under a passenger car where a number of the strike breakers were living while working for the *New England Navigation Company*. As some time has elapsed since this trouble occurred, have been unable to get any names of the ringleaders from the police as there were no arrests made.

Special Employe [sic] ascertained that about six months ago, one *Michael Fernandes, a Brava,* was arrested for an assault which took place while a strike was in progress at the erection of the new building of the *R.I. Hospital Trust Company.* There is practically no evidence at hand to show that *Fernandes* was an *IWW* except that the officer who arrested him states that the heard *Fernandes* was an *IWW.*

It is customary for the *Bravas* to use several names and it may be that *Fernandes* was one of the two subjects mentioned and has disappeared from *Providence.* A careful search fails to reveal the name of *Fletcher* or *Avila* of having been mentioned in *Providence,* at any time during the local strikes in which the *Portuguese Negroes,* commonly known as *Bravas,* were the parties.

■ Ben H. Fletcher, Case Number 29434, Investigative Case Files of the Bureau of Investigation.

22

The Search for Fletcher Continues

The federal government was gearing up for its huge trial of approximately one hundred Wobblies including five connected to Local 8: Fletcher, E.F. Doree, Walter Nef, Manuel Rey, and Jack Walsh. In doing so, the true purpose of the arrests was revealed—to crush the IWW—considering that the US Department of Justice did *not* consult the relevant officials in Philadelphia, about Fletcher and Local 8, in advance of the raids or indictments of the IWW in September 1917. Had federal officials in Philadelphia been asked, they would have indicated there was no evidence that the longshoremen were disloyal. Perhaps surprisingly, even the navy did not see Local 8 as a threat considering the Philadelphia Navy Yard exclusively employed members of Local 8 before and after the raids, indictments, and arrests. Instead, five months after the raids, US Assistant Attorney General William C. Fitts wrote to the secretary of the navy requesting evidence of Fletcher's guilt. In fact, no evidence existed that the US war effort had been subverted by the IWW, in Philadelphia or elsewhere, or that a general strike was being planned.

Fletcher, with his wife and stepchild, had moved back to his hometown sometime in fall 1918, though he might have made a trip to Baltimore, a frequent organizing destination for Fletcher.

... to show that the needs of the Navy of the United States, with respect to preparation for participation in the war, were materially interfered with and retarded by the unrest fomented and low-down methods injected into the situation during the spring and summer of 1917 by the IWW.

■ Assistant Attorney General William C. Fitts to Secretary of the Navy, January 3, 1918, Box 2219, *US v. Haywood et al.,* File 188032, Straight Numerical Files, Records of the Department of Justice.

Agent: J.F. McDevitt
Place report made: Phila. Pa.
Date report made: January 30, 1918
Period report made about: January 29th

"Re—BEN FLETCHER: IWW Activities"

At Philadelphia:
Under instructions of Agent Spates I investigated a letter received from Division *Superintendent Clabaugh* under date of January 26, 1918, and have to report that I visited different IWW meeting places and made inquiries at police headquarters but was unable to get any information other than, that the last heard of Fletcher he was in Baltimore, Md.

I had Agent in Charge write to Supt. Clabaugh, advising him of the above fact.

■ Ben H. Fletcher, Case Number 29434, Investigative Case Files of the Bureau of Investigation.

23

The Chase Is On

The federal investigation of Fletcher involved agents in Boston, Chicago, Philadelphia, and almost certainly beyond. After months of searching, Fletcher was found to be working at the Pennsylvania Railroad's sprawling railyards in the western edge of South Philadelphia. He lived within blocks of the yards in the Grays Ferry neighborhood, a heavily working-class area then home to many Irish Americans and African Americans.

Agent: Schmid
Place report made: Boston, Mass.
Date report made: February 11, 1918
Period report made about: February 9, 1918

"In re: Ben Fletcher: IWW Matter"

At Boston, Mass.:
Deputy US Marshall Bancroft of Boston, reported to this office that he has reliable information from *George O'Brien*, Probation Office, City Hall, Philadelphia, Pa., to the effect that *Ben Fletcher* is at present living at 1329 South Grove St., and is employed by the Pennsylvania Railroad company, at 36th and Grays Ferry Avenue, Philadelphia, Pa., as a laborer.

Agent sent the following telegram:

Boston, Mass. Feb. 9, 1918.
Clabaugh,
Federal Building,
Chicago, Illinois
Have information number forty-five IWW list accompanying your letter September twenty-sixth nineteen seventeen now living thirteen twenty-nine South Grove St. Philadelphia employed laborer Pennsylvania Railroad company, at Thirty-sixth and Grays Ferry Avenue that city.
(signed) Schmid

Agent: J.F. McDevitt
Place report made: Phila. Pa.
Date report made: February 14, 1918
Period report made about: February 9th

"Re—BEN FLETCHER: No. 45 (IWW Activities)"

At Philadelphia:
As per my previous reports I today continued my search for the above named man and learned from a *Miss Slocum,* representing *Miss White,* Supervisor of the South West District S.O.C. Society for Organizing Charity, 1315 S. 22nd St., that the wife of *Fletcher* has applied to them for aid and before doing anything they wanted to know something of the husband.

Miss Slocum was very anxious, almost to a point of commanding me to give her what information I had in regard to him but was unwilling to give me any information. She would not even tell me the address of the wife, other than it was South Grove Street.

As this street is in the Grays Ferry section I proceeded there but was unable to get any information except that there was a man by that name in the neighborhood.

I shall continue my search.

■ Both from Ben H. Fletcher, Case Number 29434, Investigative Case Files of the Bureau of Investigation.

24

Fletcher Arrested (Finally)

The first three reports come from two of the federal agents who arrested Fletcher, revealing how much attention the government devoted to Fletcher's case alone—in Chicago, Philadelphia, and even upstate New York—but also how ineffective they had been as Fletcher "hid in plain sight" for about four months. The fourth document, a clipping from an unknown newspaper, was included in military intelligence files on Fletcher under the heading "Labor IWW Strikes." A telegram indicated that Fletcher finally planned to travel from Philadelphia to Chicago, in late March, for the trial which also is the subject of a humorous story (Document 73).

While $10,000 bail is a lot of money in 2020, according to the US Bureau of Labor Statistics' "inflation calculator," Fletcher's bail would come to about $160,000, suggesting just how dangerously the government viewed Wobblies like him.

Agent: J.F. McDevitt
Place report made: Phila. Pa.
Date report made: February 15, 1918
Period report made about: February 10th

"Re—BEN FLETCHER: No. 45 (IWW Activities)"

At Philadelphia:
This morning I was given a telegram from *Division Superintendent Clabaugh* of the Chicago office which stated that the above named many was living at 1329 South Grove Street and that he was employed by the Pennsylvania Railroad as a laborer, at 36th and Grays Ferry Road and that he should be arrested and Chicago notified.

I have to report that I called at the address given and satisfied myself that the information was correct but *Fletcher* was not at home.

In the evening in company of *Agent McHenry* and *Capt. Griggs* of the Penna. R.R. Police I returned to the home of Fletcher and in the roll [*sic*] of an agent of the Society of Organizing Charity gained admission, he was waiting for me at the request of his wife. He is a very black Negro while his wife is a white woman. He admitted in the presence of McHenry and myself that he was the man that I wanted and that he was a member of the IWW for seven years and an organizer since a year ago last October.

I placed him in the City Hall until the morning.

★

Agent: Joseph F. McDevitt
Place report made: Philadelphia, Pa.
Date report made: 2/15/18
Period for which report made: 2/11/18

"Benj. Fletcher #45 (I.W.W.)"

At Philadelphia:
Referring to previous reports in the above entitled case, I went to City Hall this morning before reporting at headquarters and brought *Benj. Fletcher* to the office. US Commissioner *Long* held him under $10,000. Bail for his appearance in Chicago.

I also notified the Chicago office.

★

Agent: Roy C. McHenry
Place report made: Binghamton, N.Y.
Date report made: Feb. 23, 1918
Period report made about: Feb. 10, 1918

"Ben Fletcher, 1529 South Grove St., Philadelphia, Pa. IWW Activities, indicted in Chicago with Wm. D. Haywood et al."

At Philadelphia, Pa.
At the request of *Agent McDevitt*, I accompanied him and Captain *Griggs*, of the Pennsylvania Railroad police, to arrest Ben Fletcher, who is No. 45 in the list of defendants of the IWW indictment at Chicago. McDevitt left me posted outside while he entered the house, and Capt. Griggs guarded the back way out. For details of the arrest see McDevitts [sic] hereon.

After the arrest was made, McDevitt called me in and went out in search of Capt. Griggs, who came back with him. While he was gone I had a talk with Fletcher, who admitted his identity, said he knew all the IWW leaders in Philadelphia and was aware that he had been indicted.

He said he had not given himself up in response to the directions of the attorney for the IWW's at Chicago because he did not want to be put in jail. Later, when we took the car for downtown he said he had been a member of the IWW for 7 years and had been an organizer since a year last October. When arrested he was employed at the Pennsylvania roundhouse at Gray's Ferry. He said he had been in Philadelphia since September, 1917 and had always lived under his own name. He said he was born in Baltimore. He impressed me as being well read and he used exceptionally good English.

This case is concluded so far as Fletcher goes, until the trial, so far as I am concerned.

★

"Negro IWW Arrested"

Alleged Organizer Is Held in $10,000 at Philadelphia

Philadelphia, Feb. 12—Benjamin Fletcher, colored, an alleged organizer and worker among the negroes of the United States for the Industrial Workers of the World, was arrested here yesterday and held in $10,000 bail for his appearance in Chicago, where he is under a Federal indictment on charges of sedition.

Office Chief of Staff, War College Division, War Department.

★

Philadelphia, Pa., March 27, 1918

Clabaugh
Federal Bldg Chicago

Sunned [summoned?] Ben Fletcher made bond here on March thirteenth for his appearance in Chicago forthwith. Bond and all papers forwarded Clerk District Court there.

Garabino

■ First three and final entry in Ben H. Fletcher, Case Number 29434, Investigative Case Files of the Bureau of Investigation.

25

Fletcher on Trial

One hundred sixty-six Wobblies were indicted by a federal grand jury in September 1917. On April Fool's Day, 1918, Fletcher and another ninety-two Wobblies' federal trial began in Chicago, the headquarters of the union. The trial received extensive coverage in mainstream media for the next four months. The caption accompanying this sketch of Fletcher, in the *Chicago Tribune*, read as follows and spoke volumes: "Ben Fletcher, only Negro on trial, quite the pet of some of the brothers—one hugged him openly in court." The second article excerpted reconfirms the antipathy of the "mainstream" press as well as the antiracist bonafides of IWW members with backhanded compliments.

. . . As the men entered the courtroom the handcuffs were taken from them and tossed into a corner. Otto Justice of Detroit, and Ben Fletcher of Philadelphia, both out on bond, were reported late, due to delayed trains.

Fletcher, the color of blackest ebony and the only Negro indicted in the lot, was then announced. He shuffled into the room, a beaming grin on his face, and a dozen of the comrades stretched out glad hands to welcome him.

■ "Shaven IWWs Kiss as Trial Is Postponed," *Chicago Tribune*, April 2, 1918, 7.

I.W.W. BEAUTIES TO DAZZLE JURY FROM FRONT ROW

Whiskers and Age Must Go Away Back and Sit Tight.

Beauty came into its own yesterday at the I. W. W. trial. The value of getting the best face foremost was recognized. There was a reasserting of a meeting. Whiskers and mussy hair were moved back.

When the voice of I. W. W. authority made the men obeyed. When the defendants, 112 strong, filed into the courtroom the scene of previous days was changed. Those with regular, barbered features took the front row.

Rebellious locks and offending garb were ambushed in camouflage of more plebeian brothers. It was the theory that puts the fairest chorus girl at front.

"Third Bill Red" Doran, water front spellbinder from Seattle, is reported to have given livid protest. First row on other days, he found himself in the fifth. Carl Ahlteen whose pink whiskers show an undulating ripple, moved back one row. Generally speaking, the arrangement seemed to be smooth faces front, next mustaches, Bolshevist beards in the rear.

Faces showing the erosion of time were likewise harder to find from back front, where the jury sits.

Four Tentatively Accepted.

Four jurymen have been accepted tentatively. Any or all of them may yet be challenged. The four are:
A. J. McKEE, Morris, Ill.
WILLIAM MALLOW, 4342 Lincoln avenue.
ADOLPH KUECKEN, 2928 Cottage Grove avenue.
WILLIAM H. McDONALD, 1952 West Madison street.

Kuecken, a contractor, admitted his German ancestry, but declared himself purely American in his sympathies. He told of a visit to Germany, remaining there one year to complete his university studies. He also said he had read some I. W. W. and Socialist literature.

The morning session of the trial was canceled because McKee failed to appear. Rumors of kidnaping and violence vanished when he arrived much embarrassed after dinner.

"Did any accident befall you?" asked Judge Landis.

"No, sir," he replied. "I overslept."

"I'm glad, sir," replied the "court, glad that that was all. I want a jurors to get every bit of sleep you need, but I want the sleeping done between 5 o'clock in the afternoon and 11 o'clock in the morning."

Given More Food.

As a result of a protest, careful written and signed by the eighty-eight men held in jail unable to make bond the court ordered that they be given supper each day before going back to jail. They told the court that they were afraid they would be made ill and so delay the trial unless fed better.

John J. Bradley, United States marshal, was ordered to investigate the jail fare by Judge Landis and he reported the food for the day there as follows:

BREAKFAST—Bread and coffee.
DINNER—Stew and potatoes.
SUPPER—Choice of bread and coffee or bread and soup.

Judge Landis also ordered that Marshal Bradley provide shaving paraphernalia in room 603 federal building for the benefit of the men who complain of inability to spruce up properly, and failing to have a barber.

"I shall limit 'em to safety razors," commented Mr. Bradley.

Throw Away Bread, Charge.

"Good bread, at a time of wheat shortage when many need bread, has been thrown at jail guards by the I. W. W. prisoners confined in the county jail," said Will T. Davies, jailer, last night, when he learned of the food protest. He added:

"They get a wagon load of sandwiches and fruits from their organization each day. We give them more than as the other prisoners get.

"They are absolutely the worst prisoners I've got and I will be glad when they are out of here."

I. W. W. CAUGHT IN THE ACT—ON TRIAL

Defendants Sketched in Judge Landis' Court as They Watched Selection of Jurors.

Carl Ahlteen, Editor of "The Alarm" now silenced, his pink whiskers and hair add color to the assemblage. His tie is black.

"Big Bill" Haywood, daddy of 'em all and recognized brain of the "Wobblies."

"Red" Hiram, journeyman Evangelist. The Prophet in overalls.

Vincent St. John, Ex-Miners Labor agitator, Pioneer I.W.W. and a historian of the "Reds" who occasionally nods in sleep.

Jacob Martin Evers

Ben Fletcher, only Negro on trial, quite the Jack of arms of the Brothers—one hugged him openly in court.

James Keenan—a type.

Charles Hough—another type.

■ "IWW Caught in the Act—On Trial," *Chicago Tribune*, April 5, 1918, 5.

26

Fletcher and Haywood Cutting It Up

The first excerpt is the earliest reference to this joke, oddly published in the *Chicago Tribune*, a notoriously anti-union daily newspaper.

William "Big Bill" Haywood, the most prominent Wobbly, was convicted in the same trial as Fletcher. Like Fletcher, Haywood came from a working-class background so had not had the luxury of much formal education. Like most Wobblies, he came to his revolutionary industrial unionism by way of workplace experiences or, as he declared, "I've never read Marx's *Capital* but I've got the marks of capital all over my body." In 1921 Haywood jumped bail—though Fletcher and others also out on bail later returned to Leavenworth. Haywood lived his remaining eight years of life in the Soviet Union, where he wrote an autobiography which contained these humorous stories about Fletcher.

There was one Negro, Ben Fletcher of Philadelphia, who smiled as he took his ten year sentence, and said, "Judge Landis is using poor English today. His sentences are too long."

■ "Haywood Given 20 Year Term; 93 Sentenced," *Chicago Tribune*, August 31, 1918, 5.

Pontius Pilate or Bloody Jeffreys never enjoyed themselves better than did Judge Landis when he was imposing these terrible sentences upon a group of working men for whom he had no feeling of humanity, no sense of justice.

Ben Fletcher sidled over to me and said: "The Judge has been using very ungrammatical language." I looked at his smiling black face and asked: "How's that, Ben?" He said: "His sentences are much too long." At one time previous to this during the great trial in a spirit of humor, Ben remarked: "If it wasn't for me, there'd be no color in this trial at all." I might explain that he was the only Negro in the group.

■ *Bill Haywood's Book: The Autobiography of William D. Haywood*, 324–25.

27

Fletcher Sentenced

Ben Fletcher was sentenced to ten years in federal prison and fined $30,000. According to the US Bureau of Labor Statistics' "inflation calculator," that fine would be the equivalent of roughly $475,000 in 2020.

The President of the United States of America to the Marshal of the Northern District of Illinois, and to the Warden of the United States Penitentiary at Leavenworth, Kansas

Greeting:

Whereas Ben Fletcher appeared before the District Court of the United States of America for the Eastern Division of the Northern District of Illinois, on the First day of April A.D. 1918 to answer an indictment filed there—in against him for violation of Sections 6, 19 and 37 of the Criminal Code of the United States and Section 4 of the "Espionage Act" of June 15, 1917, and the said Ben Fletcher upon a trial in due form of law, having been found guilty as charged in the said indictment, and having on August 30, 1918 been sentenced to imprisonment in the United States Penitentiary at Leavenworth Kansas for and during a period of six years on count 1, ten years on counts 2 and 4 and two years on count 3, said sentences to run concurrently and to pay a fine of five thousand dollars on each counts 1 and 2 and a fine of ten thousand dollars on each of counts of 3 and 4 besides the costs in this be—half expended.

Now therefore you said Marshal are hereby commanded that you convey the said Ben Fletcher to the said Penitentiary and you the said Warden of the said Penitentiary are hereby commanded that you receive the said Ben Fletcher into the said Penitentiary and him there safely keep until the expiration of said sentence, or until he be discharged therefrom by the due course of law.

Witness the Hon. Kenesaw M. Landis, Judge of the District Court of the United States of America for the said District of Chicago aforesaid, this 30th day of August, in the year of our Lord, nineteen hundred eighteen and of the independence of the United States the 143rd year.

T.C. MacMillan, Clerk
IN THE UNITED STATES DISTRICT COURT FOR THE NORTHERN DISTRICT OF ILLINOIS EASTERN DIVISION

■ Miscellaneous Political Records, Political Prisoners, US Department of Justice Files, National Archives, in Philip S. Foner and Ronald L. Lewis, *The Black Worker*, Vol. 5.

28

Fletcher Holding Court

Big Bill Haywood recounted another story featuring Fletcher and his rapier wit. In September 1918, the convicted Wobblies, nearly a hundred in all, were held at Cook County jail before boarding a dedicated train only carrying these Wobblies to the federal penitentiary in Leavenworth. While traveling, which took about twenty-four hours, Fletcher held a mock trial that lampooned Judge Kenesaw Mountain Landis.

Ben Fletcher, to while away the time, held a mock court. His imitation of Judge Landis was laughable. He sat on the back of the seat looking solemn and spitting tobacco juice up the aisle. He had taken off his shoes, collar and tie, and his coat and vest as far as he could get them off. He grabbed at his pants to keep from falling down as the Judge had done one day in the court. Judge Landis was not a grave, black-robed individual such as judges sometimes are pictured. During the hot summer of our trial he stripped down as far as decency would permit. Fletcher gave a good imitation of the Judge's antics. He swore in the prisoners as a jury; calling the guards and detectives up to him he sentenced them without further ado to be hanged and shot and imprisoned for life.

■ Bill Haywood, *The Autobiography of William D. Haywood*, 328.

THE GENERAL STRIKE

A Wobbly artist known as "Sam," *One Big Union Monthly*, July 1919.

29

We Won't Forget

In Canada and the United States, "red Finns" made their presence known in various Left organizations, parties, and unions, particularly the IWW. In and around northern Minnesota's largest city, Duluth, as well as in the nearby "Upper Peninsula" of Michigan, Finns long played an important role. Finns were among the many ethnic groups in North America who built a robust series of newspapers and magazines in their native language. The first mention of Fletcher in the Finnish-language press, on his conviction, came in this Duluth-based magazine.

"We won't forget" has become a common phrase among us. Nowadays the working class has to give so many sacrifices that these words have been pressed into our heart's blood even more deeply. Everywhere we are seeing the victims of freedom. The closer the great turn in our society becomes the more heatedly the predators rage against us and claim victims. We are publishing below the names of all those who have in this way been convicted as victims of class struggle and are now suffering their punishment for being faithful to their humane principles and the righteous strivings of the wage workers.

[what followed was a long list of convicted "class warriors"]

Benjamin Fletcher, black Philadelphia dockworker. He told the judge before his conviction that the "IWW has done more than any other labor organization to advance their race and to lift its standard of living."

■ *Ahjo* [*The Forge*] 3, no. 4 (December 1918): 55. Translated by Aleksi Huhta.

30

Fletcher in Forma Pauperis

In addition to long prison sentences, Fletcher and other Wobblies were saddled with massive fines no working-class person ever could pay. This affidavit that Fletcher swore out testified to his inability to pay even a tiny fraction of his $30,000 fine. By the rules of the union—in stark contrast to AFL unions whose leaders got paid like employers—IWW organizers never were paid more than someone working in the field being organized; in fact, most organizers were not paid at all but instead voluntarily organized on the job or while "on the bum." When their leaders received such harsh fines, Local 8 and the entire IWW made herculean efforts to pay them as well as the mammoth legal costs involved in the many cases. The IWW also raised funds to support partners and children who lost breadwinners.

Shortly after this petition was filed, in April 1919, Fletcher and thirty-five other Wobblies imprisoned in Leavenworth were released on bond. According to lawyer and historian Dean Strang, wealthy sympathizers including Agnes Inglis (who later founded the Labadie Collection in the University of Michigan library) provided bail money.

United States of America, Plaintiff vs. William D. Haywood, et al., Defendants
Affidavit in Forma Pauperis
No. 6125

State of Kansas, County of Leavenworth SS

Benjamin H. Fletcher, being first duly sworn, on his oath says that he is a native born citizen of the United States; that on the 30th day of August, 1918, after a trial before a jury duly empannelled [sic] in the above entitled court, he was adjudged guilty of the crime of conspiracy committed as charged in the first four counts of the indictment in the above entitled cause and sentenced to imprisonment in the United States penitentiary at Leavenworth, Kansas, for the term of ten years and to pay a fine of $30,000; that he desires to sue out a writ of error to the United States Circuit Court of Appeals for this Seventh Circuit, and to review said conviction and reverse said judgment for error; and has been advised by Mr. George F. Vanderveer and Mr. Otto Christensen, his attorneys, and verily believes that he is entitled to the redress he seeks; but that because of his poverty he is wholly unable to pay the costs of said writ of error, or to give any security for the same and therefore makes this application for leave to sue out and prosecute the same to a conclusion without being required to prepay any fees or costs or for the printing of the record in said Appellate Court and without being required to give any security therefor.

Benjamin H. Fletcher

Subscribed and sworn to before me
this 21st day of February, A.D. 1919. Thos. C. Taylor, Notary Public
My commission expires Jan. 13th, 1923.

■ Miscellaneous Political Records, Political Prisoners, US Department of Justice Files, National Archives, Philip S. Foner and Ronald L. Lewis, *The Black Worker*, Vol. 5.

31

Du Bois on Fletcher and the IWW

W.E.B. Du Bois might be the most important black intellectual in US history. Over the course of his long life, his political thinking evolved, which, for him, meant he became ever more internationalist and anticapitalist. By the 1930s, if not earlier, he was a Marxist as made clear in his magisterial *Black Reconstruction* (1935). After World War II, he continued his embrace of socialism so much so that the National Association for the Advancement of Colored People (NAACP), the organization he helped found (in 1909) and lead (for decades) forced him to resign in 1948. In 1961, he joined the CPUSA, gave up his US citizenship, and moved to Ghana. Back in 1917, however, Du Bois famously had encouraged African Americans to "close ranks" and support the war effort. Very soon after World War I, he came to appreciate that the country's white majority still did not care about black men's military service and became more critical of the war, as evident in this editorial. It also features Du Bois praising the IWW for being antiracist and includes mention of Fletcher's comments during the previous year's trial. (The journalist mentioned, David Karsner, was a socialist who covered the Chicago trial for the *New York Call*, a popular Jewish Socialist weekly.)

An editorial in the Easter CRISIS (written during the Editor's absence) has been misunderstood and was, perhaps, itself partially misleading.

Mr. F.H.M. Murray of Washington, D.C., writes us:

"In a recent editorial in your magazine the statement is made that there are no Negroes among the Industrial Workers of the World. While I am certain that the statement is erroneous, I am not at this moment able to lay my hands on anything in print to confirm my denial, except the following from an article in last Sunday's New York *Call* magazine, by David Karsner, who reported the trial of the big batch of members of the IWW—in Chicago last summer and later the trial of the five Socialists at the same place. He is writing about Judge Kenesaw M. Landis, who presided at both trials and who imposed upon the hundred or so IWW, who were convicted, and the five Socialists, sentences aggregating over nine hundred years in prison and fines aggregating over two million dollars. Mr. Karsner says:

> There was only one defendant among the IWW, to my knowledge, who refused to believe in Judge Landis. He was Ben Fletcher, the sole Negro defendant. One day in the corridor I asked Ben what he thought of Judge Landis. Ben smiled broadly, "He's a fakir. Wait until he gets a chance; then he'll plaster it on thick." Ben was a sure-thing prophet, for the Judge plastered him with ten years, and his counsel said with not enough evidence to invite a reprimand.

"So it turns out that not only are there Negroes who are members of this militant workingmen's organization, but some—or at least one—prominent enough to be regarded as worth putting behind the bars with the leaders—Haywood, Fanning and others.

"I think that in the interest of the truth of history and for the honor of the black workers, you should correct the statement to which I refer.

"I say 'honor,' for even if we regard the IWW as visionaries (John Brown, you know, was a "visionary") however mistaken are their methods, if their methods are as generally set forth (which I do not believe) the success of the cause for which they are struggling and sacrificing and suffering should be particularly dear to our people, since in no other race or element of our population is there a larger percentage of workers; albeit, too many—what a pity!—are obliged to work in a menial, that is, a parasitic capacity."

THE CRISIS did not say or intend to say that no Negroes belonged to the Industrial Workers of the World, nor did it intend to condemn that organization. On the contrary, we respect it as one of the social and political movements in modern times that draws no color line. We sought to say that we do not believe that the methods of the IWW are today feasible or advisable. And too we believe the Socialist Party wrong in its attitude toward the war, but we raise our hats silently to men like Eugene Debs who let not even the shadow of public shame close their lips when they think themselves right.

We believe that the crushing of the monstrous pretentions of the military caste of Germany was a duty so pressing and tremendous that it called for the efforts of every thoughtful American. But we recognize that some people did not agree with us and these folk we honor for their honesty, even though we question their reasoning.

It is no credit to American Negroes if they had NO "Conscientious Objectors." It is tremendously to their credit that the vast majority of them thought straight and fought true in a mighty world crisis.

■ W.E.B. Du Bois, "The IWW," *Crisis*, June 1919, 60.

32

The *Messenger* on Ben Fletcher

This piece, the first of many the *Messenger* published on Ben Fletcher and Local 8, was prompted by Fletcher's imprisonment. A Harlem-based magazine coedited by Chandler Owen and A. Philip Randolph, the *Messenger* billed itself as the "World's Greatest Negro Monthly." It definitely was among the most radical, as made clear in this piece that praised Fletcher while eviscerating other black newspapers. Owen and Randolph were African American socialists, and Randolph went on to help found the Brotherhood of Sleeping Car Porters (AFL), forced President Franklin Roosevelt to commit to nondiscriminatory hiring practices on federal government contracts during World War II, and served as a key advisor to Martin Luther King Jr. about civil rights. The *Messenger*'s politics shared much in common with the IWW—interracial unionism as the path toward socialism—so repeatedly praised the interracial longshoremen of Local 8 and their celebrated black leader.

Negro newspapers seldom publish anything about men who are useful to the race. Some parasite, ecclesiastical poltroon, sacerdotal tax gatherer, political faker or business exploiter will have his name in the papers, weekly or daily. But when it comes to one of those who fights for the great masses to lessen their hours of work, to increase their wages, to decrease their high cost of living, to make life more livable for the toiling black workers—that man is not respectable for the average Negro sheet.

Such a man is Ben Fletcher. He is one of the leading organizers of the Industrial Workers of the World, commonly known as the IWW. He is in the Leavenworth Penitentiary, Kansas, where he was sent for trying to secure better working conditions for colored men and women in the United States. He has a vision far beyond that of almost any Negro leader whom we know. He threw in his lot with his fellow white workers, who work side by side with black men and black women to raise their standard of living. It is not uncommon to see Negro papers have headlines concerning a Negro who had committed murder, cut some woman's throat, stolen a chicken or a loaf of bread, but those same papers never record happenings concerning the few Negro manly men who go to prison for principle. Ben Fletcher is in Leavenworth for principle—a principle which when adopted, will put all the Negro leaders out of their parasitical jobs. That principle is that to the workers belong the world, but useful work is not done by Negro leaders.

We want to advocate and urge that Negro societies, lodges, churches, NAACP branches and, of course, their labor organizations begin to protest against the imprisonment of Ben Fletcher and to demand his release. He has been of more service to the masses of plain Negro people than all the wind jamming Negro leaders in the United States.

■ Philip Randolph, the *Messenger*, August 1919, 28-29.

33

Fletcher's Prison Letters

It was standard operating procedure for political prisoners to have their mail, incoming and outgoing, catalogued, read, and transcribed, and so it was with Fletcher's correspondence in Leavenworth. While some may consider such actions to violate the civil liberties of prisoners, ironically, such "censorship" (one agent's term) provides incredibly useful resources for historians. It is fascinating to observe the inner workings of government spying on Fletcher and all Wobbles in Leavenworth.

The second document is particularly illuminating, first, to see Fletcher's correspondents: Wobbly leaders such as Flynn and Haywood; A. Philip Randolph and other black socialists; family including his sisters, Helen Braxton and Laura Johns, both of whom had married; Charles Carter, an African American, and others in Local 8. Of course, it also is interesting to read actual letters, as in the next three documents—one to his friend and fellow Local 8 leader, Walter Nef, and the last two to the person who put up the substantial amount of money required, as a bond, for Fletcher's release.

Alas, little is known about Mary McMurtrie. According to the 1910 census, she ran a boarding house at 1104 Spruce Street in the heart of South Philadelphia, which is where his first letter was sent. She was white and middle-aged. Fletcher's second letter to her, after he returned to Leavenworth, checked in to ensure she had not been unfairly taxed by the government for her bond. His second letter, interestingly, went to an address in another part of the city, Chestnut Hill, a very wealthy area traditionally home to many "old," elite families. While perhaps she had moved, quite possibly she owned multiple properties as it seems extremely unlikely that Fletcher wrote to two women with the same name. McMurtrie's Chestnut Hill residence explains how she posted the enormous bond, $40,000, required for Fletcher's release. She later signed a petition for his release, too. Quite possibly, she was a left-leaning sympathizer for which there even existed a term, "parlor Bolsheviks."

August 23, 1919

C.E. Argabright, Esq.
Leavenworth, Kansas
Dear Sir:

I am inclosing herewith a photostat copy of a communication received in this office. You will notice that mention is made of BEN FLETCHER, a negro now serving time at Leavenworth. It is suggested that his correspondence be watched and possibly something may be learned relating to the negro agitation.

Kindly give this matter your attention.

Very truly yours,

Acting Chief

★

September 2, 1919
Mr. Frank Burke,
Assistant Director and Chief
Bureau of Investigation
Department of Justice

Dear Sir:

In re: Ben Fletcher
Negro IWW Agitator

Responsive to your letter of August 23rd, suggesting a censorship of the mail of this man, who is imprisoned in Leavenworth penitentiary. I have to advise you that in our IWW censorship, already established at Leavenworth prison, we have been covering this man's mail. Under date of August 1st, I forwarded you a copy of a letter written by him to John J. Jones, 601 E. 17th Street, New York City.

On August 14th I furnished you a copy of a letter written by him to A. Phillip Randolph, 2305 7th Avenue, New York City.

On August 15th I furnished you a copy of a letter written by him to John L. Metzen, 105 No. Clark Street, Chicago, Ill.

On August 18th I furnished you a copy of a letter written to him by Charles Carter, Southwark Station, Philadelphia, Pa.

On August 20th I furnished you a copy of a letter written by him to Wm. D. Haywood, Chicago, Ill.

On August 22nd I furnished you a copy of a letter written to him by Helen F. Braxton, 1613 So. 9th St., Philadelphia, Pa.

On August 23rd I furnished you a copy of a letter written by him to Joseph J. Jones, 559 Shawmut Avenue, Boston, Mass.

On August 20th I furnished you a copy of a letter written by him to Elizabeth Gurley Flynn, 511 E. 135th Street, New York City.

On August 26th I furnished you a copy of a letter addressed to him by "Laura" 1613 So. 9th Street, Philadelphia, Pa.

All of these copies were forwarded to you under the title "In re: Leavenworth Penitentiary, Censorship of IWW and Radical Mail."

This censorship will be continued and doubtless other letters from him which contain matters of importance will be forwarded.

Respectfully,

Arthur T. Bagley (signed)
Division Superintendent

★

Kansas City, Missouri
January 16, 1920

E.J. Brennan, Esq.,
Box 485
Chicago, Illinois

For your information there follows a copy of a letter written by Ben H. Fletcher, an IWW (Colored) Prisoner recently confined in the Federal Penitentiary at Leavenworth, Kansas—addressed to Mr. W.T. Nef, 710 North Franklin Street, Philadelphia, Pennsylvania—

> Jan. 14, 1920
> Fellow Worker:
> Am acknowledgment herewith yours of sometime ago with the twenty-five dollars donated by Philadelphia branch of Local 8 enclosed therein.

I received the bond from Attorney Metzen on the 17th ultimo—signed and returned same to him that date. Have no tidings from him to date, and presume that the investigation is still on by District Attorney in Chicago.

With best wishes. Yours for Industrial Freedom

(signed) Ben H. Fletcher

Please regard the source of this information as confidential.

Very truly yours,

Arthur T. Bagley,
Division Superintendent

★

Kansas City, Missouri
January 29, 1920

Todd Daniel, Esq.,
P.O. Box 451
Philadelphia, Pa.

Dear Sir:

For your information, we are sending you copy of a letter written January 27, 1920 by Ben H. Fletcher, a colored IWW Prisoner confined in the Federal penitentiary at Ft. Leavenworth, to Miss Mary McMurtrie, 1104 Spring (?) or Spruce St., Philadelphia:

> "Six weeks ago tomorrow, I received the bond you entered before the US Dist. Court clerks for my release on bail, pending the disposition of the case of the US vs. Wm. D. Haywood, et al, and pending an appeal before the Appelate [sic] Court in Chicago.
>
> In the absence of any result today, am writing you as follows: You should have your attorney ascertain the cause of the delay of Mr. Chas. F. Clyne, US District Atty at Chicago, after getting a line on the bond status at the Dist Attorney's Office in Phila.
>
> Personally, I am sure that politics and the absence of cordial relations between the attorney handling the matter at the Chicago end of the line is now a factor in the delay, therefore, it might be

necessary to secure some one there who can get the bond accepted. Am recently advised that Attorney Metzen who is handling the matter has been disbarred but has appealed to the Supreme Court. If such is the case, it is probably another reason for the present situation. Have gone at this length on the subject matter with you, first because the fact that you are my bondsman and are as much interested as myself; second, under date of December 17, 1919, Mr. Nef advises me of your intention to take care of the matter fully."

Please regard the source of this information as confidential.

Very truly yours,

Arthur T. Bagley,
Division Superintendent

■ All from Ben H. Fletcher, Case Number 29434, Investigative Case Files of the Bureau of Investigation.

June 15th, 1921

Mr. Walter C. Foster
Postoffice Box 451
Philadelphia, Pennsylvania

Dear Sir:—

For your information there follows a copy of a letter written under the date of June 12th, 1921, by one *Ben H. Fletcher*, an IWW Prisoner confined in the Federal Penitentiary at Leavenworth, Kansas, addressed to *Miss Mary McMurtrie*, Norwood and Sunset, Chestnut Hill, Philadelphia, Pennsylvania:

"Please let me know at your earliest convenience if the property bond you posted for my release has been released, and if it has whether you had to pay any tax or assessment on same.

Am recently advised that the Government assessed a tax of one per cent on the Liberty Bonds posted for one of the Phila. Defendants. I hear from Philadelphia weekly and believe I am fairly well informed on matters pertaining to our case.

As for the daily happenings reflecting, life, trend and doings in the Quaker metropolis, am kept posted by such premier news purveyors, as the Public Ledger and Inquirer."

Kindly regard the source of this information as strictly confidential.

Yours very truly,

Oscar Schmitz
Special Agent in Charge

■ Case #4-2-3-14, "Old German Files," Record Group 65: Department of Justice, National Archives.

34

Fletcher's Black Radical Networks

Joseph J. Jones, a left-wing black radical, met a tragic end just a few months after Fletcher wrote this letter which opens the door, if slightly, to Fletcher's wider networks. Born to an Irish mother and black father, Jones never knew his father and was abandoned by his mother at the age of five. He grew up in an orphanage in Boston's black neighborhood, Roxbury (where Malcolm Little, later Malcolm X, lived before being imprisoned). Jones fought in the Spanish-American War of 1898 and was about twenty years older than Fletcher. They apparently met in Boston in 1917, where Fletcher may have radicalized Jones and introduced him to William Monroe Trotter, the militant black publisher who ran the Boston-based *Guardian* for decades. After Fletcher left Boston, in fall 1917, Jones embraced the Bolshevik Revolution (as all Wobblies did in 1917), distributed Wobbly literature including the *Industrial Worker*, and more. Jones also was connected to—likely introduced by Fletcher—A. Philip Randolph and Chandler Owen.

On May Day, 1919, many cities, including Boston, experienced large pro-tests led by Socialists and joined by many thousands of others. In some places, anarchists blew up government buildings and, in Boston, Jones was suspected to be part of these actions. By fall 1919, and likely sooner, Jones was being sur-veilled by federal agents. In mid-November, he was detained by police after a raid on an IWW hall in New York City, where he had relocated. A few days later, under emotional stress and perhaps severe mental troubles, Jones shot and killed Theresa Klein, his roommate and partner (political and maybe romantic). He proceeded to kill himself.

The mention of Trotter in this letter further reveals Fletcher's black radical circles—not just IWW, Socialist, labor, and leftist circles but also black national-ist. Fletcher was well networked in Boston as well as New York City, Philadelphia, Baltimore, Norfolk, and elsewhere.

In re: Joseph J. Jones
Agent West
Oct. 3, 1919

Under date of August 21st Ben H. Fletcher, an IWW prisoner at
Leavenworth Penitentiary, wrote Jones as follows:

"Fellow worker:

Yours of the 18th is just in hand and I note your willingness to
assist me in proffering [?] my bond. Many thanks for the interest
you have already invested. Articles you mention have been noted
with much elation. On my solicitation Haywood has instructed
Carter of Local 8, IWW Phila. Pa., to attend the coming Negro Labor
Convention held in Wash., DC, on Aug. 25th and there try to enlist
their support on my behalf. It is needless for me to state here that
I am sorry that you will not be in attendance to help nurse things
along here. Have written both Owen and Randolph apropos to
the proposition but to date no reply. I think that either Phila. Or
Chicago would have been better field for you. Jack rec'd Mrs. K's
picture from Chaplain who is now in Chicago, and forwarded home
to her Monday. It is a fine copy of the original.

You should drop in and see Trotter of 34 Cornhill. Maybe he
would be willing to assist. Write soon. Would suggest that you
write to Haywood at Gen. Hdqts., 1001 W. Madison St., Chicago, if
you think you can line up anybody on my bond. With best wishes,
am yours for Ours,

Ben H. Fletcher

P.S. My folks have moved to 1613 So. 9th St., Phila. My brother has
returned from France OK.

B.H.F.

■ Case #36727, "Old German Files," Record Group 65, National Archives

35

Fletcher Reflects on Past and Future

In these letters written to a confidante, just before his release from Leavenworth on bond, Fletcher revealed some tantalizing information. For one, it is the only instance in which Fletcher mentioned he had belonged to the Socialist Party, almost certainly in the early 1910s when Haywood and other Wobblies also belonged; clearly, he had long left the SPA. Fletcher also noted that he did not believe the path to socialism lay via elections but also that he was not opposed to those who voted. In the first letter, Fletcher referred to the victory of SP member Victor Berger, who represented Milwaukee in the US House of Representatives for several terms. Milwaukee, with its large, progressive German American community, was the largest city in the country to elect Socialists to serve in Congress as well as its mayor's office. Quite likely, Othelia Hampel was part of that scene.

Alas, almost nothing is known of Hampel, though she must have been a kindred spirit considering how much Fletcher shared with her and that they corresponded at all. She was born around 1902 in Milwaukee. Her family name is German, and her father immigrated from Germany to the US, while her mother was born in Wisconsin. During and after the big IWW trial in 1918, a broad coalition of liberals and leftists organized to assist in mutual aid and secure the IWW prisoners' release. It seems Hampel was one such person, likely a member of the SP. Fletcher's commitment to the IWW and, more broadly, his hopes of advancing beyond capitalism also shine through.

Kansas City, Missouri
January 1st, 1920

H.H. Stroud, Esq.,
Box 663
Milwaukee, Wisconsin

Dear Sir:

For your information, there follows a copy of a letter in part, written under date of December 31st, 1919 by Ben H. Fletcher, a Colored IWW

Prisoner confined in the Federal Penitentiary at Leavenworth, Kansas, addressed to Othelia Hampel, 545 25th Street, Milwaukee, Wisconsin:

"I join you in your elation over the recent victory in the Fifth Congressional District, it is a vindication. If as the opposition slain, the ballot box result is a barometer of our desires and intentions (political) then, it goes beyond questioning that so far as the Fifth Congressional District of Wisconsin is concerned the enfranchised are tired and disgusted with the Reactionary conduct of our Nation's affairs.

"Personally, I am of the opinion that between now and this time next year not a few similar signs of change will be recorded. We are living in momentous times, even the air seems supercharged with the spirit of the coming charge. None of us are so gifted with the power "clairvoyancy" [clairvoyance] as to be able to fortell [sic] the day or the hour, therefore the first and most important duty is for all of us to prepare ourselves for the final chapter in the life of Capitalism.

"But, excuse me, your [sic] a socialist and here I am getting off a "spiel" just as if you were not. Yet an IWW was never known to do otherwise.

"I signed my bond two weeks ago and am waiting for its approval (which will be a little while yet. After my release expect to go hunting and trapping in Maine. Do you in attend school.

"The class-conscious movement of Labor is the most purposeful Ideal that was ever known. I don't worry and am serenely confident that our cause will eventually triumph. Until she does, I know that the road to Industrial Freedom is going to be rocky, but if each does his bit and stick to the task, it won't be rocky long."

Please regard the source of this information as confidential.

Very truly yours,

Arthur T. Bagley,
Division Superintendent

Kansas City, Missouri
January 24, 1920

T.H. Campbell, Esq.,
Box 275
St. Paul, Minnesota

Dear Sir:

For your information, there follows a copy of a letter written by Ben H. Fletcher, a Colored IWW Prisoner now confined in the Federal Penitentiary at Leavenworth, Kansas, who is soon to be released on bond—addressed to Miss Othelia Hampel, 545 25th Street, Milwaukee, Wisconsin:

"January 22, 1920
"Dear Comrade:
"Yours truly came duly to hand and needless to state I was glad to hear from you. Owing to some oversight in the execution of my bond my release has been delayed, temporarily. You ask where I hail from, well, I am from Philadelphia, Penn. The city of Brotherly love. While that might sound facetious it is a fact nevertheless, that a little more unity has prevailed there during the present maelstrom of Labor oppression, than in most cities. The IWW is very strongly represented in the Marine Transportation Industry of Phila—We have about seven thousand longshoremen and seamen, there.

"Have been a member of the Socialist Party in Phila, the Messenger is making strides there among the Negro. Do you read it? Like yourself, I suppose I was born a rebel, though I have had varied experiences some which would have caused me to align myself with the employing class if I could have forgotten the place from which I sprung. While I do not countenance against the working class striking at the ballot box, I am firmly convinced that foremost and historical mission of Labor is to organize as a class, Industrially, train and develop our own technicians "scientific" men and woman and thereby prepare ourselves to successfully continue the operation of Industry, when capitalist Society [dies it will be] of 'dry rot.' Of course any political gain, redress or concession that we can secure is the meanwhile and should not be ignored. And so political unity follows industry unity, being it's [sic] shadow—we go marching onward to certain victory.

"We are living in stirring times. Personally I don't think we have anything to fear in the New York Assembly situation, 'Big Business' will not permit the matter to hold, because it would establish a precedent whereby any minority party could be barred from holding office because it held views and opinions differing from the majority Party of parties.

"Heard from a former college Pal of mine recently who went "over the top" he mentioned that since being demobilized he never saw the serious attention given to discourse on Social Topics among the negro workers as now obtains, knowing the psychology of the American capitalist as do I, this is good news because the especially big interests, are banking on the negro as the American 'White guard' when the break down comes.

"The report I mentioned together with numerous others, I've received, met including the many papers we, the Negro, are now publishing—presenting the cause and remedy buoys me up, and this ten year sentence doesn't weigh so heavy. Must ring off, have served 1 and 1/2 years."

Please regard the source of this information as confidential.

Very truly yours,

Arthur T. Bagley,
Division Superintendent

■ Both from Ben H. Fletcher, Case Number 29434, Investigative Case Files of the Bureau of Investigation.

36

Fletcher Out on Bond— Still Troublemaking

The first, brief IWW article announcing Fletcher's release from Leavenworth includes another mention of Fletcher's joke and suggests the wide circulation of this vignette. The IWW publication *New Solidarity* evolved out of *Defense News Bulletin*, also published in Chicago.

Fletcher corresponded with James Phillips, a Finnish-born, Boston-based, IWW seaman and Fletcher's primary point of contact when he organized there in 1917 and, quite possibly, earlier. Like Fletcher, Phillips was caught up in the wartime dragnet of Wobblies and found guilty in the same mass trial. Phillips was sentenced to five years in prison and served most of that in Leavenworth where they would have had plenty of time together. According to historian Stephen M. Kohn, Phillips was deported after getting out of prison.

The Sandgren named by Fletcher in his letter referred to John Sandgren, editor of the IWW magazine *One Big Union Monthly* in 1920. Sandgren was an anarchist who, like Fletcher, was highly suspicious of the growing Communist presence in the IWW and used his position accordingly. He later was removed from his position for being too stridently anticommunist.

Fletcher's letter to his father, Dennis, is the most unusual as almost nothing is known about his father. The reference to Penrose was to US Senator Boies Penrose (Republican) who dominated Pennsylvania state politics, including Philadelphia, for the first two decades of the twentieth century. Bob McKenty was the well-known warden of the Eastern State Penitentiary, a notorious prison located in Philadelphia. In Fletcher's letter to Phillips, Harold Lord Varney was a Wobbly and writer.

Ben Fletcher, the only colored Fellow Worker tried and convicted on the Chicago federal indictment, was released from Leavenworth on bond last week pending the outcome of the appeal. Fellow Worker Fletcher received a ten-year bit and, it will be remembered, commented that Judge Landis' literary style was going on the blink: he was pronouncing such long sentences. Fletcher's home is in Philadelphia, where he was an organizer for MTWIU No. 8, and he expects to go there this week.

■ *New Solidarity,* February 14, 1920, 3

Kansas City, Missouri
February 4, 1920

Todd Daniel, Esq.,
P.O. Box 451
Philadelphia, Pa.

Dear Sir:

There follows, for your information, excerpts from a letter written by Ben H. Fletcher, an IWW prisoner confined in Leavenworth Penitentiary, to Dennis Fletcher, 1613 South 9th St., Philadelphia, Pa.

> "Have not succeeded in getting headed East, yet, why I do not know. I wrote my Bondman last week relative thereto, may be something will be forthcoming shortly."
>
> . . . [in original]
>
> "Penrose is the boss again Philly—has anybody been rewarded in our District? One of our boys here is a personal friend of Billy McComeh who was Captain so long ago, and Bob McKenty. There is a bunch of us here from Philly, and now and then we get together and pop off about the various happenings places and people. One thing we are agreed on is that this Western country is a h of a place. Would you believe this, that men are working here as guards for as low as $75 a month—about a hundred is the highest now don't laugh, because I know when you worked for our dear old Uncle your graft was more than that. It's time to go to rest and I must ring off."

Please regard the source of this information as confidential.

Very truly yours,

Arthur T. Bagley,
Division Superintendent

★

Kansas City, Missouri
February 14, 1920

R.B. Spencer, Esq.,
Box 987
Pittsburg [sic], Pa.

Dear Sir:

For your information there follows a copy of a letter written by Ben H. Fletcher, a recently released colored IWW Prisoner on bond from the Federal Penitentiary at Leavenworth, Kansas, addressed to James Phillips, an IWW Prisoner now confined in the above mentioned institution. The letter is postmarked Pittsburg [sic], Pennsylvania; February 11, 1920:

"Dear Jim:

"My Phila address is 1613 So. 9th St., and I am leaving here for there tonight, write me there apropos to your personals in NY. Halls are open here. Business as usual. Monster meeting protesting against recent raids the Sunday, at the Coliseum (10,000) in attendance.

"Robli Magnes of NY went down the line in Royal style. No trimming. Keynote of speech Industrial Organization of labor to get the power to enforce Justice and realize Industrial Freedom. Byers is out. Looks bad all are out except Bloom and one or two others.

"Over 100 more jailed much furniture smashed etc. Case came up yesterday for preliminary hearing was postponed until April 8. Dist Atty. Claiming Indictments not being perfected yet. It has been a pretty hard struggle yet there is much room for improvement. Members are standing firm and resolute, however. Fox is missing.

"Harold Hood Varney is no longer pulling for us. IWW is too conservative is his excuse—whatever that means. My opinion is its cold feet. Had a talk with Sandgren and he is on the level. Thoroughly understands that the IWW is not to be swamped by mass action nonsense or other villetenti [?] movements.

Yours for Ours,

(signed) Ben H. Fletcher"

Please regard the source of this information as confidential.

Yours very truly,

Arthur T. Bagley
Division Superintendent
Bureau of Investigation
Department of Justice

★

Kansas City, Missouri
February 23, 1920
Todd Daniel, Esq.,
P.O. Box 451
Philadelphia, Pa.

Dear Sir:

For your information this letter is to advise you that Ben H. Fletcher, 1613 So. 9th St., Philadelphia, a colored radical IWW prisoner recently released on bond from the United States Penitentiary is corresponding with IWW prisoners confined in the penitentiary at Leavenworth. From the contents of the correspondence he is evidently to be engaged in radical-IWW work.

Kindly regard the source of this information as confidential.

Very truly yours,

Arthur T. Bagley,
Division Superintendent

■ Last three from Ben H. Fletcher, Case Number 29434, Investigative Case Files of the Bureau of Investigation.

★

Agent: J.F. McDevitt
Place report made: Philadelphia, Pa.
Date report made: 2/15/18
Period for which report made: 2/21/20

"Radical Activities—Philadelphia District" (excerpt)

Ben Fletcher, the IWW Negro Organizer, whom I arrested as a result of the big IWW raids in 1917 and who was afterwards indicted with the 166 in Chicago, has just been released and has returned to Philadelphia and taken up his old work as an active IWW.

■ #202600-1617, "Old German Files," Bureau of Intelligence, Record Group 65: Department of Justice, National Archives

37

The Price of Progress

Despite the risk of being sent back to Leavenworth for the slightest infraction, once released Fletcher gave numerous public speeches. In classic Wobbly style, Philadelphia IWW's organized a weekly meeting on a street corner in South Philadelphia—a longstanding, multiethnic, working-class community and just a mile from the waterfront. The title of Fletcher's talk surely was a topic he had pondered while in prison.

PHILADELPHIA WOBS ATTENTION

KNOWLEDGE IS POWER

Come to the Open Forum of the Industrial Workers of the World, held every Sunday, 2 P.M. at SE Cor. 8th and McKean Sts. And increase your knowledge on current events, economics, Industrial Unionism, etc.

Sunday, March 21, 1920
Subj: Economics
By J. Cleary

Sunday, March 28, 1920
Subj: Dictatorship of the Proletariat
By William Stockinger

Sunday, April 11, 1920
Subj: The American Bastille
By G[iovanni] Baldazzi

Sunday, April 18, 1920
Subj: Revolutionary Progress
By E. Abate

Sunday, April 25, 1920
Subj: The Price of Progress
By Ben Fletcher

Admission Free. Open Discussion

■ *New Solidarity*, April 2, 1920, 4.

38

The Abolition Movement of the Twentieth Century

This article by Fletcher, possibly a letter to the editor, is incomplete but still quite instructive about Fletcher's knowledge of US labor and race relations and passion for the IWW. In particular, Fletcher explored—for a black readership—why so many black workers chose to replace unionized workers on strike (i.e., to scab): namely, those unions, most part of the AFL, were racist in that they denied membership to black members or, at best, segregated them. In this regard, Fletcher confirmed why Booker T. Washington, the most prominent African American of the late nineteenth and early twentieth centuries, encouraged black people to act as strikebreakers. Another outcome of the racism of white workers and most unions was that black workers considered white employers as their allies rather than their fellow (white) workers. In such a scenario, the primary beneficiaries were employers who divided and, thus, weakened workers resulting in lower wages for workers and higher profits for bosses. To Fletcher, the solution for black workers was obvious: join the IWW. In the short term, that would result in material benefits, but he also was clear that the long-term goal was to abolish capitalism. The means was industrial unionism which he explains quite effectively using an example from the construction industry, which was—and remains—plagued by craft unionism.

Since the founding of Local 8, in 1913, organizing workers in the port of Baltimore had been a priority. Similar to Philadelphia, dockworkers in Baltimore consisted of many African American, Irish, and Polish men. Its white and European immigrant workers belonged to the ILA but were weak. Fletcher and other Wobbly organizers repeatedly were dispatched to line up the longshoremen who remained an elusive prize. Local 8 was to commence its largest strike a few months later so ensuring that Baltimore longshoremen did not unload "hot cargo" was a high priority for Local 8.

The *Baltimore Afro-American* was the main black newspaper in a city that, alongside Washington, DC, had the largest black population in the South. Established in 1892, it remains in operation and in recent years has been nicknamed the *Afro*.

... When this situation was brought to the attention of the rank and file of these organizations and they, in any instance, took steps to stop this union scabbing tactics in order to present a united front in their struggles for a better life in industry, their officials immediately drove home the fact that they had a contract and agreement with the employer and must not violate same even to secure solidarity of labor.

Thousands of strikes and hundreds of labor unions were lost as a direct result of this situation. Then aside from this organized scabbery there was another factor that prevented a successful outcome of the trade unions' attempts to get results worthwhile. This factor was the Negro worker who constitute 15 per cent of the actual wage workers in these United States and produce three fifths of the wealth in the South.

It is common knowledge to the readers of this paper that the Negro worker was almost completely divorced and ignored by the trade unions, mostly affiliated with the American Federation of Labor. The leaders of the American Federation of Labor are for the most part as bitterly opposed to the Negro worker becoming a factor in the affairs of the labor movement as the Employer himself. Naturally the Negro worker welcomed any opportunity to take the places of members of this organization that was so hostile and prejudiced against the Negro.

Therefore the founders of the IWW having obtained these facts from their inquiry were determined that the organization they would put on foot would meet these issues squarely and solve them. Hence, the IWW was organized as an Industrial Union, it being the avowed aim of the organization to assemble Labor in the Union as is assembled on the job.

Instead of organizing the hod-carriers, bricklayers and carpenters on a building as separate organized workers—organize them as Building Construction Workers.

Second, the IWW was to organize Labor regardless of its race, color or trade. It was held then that race prejudice must not and will not be permitted to play any part in the IWW. Needless to state these principles have never been compromised; and that is the REASON WHY the IWW is damned, persecuted and lied about by the employing class and their minions.

That is why Haywood and ninety-three others including the writer (who is now at liberty on $40,000 bail) were sentenced to terms of years as high as twenty years.

Concentration of industry makes the American Federation of Labor unable to cope with the growing power of trust magnates. The IWW by organizing the workers, regardless of race, color or trade is forming the structure of another society. Not being organized to just secure more wages the IWW holds that it is the historic mission of the working class to abolish the wage system. It is the abolition movement of the twentieth century, and if sufficient number of workers rally to its standard complete industrial emancipation will be the heritage of all us workers and we will become disenthralled from the thralldom of the rich.

Ben H. Fletcher

■ *Baltimore Afro-American*, April 2, 1920, 4.

39

Organizing the Atlantic Coast

Fletcher and Jack Walsh, another Local 8 organizer also released on bond from Leavenworth, are praised for their work organizing longshoremen along the Atlantic. Fletcher's work in Baltimore was especially important as Local 8 called a massive strike a few months later, so needed the help of workers, notably in Baltimore, to deny shipping companies that might transfer ships elsewhere. It demands repeating that their efforts were risky as they were only temporarily released from prison. For transgressions, legal or imagined, they could be sent back to Leavenworth and forfeit their bonds.

The Marine Transport Workers Industrial Union No. 8 is planning an intensive organizing campaign this spring and intends to make a big drive for membership on all fronts.

On the Atlantic Coast Fellow-workers Jack Walsh and Ben H. Fletcher old and experienced members in the Marine industry are taking charge of the Atlantic Coast drive.

Fellow-worker Jack Walsh is at present in Boston and will put in his time in New England. Boston before the war was one of our strongest ports and Fellow-worker Walsh who has formerly done good work in Boston will undoubtedly put this port again on the map as one of the strongholds of the MTW.

Fellow-worker Ben Fletcher is concentrating his efforts on Baltimore. Baltimore is the port in which we lined up 1,200 colored longshoremen in one month in 1917. And through a combination between the bosses and the AF of L our members were blacklisted and forced off the job. Fellow-worker Fletcher in a few days was able to reorganize the defunct branch and reports that prospects of a good stable organization is exceptionally good in Baltimore.

On the Lakes, Fellow Worker Kangas who has done good work last season will be placed in the same territory and we expect very good results.

As soon as we can get a competent Italian organizer we will make an organization drive in the port of New York.

With such good prospects of organization before us, with the Old Unions falling to pieces and with such good competent men in charge of the organization work No. 8 should be able to double its membership.

It is up to all *the members* to co-operate with our traveling delegates to help them in all possible ways. Remember the best organizers can do little without the earnest and hearty co-operation of the entire membership.

The MTW No. 8 has been lucky to get such old, earnest, and competent members to go into the field and do their part and we trust that all members will co-operate and help build up a strong and powerful union in the Marine Industry.

Now altogether for a 100 per cent increase in membership for 1920.

Get credentials if you have not got them. Co-operate with the traveling delegates. Get busy and pull together for a 100 per cent organization of the MTW on the waterfront.

Don't forget to send suggestions on organization work to the MTW Conference to be held May 6th at Chicago, Ill.

With best wishes, we remain, Yours for the One Big Union of the MTW

James Scott, Sec-Treas.
Elmer Kennard, Chairman, G.O.C. [General Organizing Committee]

■ *One Big Union Monthly*, May 1920, 54.

40

On the Baltimore Waterfront

Fletcher regularly visited Baltimore since its longshoremen, as in Philadelphia, consisted primarily of African Americans, Irish Americans, and Polish immigrants. In fact, he likely lived in Baltimore for a month or two during this campaign.

Ben Fletcher is doing well in Baltimore and the branch has taken on new life. A Polish organizer is needed in this port and the M.T.W. Conference will probably place one here.

—James Scott (Sec-Treas. MTW) and Elmer Kennard (Chairman, G.O.C.)

■ *One Big Union Monthly*, June 1920, 57.

41

Fletcher's Sterling Honesty and Humor

The *New York Call*, a daily newspaper published from 1908 to 1923, was affiliated with the Socialist Party of America. In 1918, David Karsner covered the IWW trial for the *Call* and, in 1920, he wrote a six-part series for its Sunday magazine entitled "The War and the IWW." Worth clarifying, for twenty-first century readers, is the phrase Haywood used to describe Fletcher: "one of the whitest men we've got." In the early twentieth century, many variations of the phrase "that's white of you" circulated in the United States. Such a saying illuminates the pervasiveness of white supremacy in that era and not just in the American South. That Haywood, who knew Fletcher well and had long organized black and other workers of color, used that phrase presumably was evidence of his awareness of racism, so his use of the term possibly was ironic—or perhaps not.

"About Ben Fletcher"

I should not wish to close this phase of the story without a word about Ben Fletcher, the only Negro defendant in the Chicago case. Fletcher was a stevedore in Philadelphia before he became an Organizer for the Marine Transport Workers at $16 a week [in 1917]. Ben's correspondence was voluminous, and most of it was read to the jury by Assistant Prosecutor Porter. There was one letter of Ben's among the batch that stood out above all the others. Ben wrote to Haywood acknowledging receipt of his weekly pay check, and replied that he was inclosing money order for one day's wages, payable to the general headquarters, because he had worked for the IWW only five days, instead of six that week, taking a day off to get married. When that letter was read lawyers of both sides and newspaper men agreed that sterling honesty of that character was very rare.

In the early stage of the trial, when the government was reading letters by the defendants almost daily, and the proceedings were exceedingly tedious, Ben leaned over to Haywood and remarked that he was "the only man who lent any color to the proceedings."

Fletcher was never jailed [during the trial]. He managed to get bail in Philadelphia as soon as he was arrested in September, 1917 [this isn't true as discussed in Documents 20–24]. He twice offended the good temper of the court, once by oversleeping and once by overeating. The last offense caused Jude Landis to cancel Ben's bail, and he spent about two weeks in the Cook County jail. Ben took his punishment good naturedly, saying that the meal with which he gorged himself was well worth the punishment. Haywood remarked to me when Ben was found prostrated by too much food: "We don't want to lose Ben; he's one of the whitest men we've got."

Judge Landis gave Fletcher 10 years. "The judge is using bad English today; his sentences are too long," remarked Fletcher, smiling when he heard his fate.

■ David Karsner, "The War and the IWW: The Extent of its Opposition to the Draft," *New York Call Magazine*, September 5, 1920, 6–8.

42

Solving the Race Problem

This detailed *Messenger* article allowed readers to glimpse at the inner workings of Local 8 from the perspective of an ally attending one of its meetings. According to a federal agent's report, coeditors Chandler Owen and A. Philip Randolph both attended Local 8's meeting on June 10, 1921. It examined how rank and file members were firmly committed to the ideology of the IWW and understood how essential interracialism and equality (e.g., in wages regardless of craft) were to their success. The author noted and condemned a black person advocating for black-only unions. In 1920, the ideal of black nationalism was quite popular thanks to Marcus Garvey and the Universal Negro Improvement Association which he led. The editors of the *Messenger*, however, were socialists who rejected black-only organizations. This article also highlighted how black workers, in particular, benefited materially from belonging to an antiracist union. In addition, due to the power and inclusive nature of Local 8, black people could walk more safely in the neighborhood and even had moved into previously white-only blocks—a fascinating bit of evidence that ran counter to the rising racism and segregation in Philadelphia and across the nation during and after World War I.

In the city of the Quakers, the Southern bugaboo—the Negro and white peoples, has been routed by the plain, unvarnished workers. In the Marine Transport Workers Industrial Union, No. 8, there are 3,500 men, three-fifths of whom are Negroes. During the war there were more than six thousand men in the organization.

Despite the affiliation of Local 8 with the IWW, no attempt was made during the war to destroy the organization, doubtless due, so it is rumored among the men, to the recognition by the boss stevedores of the fact that the union had the power to tie up the port of Philadelphia.

Another signal achievement to which the men point with great pride is that no mishaps, as explosions of any kind, occurred in their port—one of the largest and most important ports in the country, during the war, from which munitions and various materials of war were shipped to the Allies. Yet, malicious propagandists have sought to stigmatize these men as "anarchists" and "bomb throwers."

Again, the organization has been the lever with which the men have raised their wages from 25 cents to 80 cents and $1.20 per hour [for overtime]. They have also established union conditions on the job. They have overthrown monarchy in the transport industry of Philadelphia, and set up a certain form of industrial democracy, in that the boss stevedores and the delegates of the union confer to adjust differences that arise between the longshoremen and the shipping interests. This is quite a long way from the day when the boss stevedores hired and fired, and reduced wages without let-up or hindrance. Then chaos reigned on the waterfront. The longshoremen had no power because they had no organization.

"But times have changed," so one of the men assured us with a twinkle of triumph in his eyes; seeming at the same time to imply that they would never again return to the old conditions.

"We have no distinctions in this union"—another vouchsafed, "Everybody draws the same wage, even to the waterboy."

At this time, our interesting confab with the different workers standing around in the hall, was abruptly cut short by a sharp rap of a gavel reinforced a husky voice, calling for order. Men were seen, in different parts of the hall, we observed two workers, one black and one white, seated upon a platform. We inquired of their functions, and were informed that the colored worker was the chairman and the white worker was the secretary.

The chairman was direct and positive and yet not intolerant. The meeting proceeded smoothly, interrupted here and there with some incoherent remarks, giving evidence that John Barleycorn was not dead. This was taken good-naturedly, however, as the worker, in question, was known as a good union man.

The most interesting phase of this meeting was the report of a committee on a movement to segregate the Negroes into a separate union. Strange, to say, this move came from alleged intelligent Negroes outside of the union, who have heretofore cried down the white workers on the ground that they excluded Negroes from their unions.

It is interesting to note, in this connection, that the white workers were as violent as the Negroes in condemning this idea of segregation. All over the hall murmurs were heard, "I'll be damned if I'll stand for anybody to break up this organization," "It's the bosses trying to divide us," "We've been together this long and we will be together on."

Finally a motion was passed to adopt a program of action of propaganda and publicity to counteract this nefarious propaganda to wreck the organization upon the rocks of race prejudice.

Here was the race problem being worked out by black and white workers. They have built up a powerful organization—an organization which has been the foundation of a good living for the men. Many a man told us that he had been able to maintain this children in high school on the wages Local 8 had secured for him, and at the thought of anyone attacked the organization, his eyes flashed—a hissing fire of hate—regarding such an attack as an attack upon his life and the lives of his wife and children.

Colored workers told us, too, that they remember when a colored man could not walk along the waterfront, so high was the feeling running between the races. But, now all races work on the water-front. Negro families live all through that section. It is a matter of common occurrence for Negro and white workers to combine against a white or a black scab.

And the organization, Local 8 of the Marine Transport Workers Industrial Union did it all! The white and black workers were then pulling together. Why should they now pull apart? What they have done, they can do, and even more, if only the workers of races realizes their power lies in solidarity—which is achieved through industrial organizations.

■ *Messenger*, July 1921, 214–15.

43

The Forum of Local 8

Another fascinating and all too rare peek at the inside of a Local 8 meeting. Since the federal government confiscated all of the union's records through September 1917 and postwar ones apparently have not survived, either, this report is precious. It discusses two of the most important issues Local 8 dealt with after World War I: ferocious competition with the AFL's International Longshoremen's Association (ILA) and the rise of Marcus Garvey's Universal Negro Improvement Association, the latter referred to obliquely for advocating voluntary segregation which the *Messenger* editors vigorously opposed. The editors praised Local 8 for attacking racial divisions among its membership through educational forums which organized discussions on topics including the resurgent Ku Klux Klan and the Tulsa Race Riot of 1921. Lastly, this piece recalls an era when workers frequently met at their union halls for political and social discussions.

The meeting was called to order at 8:30 P.M. sharp. Immediately the gavel sounded, a hall of six or seven hundred eager-eyed workers doffed their hats and sat up erect—a picture of attention, interest and enthusiasm. It was the beginning of an innovation among workers.

It was a conscious and deliberate effort of the Marine Transport Workers to conduct a systematic forum for self-education.

Rumors had been floating in the air about the rise of a dual union. It had been reported that agents of the ILA were operating along the waterfront, seeking to sow the seeds of discord and dissension among the rank and file of the organization. Alleged Negro leaders masquerading in the guise of race loyalty, had been preaching the nefarious and dangerous doctrine of race segregation to the Negro members of Local 8. Negroes were made all sorts of fictitious and fraudulent promises about their receiving sick and death benefits. To these sugar-coated, empty and unsubstantial pledges, the militant, class-conscious and intelligent Negro workers turned a deaf ear. They meted out to the self-styled and self-appointed ILA saviors of the Negro workers, curses instead of blessings.

It was to reinforce and fortify the brains of Local 8 that this forum was organized. Only those men of the organization were deceived by the notorious misrepresentation of the paid agents of the bosses who were "strong in class the back and weak in the head." But always alert, active and conscious of its class interests, Local 8 proceeded to formulate plans to break down the insidious, antilabor solidarity propaganda of the ILA.

The subject of the lecture of the first meeting was "The Relation of Organized Labor to Race Riots."

The speaker attempted to show that inasmuch as labor fights race riots just as it fights the wars between nations, only labor could stop race riots. He pointed out that just as the bosses of the workers profit from national wars, so the bosses of the workers profit from race wars; that it was to the interest of the capitalists to keep the workers divided upon race lines so that they could rob them more easily and successfully. He stated that: "If the white and black working dogs are kept fighting over the bone of race prejudice, the artful, hypocritical yellow capitalist dog will steal up and grab the meat of profit." It was explained how race riots served the interests of the employers of labor, by keeping the workers divided, at daggers points. He indicated how the ILA was serving the interests of the Stevedores and Shipping Interests by preaching a race-riot doctrine of segregation.

Brief, pointed and enthusiastic questions and discussions followed the lecture.

There was an evident passion to talk among the fellow workers. The forum afforded them an ideal opportunity to vent their grievances against the ILA and the entire tribe of anti-labor forces in the country.

Although the verbs and nouns seldom lay down in harmony and peace, the clear economic thinking of the fellow workers was marvelous and evident to any one.

Each speaker deplored and condemned the Tulsa race riot in Oklahoma. With a sound working-class instinct they laid the cause of the Tulsa massacres at the door of the labor-hating, profiteering, conscience-less Ku Klux Klan predatory business interests of the South.

Here, too, was a living example of the ability of white and black people to work, live and conduct their common affairs side by side. There were black and white men and black and white women in this meeting. No rapes, no lynchings, no race riots occurred! Isn't it wonderful! Let the Southern press together with its northern, eastern and western journalistic kith and kin, bent upon their base, corrupt, wicked and hateful mission of poisoning the wells of public opinion with the virulent spleen of race prejudice, taken note!

The second forum meeting discussed the interesting subject of "Labor Preparedness for the Next War." "Industrial Unionism, the Only Hope of the Workers" provided an enthusiastic and lively discussion. John Barleycorn wormed his way into the stomach of one fellow and upset his head, thereby necessitating a discussion of the "Relation of Liquor to the Labor Movement." Searching and discerning questions on the economics of the Prohibition Movement were hurled at the speaker. "Was the abolition of the liquor industry which increased unemployment to the interest of the workers?" was asked. The speaker answered that, "there was no more reason for advocating the sale of liquor, a recognized poison, on the ground that it afforded employment to workers than there was to advocate war, or the building of houses of prostitution on the grounds that such would afford employment to the workers."

This meeting was followed by a lecture on the "Open Shop Campaign— the Remedy: Trades or Industrial Unionism."

The Forum meets every Friday evening in Philadelphia.

Here the workers are trying to democratize knowledge, for they, too, are learning that knowledge is power and that if the capitalists control all the knowledge, they will also control the world.

■ *Messenger*, August 1921, 234.

"Protect yourself from this menace: The Ku-Klux-Klan," IWW poster, c. 1924. University of Michigan Library (Special Collections Research Center, Joseph A. Labadie Collection).

44

The Task of Local 8

In the *Messenger*, coeditors Owen and Randolph regularly critiqued global capitalism and praised the IWW. They went out of their way to highlight how Local 8, in particular, stood at the vanguard of interracial unionism, citing specific examples of how it organized its meetings and directly attacked the matter of racism at educational gatherings.

Labor, the world over, is faced with the task of rescuing humanity from the wreck of capitalism. In England, France, Italy, Germany, and America, the laboring element are the chief victims of the impasse, precipitated in industry, by the present masters of the world.

The industries, built up by labor and operated for the production social necessities, are now idle. As a result of the inability of the high priests of capitalism to carry on production without interruption, unemployment, want and misery blight the lives of millions of willing workers in every land where the system of private ownership in the social tools of production, obtains.

For the work of taking over the business of running the world, the toilers need to prepare. In every country, and in every industry, the workers are confronted with the task of preparing themselves. This is the most immediate phase of their work. To this task, be it said to the credit of the Industrial Workers of the World, Research Bureaus have been established. Their purpose is to investigate the processes of industries, such as mining, manufacturing, feeding, shipping, railroading, banking, farming, etc.—with a view to placing, at the convenience of labor, a body of scientific knowledge essential to an efficient control, operation and management of the world's work.

The plan of scientific-knowledge-research-bureaus is a direct and necessary outgrowth of the industrial union form of organization. In an industrial democracy, the industry will naturally form the unit of society, and, hence, a knowledge of its organization, processes, and technique of management becomes, at once, the primary prerequisite to those in whose charge the industrial mechanism will fall. In anticipation of the trend of the industrial life of the world, labor unions, in all of the various countries are turning their attention to problems of industrial control, operation, and management. In England, the recognition by the workers of the need for greater knowledge of the machinery of production and exchange is manifest in their development of the "shop stewards' movement." In Germany, Italy and France similar movements are in process of development.

As a result of this new urge for knowledge, workers' colleges, papers and magazines, forums and churches, have grown up. They are mobilizing an army of educators to conduct their educational efforts. The class struggle has, at last, driven the proletariat to see that education, organization and agitation must go hand in hand, and that not until the workers have achieved a working class solidarity based upon scientific knowledge, will they seriously struggle for emancipation. This, of course, does not mean that each worker must be a political economist, but it does mean that the workers must understand the nature of the class organization of society; they must realize what a menace to the interests of the workers, divisions upon race, religion, color, sex, nationality and trade, constitute. Needless to say, that economic understanding must come both from the struggle between labor and capital, and the conscious educational efforts of organized labor. For a long time labor has received its training, in toto, from the school of industrial war, and such was the logical and inevitable thing to happen; for the material conditions of strife and conflict alone could effectively convince the workers of the necessity of their employing the same weapons of offense and defense that are employed by the employing class. A capitalist press, school, forum, church, stage and screen can only be counteracted by a labor press, school, forum, church, stage and screen. As capitalists are organized upon the basis of the industry and several industries are integrated, and centralized into One Big Union of Capital, so labor must organize upon the basis of the industry and integrate and centralize its industrial units into One Big Union. This logic, of course, applies to the questions of race, color, religion, sex or nationality. They fan and enkindle the sinister flames of religious, race, color and nationality prejudice in order that the poor, gullible, credulous, well-meaning but misguided "Henry Dubbs"—the slaves, will fly at each other's throats, for while they, the workers, fight among themselves, the Bosses rob them all.

To offset the separation tendency among the workers, the Marine Transport Workers of Philadelphia, Pennsylvania, have entered the vanguard of American labor. When the spirit of race prejudice between the black and white workers, on the waterfront in Philadelphia first manifested itself, Local 8 proceeded to conduct an educational campaign in leaflets and forum lectures. This forum was attended largely by both black and white workers. The lecture course covered a wide range of subjects, touching upon national and international topics. The questions and discussions from the floor were pointed, well put and intelligent. Chiefly the economic aspect of the topics discussed, was stressed by the workers.

The leaflets which were issued by the organization dealt with some subject vital to the interests of the workers. Local 8 is working out the methods in its special industry which will equip the toilers for the task of workers control and management. No finer spirit of brotherhood can be found anywhere than exists in the organization. Upon entering the hall, during meetings, one is met with the fact of a Negro chairman and a white secretary sitting side by side conducting the meeting. From the floor, white and colored workers rise, make themselves heard, make motions, argue questions pro and con, have their differences and settle them, despite Imperial Wizard Colonel William Joseph Simmons' and Marcus Garvey's "Race First" bogey. At picnics, the workers also mingle, fraternize, dance, eat and play together. Nor do the Negro workers dance, eat and play only among themselves; but both white and black men, white and black women, and white and black children eat, play and dance together just as they work and hold their meetings together.

Local 8 is setting the example which labor groups throughout the country must emulate if the Ku Klux Klan which is behind Tulsa, is to be destroyed, and if the open shop campaign is to fail.

The *Messenger* and its editors have been trying to spread this "Brotherhood" propaganda among the white and black workers, wherever and whenever possible. Glad to say, the Marine Transport Workers is one of the few labor organizations which has given whole-hearted support, moral and financial.

When the workers, in America, are able to build Local 8's in every section of the country, the 100 per centers, the Open Shoppers, the combined manufacturers and capitalists of America, will not dare to institute an assault upon labor in the guise of the "American Plan."

■ *Messenger*, October 1921, 262–63.

45

Advice from a Black, Radical Friend

This letter from Chandler Owen, coeditor of the *Messenger*, is instructive in exploring the debate within and around the IWW over whether prisoners should request a pardon from the US president or make any deal whatsoever to have their sentences reduced or commuted. The debate also raged among and divided those imprisoned. As for Local 8 members in Leavenworth, Fletcher, Doree, and Nef were among those wanting to get out as soon as possible and not caring how it was done—basically for the reasons listed by Owen. A smaller group perceived that any request implied admission of guilt, however, and such irreconcilables included Walsh. From this letter, one may also infer that Fletcher and Owen (and Randolph) regularly corresponded, which fits with the numerous statements and articles about Fletcher and Local 8 published in the *Messenger*.

October 15, 1921

Mr. M.J. Brennan
P.O. Box 241
New York, NY

Dear Sir:

For your information there follows a copy of a letter written to *Ben Fletcher*, Negro prisoner, IWW, confined in the United States Penitentiary at Leavenworth, Kansas, on the stationary of *The Messenger Magazine*, 2305 Seventh Avenue, New York City, October 11th, 1921. Telephone Morningside 1996. Editors: A. Philip Randolph, Owen Chandler, the letter was being written by *Chandler Owen*:

> Dear Fellow Worker Fletcher: How are you these days? We are out here fighting very hard for the boys inside. The enclosed release expresses the position of the Department of Justice on your cases. I am very anxious that you men shall take advantage of whatever opportunity is afforded in your cases and not be tied down by some

abstract conception of principle. As I see it no new question is raised, anyhow. You men have never stood for destroying property, did not impede the war, or any of those alleged offenses. What the Government is trying to do is to save its face by a technicality, and you men don't need to sacrifice your lives and entire pleasure over the technicality. The reason I write so definitely and frankly is because I realize that you fellow-workers are very desirous not to go back on anything you regard as principle. Here, however, you don't have to, because you have never done any of the things charged. The enclosed release of the Civil Liberties Bureau [later renamed the American Civil Liberties Union or ACLU] expresses our attitude also. Write me if there is anything we can do for you. Excuse short letter since I am hurrying this to you. Your steadfast friend, (signed) Chandler Owen.

The above mentioned release appears to have been taken from an IWW Bulletin and the article referred to is entitled "IWW Pardons Defend on Views Attorney General's Office Doesn't Require Repudiating."

■ Case #4-2-3-14, "Old German Files," Bureau of Investigation, Record Group 65: Department of Justice, National Archives.

46

A Miscarriage of Justice

Walter Nef, a German Swiss immigrant and IWW leader, wrote this article. Nef played a central role in the creation of the Agricultural Workers Organization, which proved pivotal in the resurgence of the IWW in the mid 1910s. Nef then moved to Philadelphia and became active in Local 8. Nef discussed his views on the federal government's wartime persecution of the IWW that resulted in his arrest and that of other Local 8 stalwarts: Fletcher, E.F. Doree, Jack Walsh, and Manuel Rey. One additional point: the $20,000 fine Nef received, according to the US Bureau of Labor Statistics' "inflation calculator," would be about $320,000 in 2020.

On July 16, 1916, I left the office in Philadelphia and went to work as a longshoreman and worked most of the time on ammunition and powder, general cargo for Murphy, Cook & Co., and sometimes on lumber, to which I can get many members to testify. There have been no explosions on the docks of Philadelphia or on any ships out of that port and all the ammunition was loaded by members of the IWW and there were no guards on the docks. The head foreman, called "Billboro," can testify to my work as a longshoreman. Besides there are many members who can testify to my position in regard to Germany and the war.

As I stated before Honorable Judge K.M. Landis before sentence was passed, I knew of no conspiracy and if there had been a conspiracy against the government then explosions and obstructions would have taken place. But there were none. We had lots of members on the Panama Line, which is under government control, and there was no trouble. Besides the members liked to work on those boats and no time was lost on any trips. The Bulletins testify to this, I think. The Bulletins were published in "Solidarity," I think, and "Solidarity" was introduced into evidence.

I was arrested on September 29, 1917, about 8 o'clock in the morning at home, having just returned from work for Murphy, Cook & Co., at Wilmington, Delaware. The federal officers were at the house Friday night, about half an hour after I had left, and were asking for me. I read in the paper the following morning that Doree was arrested and that others

IWW prisoners, who had been out on bond, returning to Leavenworth.

were looked for. I got off at West Philadelphia station, where I always get off going home, and was told that I was wanted. I then started to wash and get breakfast then US Deputy Marshal McDevitt came in and told me to come with him. Had no one come when I finished my breakfast then I would have gone to the Federal Building myself.

After being released on bonds I went to work again on the waterfront and worked two days when we were told we had to go to Chicago to appear there. When we got there we were told that we were not wanted, that it was a mistake.

In the evidence on the General Executive Board, presented by the prosecution, I am on the list for prospective secretary-treasurer of the IWW, and it looks as if I were convicted on this account, and will state that I have never known of it as I was not notified by Wm. D. Haywood at any time. I have never been consulted in this respect. It was a complete surprise to me.

Now I will state that the federal officers took several copies of "The Deadly Parallel" from the store room at Philadelphia. When these leaf-lets were received I never sent any away as I did not agree with the comparison made with the AF of L, but believed that there should have been comparison made, from the standpoint of principle, to the German Social Democrats on the Sub-Socialist Congress. The declaration of the IWW was made before the AF of L declaration and not in comparison with the AF of L declaration.

There were no pamphlets of [French syndicalist] Gustave Herve's in Philadelphia. We never had any there and would not handle them. The records should show that there never were any.

Now, in regard to strikes, I have stated before the Honorable Judge K.M. Landis that there were none to oppose the government that I know of and would not take part in any. There were small strikes, however, along the coast. When I came to the East in December, 1916, there were strikes almost continually on boats in the different ports for more wages, some asking for a 25 per cent bonus, some 50 per cent, 75 per cent and others 100 per cent of wages paid. The members of the International Seamen's Union were talking of striking in the spring for a raise in wages. The increase in the cost of living made a raise necessary. The shipping companies, refusing to recognize a union, made a chronic condition that union men were fired when non-union men could be secured. This brought on strikes, one after another, all winter of 1916 and 1917. In order to stop this I had written to Norfolk and other places that a $10.00 flat raise would be better than continually one crew after another asking for different bonuses, and would be more lasting in the long run, besides it would be best for an organization of labor.

On about April 10th or 20th, 1917, I wired to the different ports to ask for $10.00 flat increases on all ships, as members in Boston were already on strike for a $10.00 raise and they got it. This was practically settled. Then on May 1 the International Seamen's Union asked for a $15.00 raise, $60.00 a month, and we asked for $60.00 a month also. This second raise was forced by the International Seamen's Union of the AF of L and was for better conditions and not to oppose any government.

During the latter part of August, 1917, I was called to Boston by the members of Boston to try and help settle a strike there. I was in Boston four days and appeared before a state official at the Capitol Building, and no settlement could be effected. I left the next day and went to work again in Philadelphia on the waterfront. James Phillips may know the names and can testify to this. This strike was not to oppose any government. There were no other strikes to my knowledge during war time and absolutely none in opposition to the war program.

There is one other matter. I heard a telegram read by Honorable Judge K.M. Landis, dated August 4, 1917, to someone in Arizona, stating that the lumber workers and agricultural workers were on a general strike and that the MTW reports action. This is as big a surprise to me as the news that I was on the list for secretary-treasurer in case Haywood should be arrested. I was not in the office in Philadelphia from July 16, 1917, except to visit there three or four times, and do not know of any strike which should have taken place nor of anyone taking any steps to call a strike. I know that I would not have approved of such a strike.

This is about all I can think of now. In conclusion I wish to state that I have been found guilty and given a sentence as follows:

Six years and a fine of $5,000 on the first count;

Ten years and a fine of $5,000 on the second count;

Two years and a fine of $5,000 on the third count;

Twenty years and a fine of $5,000 on the fourth count.

All the above sentences to run concurrently, making it a twenty-year sentence in the Federal Prison at Leavenworth, Kansas, and a $20,000 fine.

I feel that I am absolutely innocent of obstructing the federal government and the state government in the prosecution of the war program, military or otherwise.

If I have to serve, in view of the foregoing, twenty years in prison for obstructing or even having in mind to obstruct the government, then I can go to the penitentiary with a clear conscience of being "Not Guilty" and being innocent of the charges I was convicted on.

Walter T. Nef, UNITED STATES OF AMERICA VS. HAYWOOD, et al.

■ *Messenger,* November 1921, 282–83.

47

Feds Oppose Releasing Fletcher

In 1919 and early 1920s, the IWW and its many affiliates around the nation, including Local 8, pushed hard to get their members released from prisons. Alongside the IWW in the fight to get Fletcher pardoned stood the *Messenger*. Wobblies, Socialists, and allies encouraged people to write letters to US President Harding and organized petition drives for the same purpose. Accordingly, the pardon attorney's office of the Department of Justice considered Fletcher's case and its internal records make for interesting reading. Nevertheless, the federal bureaucracy resisted such calls. In December 1921, the Department of Justice's "Report on All War Time Offenders Confined in Federal or State Penitentiaries" recommended to the attorney general that Fletcher not be granted executive clemency. What is curious is that, for a change, the government explanation was simple and honest: Fletcher had tremendous influence among marine transport workers, especially black ones.

He was a negro who had great influence with the colored stevedores, dock workers, firemen, and sailors, and materially assisted in building up the Marine Transport Workers Union which at the time of the indictment had become so strong that it practically controlled all shipping on the Atlantic Coast.

■ Miscellaneous Political Records, Political Prisoners, Department of Justice Files, Dec. 10, 1921, TAF/c2c, National Archives, Washington, DC, in Philip Foner, "The IWW and the Black Worker," 59.

48

A Call to Solidarity

This leaflet, issued by Local 8 and printed in the *Messenger* (and reprinted in its April 1922 issue), laid out the core values of the organization: open to all workers regardless of racial or ethnic heritage, organized industrially, and firmly committed to the "class-war."

Local 8 of the Marine Transport Workers of Philadelphia, affiliated with the Industrial Workers of the World, call to the workers of all races, creeds, color and nationality to Unite.

If we would maintain our standard of living, and prepare for the final emancipation of the workers, we must organize our labor power upon an industrial basis.

We are the only organization in America which has a uniform wage for engineers, holdmen, truckers, riggers, and water boys.

Of our three thousand and five hundred members, over two thousand are Negroes.

In this period of industrial depression and black reaction, only solidarity can save the workers.

Let workers of all races, creed, color and nationality, organize to liberate the class-war and political prisoners. Let us organize to build up a new Brotherhood for mankind where there is no race, class, craft, religious or nationality distinctions.

Workers: Organize, Agitate, Educate, Emancipate!

MARINE TRANSPORT WORKERS
INDUSTRIAL UNION, NO. 8
Industrial Workers of the World (IWW)
121 Catharine Street, Philadelphia, Pa.

■ *Messenger*, February 1922, 360.

A Call to Solidarity!!

Local 8 of the Marine Transport Workers of Philadelphia, affiliated with the Industrial Workers of the World, call to the workers of all races, creeds, color and nationality to Unite.

If we would maintain our standard of living, and prepare for the final emancipation of the workers, we must organize our labor power upon an industrial basis.

We are the only organization in America which has a uniform wage for engineers, holemen, truckers, riggers, and water boys.

Of our three thousand and five hundred members, over two thousand are Negroes.

In this period of industrial depression and black reaction, only solidarity can save the workers.

Let workers of all races, creed, color and nationality, organize to liberate the class-war and political prisoners. Let us organize to build up a new Brotherhood for mankind where there is no race, class, craft, religious or nationality distinctions.

Workers: Organize, Agitate, Educate, Emancipate!

Marine Transport Workers
Industrial Union, Local No. 8

INDUSTRIAL WORKERS OF THE WORLD (I. W. W.)

121 Catharine Street, Philadelphia, Pa.

49

Free the Local 8 Four!

Again, the *Messenger* served as a vehicle for Local 8 and the IWW to share its message. In this instance, Local 8 members endorsed a resolution to US President Warren Harding asking him to explain why four members of Local 8 (Fletcher, Doree, Nef, and Walsh) were imprisoned. The article pointed out that Local 8 never disrupted the war effort, thereby disproving the central claim of the Department of Justice that the IWW acted treasonously during World War I. While many, quite likely most, Wobblies opposed the war, the organization as a whole intentionally refused to take a stand, leaving it up to the individual consciences of its members. As this document shows, most in Local 8 supported the war or did not actively oppose it. That they did so and still saw their leaders, including Fletcher, swept up in the national raids provided strong evidence that the federal government wanted to destroy the IWW, using the war as the excuse to do so.

Open Forum
Philadelphia, February 8th, 1922

To the President of the United States:
 We the members of the Marine Transport Workers Industrial Union Philadelphia Branch No. 150 formerly Local No. 8 Branch No. 1 of the Industrial Workers of the World numbering about 2,500 Members at a regular meeting assembled February 7th, 1922 adopted the following resolutions:
 WHEREAS:—Four of our Members are serving terms aggregating Fifty (50) years in Leavenworth Penitentiary, Three (3) Ten and One (10) Twenty years for alleged violation of the Espionage Act and Draft Act and
 WHEREAS:—The record of our Organization during the war shows that it was at all times loyal to the Government and tried its best to be as efficient as possible in carrying out the Government's war program, as will more fully appear hereinafter; and
 WHEREAS:—These four men took an active and loyal part in this work of the Organization and never had any intention whatsoever of violating either the Draft Act or the Espionage Act and

WHEREAS:—We know and can prove by the records of the Organization part of which are set forth herein, of which Organization these four men were Members that they never conspired to obstruct the draft or interfere with the United States Government in its war with the Central Powers for if the object of these Men had been to obstruct the Government in its War work they had ample opportunities for doing so morally and physically, since some of them worked on high explosives themselves, and

WHEREAS:—This Organization loaded all explosives that left this Port before and after the United States entered the war with Germany and not a single accident of any kind took place at the docks or on the ships loaded by our Organization, and ammunition was loaded at Pigeon's Point, Wilmington, Carney's and Thompson's Points and also 90 per cent of the General Transportation was loaded and unloaded by Members of our Organization. A Transport Steamer after being loaded at the Port of New York took fire at sea and was brought back to the Philadelphia Navy Yard and Members of this Organization handled that Steamer. The Buttons of our Organization were recognized by the United States Government on the river front and Navy Yard in many instances as a River Front Passport, and

WHEREAS:—We had from 500 to 1000 Members working at the Navy Yard every day in the week, during the war both day and night and

WHEREAS:—Every Member of the Organization in the draft age registered and between 700 to 800 Members went to war and saw actual service. Every Member in the Army or Navy was considered in good standing in the Organization until he returned and was exempted from paying dues to the Organization. 1000 Members of this Organization working at the Navy Yard purchased between $50,000 and $55,000 of Liberty Bonds, Members working for Murphy Cook Co. purchased $25,000, Members working for S.C. Loveland purchased $15,000 and miscellaneous about $20,000 totaling all told in Liberty Bonds by Members of this Organization $115,000.

To prove what the spirit and action of our Organization actually was we shall quote resolutions from the minutes of our business meetings while we were at war with Germany.

Meeting of December 30, 1917.

Resolved:—That every Member of Local No. 8 become a Member of the Red Cross Society.

Meeting of December 30, 1917.

Resolved:—That our Financial Secretary be empowered to get in touch with the Red Cross Society.

Secretary wrote up all Members for Red Cross.

Meeting of February 26, 1918.

Resolved:—That any Member of our Local Union who has been in the United States Army or Navy service and shows an Honorable discharge when he returns, his book be straightened up.

Meeting of April 9, 1918.

Resolved:—That we get a Liberty Bond of $1,000.

Communication came here asking to buy Liberty Bonds from USA.

Meeting of April 16, 1918.

Resolved:—That we get a Service Flag.

Meeting of April 9, 1918.

Resolved:—That we postpone the Celebration of the 15th of May which is our legal holiday ever since our Organization is in existence so as not to hamper the war work of the Government.

ALL THESE MOTIONS WERE CARRIED OUT.

On the strength of the facts mentioned, we the Members of this Organization want to know why our Members are kept in prison?

When the United States Government appealed to us for our support during the war, we faithfully and generously complied with their appeal as we considered it our duty to our Government to do our utmost so that success may be with us. Now we appeal to you Mr. President and Mr. Attorney-General, for your kind and immediate consideration for the unconditional release of Walter T. Nef, Edward F. Doree, Benjamin H. Fletcher and John J. Walsh being that these Men never violated any law or intended to interfere in any way at all with the war program of the Government when at War with Germany, and be it further

RESOLVED:—That a copy of these resolutions be sent to the daily press so that the Public as well as the government may know the actual records of our Organization.

■ *Messenger*, March 1922, 377.

50

Feds Can't Figure Out Why They Imprisoned Fletcher

The US pardon attorney assigned the cases of Local 8's leaders wrote that he had "considerable difficulty" in "ascertaining just what" these longshoremen had done "that constituted the offense of which they were convicted." In fact, numerous federal agents, including the one who conducted the raids on Local 8 in 1917, later admitted, "I personally do not know of any crime that he [Nef] has committed against the country." Even the US Attorney for eastern Pennsylvania (during the war) wrote on behalf of the Local 8 prisoners, encouraging President Harding to pardon them.

April 8, 1922
Memorandum for Mr. Burns,
Chief, Bureau of Investigation

This office is making further investigation concerning the facts in the cases of Walter Neff [Nef], Edward F. Doree, Benjamin Fletcher and John Walsh. Marine transport workers at Philadelphia, who were co-defendants with Haywood and convicted with him and others in the IWW cases at Chicago, in August 1918.

These defendants seem to be on a different footing from many of the other defendants in that case in that there was no interruption of the Marine Transport Service at Philadelphia during the war and that the war record of these defendants seems to have been good.

I am informed that [redacted words, perhaps Walter C. Foster, "Special Agent in Charge" of the 1917 raids and arrests of Philadelphia Wobblies] one of your present operatives in the Bureau of Investigation, had charge of the investigations against the IWW in Philadelphia during the war. We are having considerable difficulty in ascertaining just what these Philadelphia defendants did that constituted the offense of which they were convicted and it occurs to me that [redacted words, likely an informant or spy] can probably furnish the Department some valuable information with regard to these defendants.

I have before me just presented a petition for executive clemency on behalf of Doree and there are circumstances in the case [his young son was very ill] which make it desirable that prompt action be taken. Will you be kind enough to ask [redacted words] to submit to the Department a statement concerning the activities and attitude of these Philadelphia defendants during the war, including a statement of any grounds justifying the conviction and also an expression of his view as to what action, if any, is justifiable at this time looking to an extension of executive clemency, treating each defendant individually and particularly at this time Doree and Neff.

Respectfully,
(Signed) James A Finch,
Pardon Attorney

■ US Pardon Attorney James A. Finch, "Memorandum for Mr. Burns, Chief, Bureau of Investigation," April 8, 1922, JAF-CZC, File no. 37-479, Box 985, 1853–1946, Record Group 204: Records of the Office of the US Pardon Attorney, National Archives, Suitland, Md.

51

Why Should These Men Be Released?

The campaign to free the IWWs languishing in federal prison was a long one. Other leftists and some progressive people also supported this struggle. Interestingly, one of the long-lasting consequences was the creation of the American Civil Liberties Union. This document is yet another example of the support that the black socialist magazine the *Messenger* gave to this cause. Curiously, even though the IWW claimed that the US judicial system was inherently biased in favor of preserving the capitalist status quo, many of its members continuously dealt with the legal system in a rational way—somehow believing that if only the IWW could demonstrate the logic of its arguments, its members would be freed from jail.

The purpose of this appeal is endorsed by: Mrs. George Biddle, George Burnham Jr., Miss Fanny T. Cochran, Pres. W.W. Comfort, Dr. Franklin Edgerton, Samuel S. Fels, Mrs. Edwin C. Grice, Dr. Jesse H. Holmes, Dr. Rufus M. Jones, Frances Fisher Kane, Rabbi Jos. Krauskopf, Mrs. Wilfred Lewis, Mrs. Ellis D. Lit, Mrs. S.G. Morton Maule, Harrison S. Morris, Miss Sarah G. Tomkins, Col. S.P. Wetherill Jr., Mrs. James D. Winsor, Dr. Lightner Witmer.

In the name of Justice they ask President Harding to pardon four Philadelphians unjustly convicted and now serving long terms in Leavenworth Prison.

Edward F. Doree, sentenced to 10 years, Benjamin H. Fletcher (Negro) sentenced to 10 years, Walter T. Nef, sentenced to 20 years, John J. Walsh, sentenced to 10 years.

Philadelphia Civil Liberties Committee, E. Lewis Burnham, Chairman, 1400 Morris Building, Edward W. Evans, Mrs. Eliza Middleton Gope, Miss Mary H. Ingham, Edmund C. Evans, Miss Sophia H. Dulles.

1. *Because they stand convicted under war-time legislation only.* Even if they were guilty, they should now be released, since we are at peace. The activities charged against them would not now be crimes. England, France, Italy, Germany and Austria have released their offenders against war-time laws. All the German spies, such as F. Von

Rintelen, caught red-handed in acts of violence against the United States in war-time, have been released. All conscientious objectors and Eugene V. Debs, who admitted making a speech against the draft and the war-policy of the government, have recently been released. On no principle of reason or justice can these Philadelphians be held to be more guilty than those men, even if the government's contentions be admitted.

2.   While a Jury's verdict has declared these men guilty of violating the Selective Service and Espionage Acts, we shall produce evidence to show that their actual intent was quite the contrary. They were convicted because the jury implied that they approved of the acts of others which in fact they never approved of. Morally they are certainly not guilty of anything of the sort. A careful search through the printed record of the trial, fails to convince an impartial inquirer that any of these four men ever advocated opposition to the Government's war policy, or any of the laws of the land.

3.   On the contrary, two of these men, Nef and Doree, repeatedly counseled their friends and acquaintances, orally and in writing, to accept service under the draft and not to oppose the war or any war-time legislation. They were asked to take part in meetings opposing the war and the draft; and they refused to do so.

4.   The labor unions of which these four men were leaders did valuable service to the government during the war. Their war-record is striking proof of the innocence of their leaders.

5.   The atmosphere and circumstances of the trial were serious obstacles to a fair and just verdict. The men were tried in the summer of 1918, during a period of War Hysteria. *"The verdict rendered was a foregone conclusion from the beginning in obedience to a public hysteria and popular demand."* The trial lasted for a month; the printed record of the case covers nearly 3,000 pages, besides which there are enormous quantities of exhibits that were never printed. Yet, the jury took just *twenty-five minutes* to "consider" this evidence and find 98 defendants (including these four) guilty on all four counts of the indictment. Before the trial various agencies of the government by illegal means seriously hampered the work of preparing the defense, and so in effect deprived these men of their "day in court."

IN SUPPORT OF THESE STATEMENTS
We submit the following condensed account of the case. The facts are based upon a careful investigation and are supported by reliable

evidence. The evidence can be verified by anyone who wishes to take the trouble to do so.

Walter T. Nef, a native Swiss, but a naturalized American citizen was Secretary-Treasurer of Marine Transport Workers Industrial Union No. 100 (IWW) of which union John J. Walsh, an American citizen, and Benjamin H. Fletcher, an American Negro, were organizers. Edward F. Doree (born in Philadelphia; his father was French, his mother Swedish) was Secretary-Treasurer of Textile Workers Industrial Union No. 1000 (IWW). All four men had their homes in Philadelphia. Nef and Doree were the most prominent and influential IWW leaders in the city. Both Nef and Doree are married; Doree has a child, a boy of five.

THE CHARGE AGAINST THESE MEN
These men were convicted of conspiracy on four counts.

But in the case of two counts—forcible hindrance, by strikes, etc., of the execution of certain federal laws, and injury to various persons in the right of furnishing materials to the United States—the conviction was reversed by the United States Circuit Court of Appeals.

The only charges of force or violence or sabotage made against these men fell under these two counts, on which the conviction was reversed.

It is therefore absolutely untrue that they stand convicted of any crime involving the use, actual or contemplated, of force or violence—whether against the government, or against any individuals.

The two counts on which their conviction stands charge conspiracy to violate war-time measures, viz., the Draft Act and the Espionage Act.

It is charged that they conspired to persuade draft eligibles not to register for the draft, or to desert after being drafted; and that they conspired to cause insubordination and mutiny in the armed forces of the United States.

POSITION OF THE IWW UNIONS IN PHILADELPHIA
The Marine Transport Workers Industrial Union No. 100 comprises long-shoremen, stevedores, sailors, and other marine dock workers. For years it has completely controlled the Philadelphia waterfront. This was true throughout the entire period of the war. Enormous quantities of war munitions were loaded from this port during the war, *all of which was loaded by members of this IWW union.* And there was not a single accident during the entire war, on any dock or ship loaded at the Philadelphia port.

Of the more than three thousand members of this union, every single one who was of draft age registered for military service; and there was not a single "conscientious objector" among them. More than seven hundred were in the army (including four captains and twelve lieutenants). Five hundred saw service in France. Several score gave up their lives for their country.

This union has a service flag, and also an Honor-List of members who had bought Liberty Bonds. Both the flag and the list of bondbuyers were hung conspicuously in the union hall during the war. The union itself, as an organization, bought with money in its treasury $1,000.00 worth of Liberty Bonds.

Remember that this is the union that was led by Nef, Fletcher and Walsh, whom the government accuses of counseling and aiding resistance to the draft and insubordination and mutiny in the armed forces of the United States.

Not a single strike occurred among these IWW longshoremen in Philadelphia in the year of 1917. If the leaders had been trying to impede the progress of the war, as charged by the government, they could easily have found pretexts for strikes that would have caused endless trouble and delay in the shipment of munitions and war supplies.

■ *Messenger*, May 1922, 404–5.

52

Free at Last!

Slowly but surely, President Harding commuted the sentences of many people still languishing in federal prisons years after World War I ended and despite growing misgivings about the unconstitutional nature of the Espionage and Sedition Acts that criminalized speech. Fletcher, Nef, and Walsh had their sentences commuted in late October 1922. Doree's sentence had been commuted almost two months earlier. Even Debs's sentence was commuted almost a year before Fletcher and other Wobblies. These World War I–era laws that launched the first Red Scare set the precedent for further witch hunts, for example after World War II when the United States engaged in a "Cold War" with the Soviet Union, which, in turn, caused a second Red Scare, sometimes called McCarthyism.

Agent: Redacted
Place report made: Chicago, Illinois
Date report made: Nov. 6, 1922
Period report made about: For week ending Nov. 4, 1922

"IWW Weekly Report: Radical Matter"
At Chicago, Illinois:

WALTER NEFF [NEF], BEN FLETCHER AND JOHN WALSH, three of the thirty-eight IWW defendants who surrendered at the US Penitentiary at Leavenworth on April 25, 1921, in accordance with the order of the Circuit Court of Appeals, Seventh Circuit, Chicago, Illinois, received Presidential commutations on October 31, 1922, conditional upon their future good behavior.

■ File No. 51-1225-25, p. 4, Federal Bureau of Investigation, "Subject: Industrial Workers of the IWW Defense Committee." Obtained via Freedom of Information Act.

53

Longshoremen Fighting for Life

This short piece discussed recent IWW longshore strikes on the Atlantic and Pacific Coasts. In Philadelphia, as the editors pointed out, Local 8 was an industrial union, interracial in character, and maintained an egalitarian wage scale regardless of occupation. Local 8, alas, lost this long, bruising lockout/strike. A combination of government repression, rising racism and xenophobia, the emergence of communism as a serious rival to the anarcho-syndicalism of the IWW, and employers pushing for the "open shop," together resulted in the end of Local 8's power which had lasted nearly a decade.

On the waterfront in Philadelphia and Portland, an intense and desperate contest is being waged by the IWW's to preserve a decent standard of living and to save their organizations from the savage and brutal assaults of the hypocritical and frightened Stevedores, the powerful steamship interests. In these struggles, be it said to the credit and honor of the IWW, the Negroes and whites are fighting shoulder to shoulder for more milk for their babies and to keep the wolf from their door, as well as to defend their organization which has been the very prop of their lives.

One great asset to the strikers is that they are industrially organized. Even the waterboy is taken into the organization for they have learned that it is impossible for labor to win while one part is scabbing on the other part, when a fight is on.

The MESSENGER bids you to hold out and hold on.

■ *Messenger*, December 1922, 538.

54

Philadelphia's Waterfront Unions

In one of his longer published pieces, Fletcher addressed the reasons why many black members of Local 8 broke from the IWW and formed an independent union, the Philadelphia Longshoremen's Union (PLU), in 1923. The split involved numerous issues but mostly local versus national control in the organization. This divisive and multifaceted topic, called "centralism" among Wobblies, not only contributed to the implosion of Local 8 but also the fracturing of the IWW, in the United States, in 1924. Well worth noting is that all of the principles that the PLU committed itself to are IWW principles. The formation of the PLU also must be understood in the context of the Philadelphia Controversy, more fully discussed in Document 69. Also notable was how Owen and Randolph labeled Fletcher. Randolph went on to gain the title here accorded to Fletcher once Randolph helped found the Brotherhood of Sleeping Car Porters, the most well-known black majority union in US history, in 1925.

By Ben Fletcher, The most prominent Negro Labor Leader in America
During the month of May, 1913, the Longshoremen of Philadelphia went on strike and re-entered the Labor Movement after an absence of 15 years. A few days after their strike began against those intolerable conditions and low wages always imposed upon the unorganized workers, representatives of both the Marine Transport Workers' Union of the IWW and the International Longshoremen's Union of the AFL got before them and presented their various arguments favoring the Philadelphia Longshoremen's affiliation. At a mass meeting they made their choice, deciding to organize into the IWW and by May 20th had become an integral part of that organization.

After nine years' identification with the IWW they have been forced to sever their connection with that organization in order to prevent the annihilation of their local autonomy by that unreasonable and inefficient Centralism that has grown upon the IWW since 1916. Since that year innumerable assaults have been made by both the Central Administration of the Marine Transport Workers and the Central Administration of the IWW upon their right to determine the local administration of the

Union's affairs. Unacquainted in a practical way with the problems arising from a job-controlling organization, numbering 3,000 members; "Foot Loose Wobblies" from the IWW Western jurisdiction, by abusing the IWW Universal Transfer System, sought to (and sometimes succeeded) acquire a determining voice and vote on any questions relating to Local job or Financial matters.

Repeatedly the IWW General Administration has attempted to force the Philadelphia Marine Transport Workers' Union to remit to the Marine Transport Workers' Central office, weekly, all net income balances above $100 and to confine all expenditures to those "permitted." Needless to state the organization consistently refused to do so. Last Fall the "Foot Loose Wobblies" succeeded in stampeding the Union into an insane attempt to wrest from US Shipping Board and Private Steamship and Stevedoring Interests the 44-hour week single handed. Immediately upon the collapse of the strike a representative of the IWW's General Administration appeared before a regular business meeting of the Philadelphia Longshoremen and delivered the following ultimatum: "You must strictly comply with the Constitution of the IWW and remit all funds except a $100 or so from now on to the Central Office, or by the authority vested in the General Executive Board your charter will be annulled and your funds seized."

Pursuant to a motion under new business, steps were taken immediately to safeguard all property and funds of the Union. Last month (April) the organization of the Longshoremen in Philadelphia became a duly chartered Independent Union, known as the Philadelphia Longshoremen's Union. As heretofore it will embrace in One Union any and all workers engaged in the Marine Transport Industry.

The history of the Philadelphia Longshoremen's connection with the IWW is one of unswerving loyalty to its fundamental principles. Some have died while hundreds of others have been jailed as its standard bearers in order to vindicate its causes. At no time during this connection was it necessary to appeal for outside aid to meet the expenses incurred in defending its jailed militants. Into the coffers of the IWW the Philadelphia Longshoremen dumped $50,000 in per capita tax alone during their affiliation, organization assessments, relief, defense and miscellaneous contributions in proportion.

Notwithstanding, the IWW was not able in that period of time with that amount of finance at their disposal to organize one supporting job control port. The Philadelphia Longshoremen are of the opinion that they and they alone can rebuild their organization, just as it was they and they alone who did the trick in the past. They are confident that the organizing of the waterfront workers strictly upon the basis of and in conformity with their class interests will eventually overcome all the slander, baseless charges and race baiting now being propagated with avidity by those who were once loudest in their praise and boast of our power and righteousness.

■ *Messenger*, June 1923, 740–41.

55

The Negro and Organized Labor

Fletcher wrote this essay, important for numerous reasons including his outspoken critique of capitalism and racism. In the twenty-first century, the term "racial capitalism" has grown more popular as a concept describing what Fletcher discussed in 1923. Many who knew Fletcher commented on his brilliant speaking style and ability to dissect both the inequities of capitalism and the racism of the mainstream labor movement (as embodied by the AFL), but this document is one of his few lengthy written treatments. Fletcher warned that for organized labor to be effective it absolutely must eliminate racism within its ranks and commit itself to racial equality: "No genuine attempt by Organized Labor to wrest any worthwhile and lasting concessions from the Employing Class can succeed as long as Organized Labor for the most part is indifferent and in opposition to the fate of Negro Labor." His description of how US unions treated African American workers remained applicable for many decades to come, and even to the present moment. Fletcher's discussion of a Negro Labor Federation predicted the formation of black caucuses inside predominantly white unions, including the Revolutionary Union Movement among Detroit's black auto workers in the late 1960s and the Coalition of Black Trade Unionists in the early 1970s. Also curious is the final sentence with a biblical reference to St. Paul (Acts 16:9), the only published reference he made to religion.

In these United States of America, the history of Organized Labor Movement's attitude and disposition toward the Negro Section of the world of Industry is replete with gross indifference and, excepting a few of its component parts, is a record of complete surrender before the color line. Directed, manipulated, and controlled by those bent on harmonizing the diametrically opposed interests of Labor and Capital, it is for the most part not only a "bulwark against" Industry of, by and for Labor, but in an overwhelming majority of instances is no less a bulwark against the economic, political and social betterment of Negro Labor.

The International Association of Machinists as well as several other International bodies of the AFL along with the Railroad Brotherhoods, either by constitutional decree or general policy, forbid the enrollment of Negro members, while others if forced by his increasing presence in their jurisdictions, organize him into separate unions. There are but a few exceptions that are not covered by these two policies and attitudes. It is needless to state that the employing class are the beneficiaries of these policies of Negro Labor exclusion and segregation. It is a fact indisputable that Negro Labor's foothold nearly everywhere in organized labor's domains, has been secured by scabbing them into defeat or into terms that provided for Negro Labor inclusion in their ranks. What a sad commentary upon Organized Labor's shortsightedness and profound stupidity. In these United States of America less than 4 per cent of Negro Labor is organized. Fully 16 per cent of the Working Class in this country are Negroes. No genuine attempt by Organized Labor to wrest any worthwhile and lasting concessions from the Employing Class can succeed as long as Organized Labor for the most part is indifferent and in opposition to the fate of Negro Labor. As long as these facts are the facts, the Negro Section of the World of Industry can be safely counted upon by the Employing Class as a successful wedge to prevent any notable organized labor triumph. The millions of dollars which they have and continue to furnish Negro institutions will continue to yield a magnificent interest in the shape of Negro Labor loyalty to the Employing Class.

Organized Labor can bring about a different situation. One that will speed the dawn of Industrial Freedom. First, by erasing their Race exclusion clauses. Second, by enrolling ALL workers in their Industrial or Craft jurisdictions, in the same union or unions, and where custom or the statutes prohibit in some Southern states, so educate their membership and develop the power and influence of their various unions as to force the repeal of these prohibition statutes and customs. Thirdly, by aiding and abetting his entrance into their various craft jurisdictions, unless he comes, of course, as a strike breaker. Fourth, by joining him in his fight in the South to secure political enfranchisement. Fifth, by inducting into the service of organized labor, Negro Labor Organizers and other officials in proportion to his numbers and ability.

The Organized Labor Movement has not begun to become a contender for its place in the Sun, until every man, woman, and child in Industry is eligible to be identified with its Cause, regardless of Race, color or creed. The secret of Employing Class rule and Industry's control, is the division and lack of cohesion existing in the ranks of Labor. None can dispute the fact that Organized Labor's Attitude of indifference and often outspoken opposition to Negro Labor, contributes a vast amount to this division and lack of cohesion.

Organized Labor Banks, Political Parties, Educational Institutions, co-operatives, nor any other of its efforts to get somewhere near the goal of economic emancipation from the thralldom of the rich, will avail naught, as long as the color line lies across their pathway to their goal and before which they are doomed to halt and surrender. Until organized labor, generally casts aside the bars of race exclusion, and enrolls Negro Labor within its ranks on a basis of complete sincere fraternity, no general effort of steel, railroad, packing house, building trades workers or any workers for that matter, to advance from the yoke of Industrial slavery can succeed. Just as certain as day follows night, the Negro will continue to contribute readily and generously toward the elements that will make for their defeat. Personally, the writer would not have it otherwise unless organized labor, majorly speaking, right about faces on its Negro Labor attitude and policy!

Signs are not wanting that men and women of vision in the ranks of organized labor, of both the radical and conservative wing, are alive to the necessity of a reformation or organized labor's attitude on the Negro, and are attempting to bring their various organizations in line with such organizations as the United Mine Workers of America, Amalgamated Clothing Workers and the Industrial Workers of the World. Negro Labor has a part to play also in changing this present day attitude of organized labor. It should organize a nation-wide movement to encourage, promote and protect its employment and general welfare. Divided into central districts and branches thereof, it would be able to not only thereby force complete and unequivocal recognition and fraternal cooperation from organized labor, but at the same time render yeoman service in procuring the increased employment of tens of thousands of fully capable Negro workers in such positions as now are closed to them because of the lack of sufficient organized Negro Labor pressure in the right direction and with the right instrumentality of intelligent vision.

This organization would by virtue of its being comprised of Negro Labor of all Industries and crafts be able to safeguard its every advance and prevent any successful attack against same. Collective dealing with the Employing Class, is the only way by which Labor can procure any concessions from them of effect and meaning. It is the only way in which to establish industrial stability and uniformity in its administration and finally Industrial freedom. This holds good for Negro as well as white labor. There are fully 4,000,000 Negro men, women and children, eligible to participate in such a Negro Labor Federation.

The beginning of such an organization a generation ago, the attitude of organized labor to the Negro would be just the reverse today. Organized Labor for the most part be it radical or conservative, thinks and acts, in the terms of the White Race. Like the preachers, politicians, who when preaching about the "immortality of the soul" or orating about the "glorious land of the free" have in mind and so explain, white folks. So with organized labor generally. To a large extent Negro Labor is responsible for this reprehensible exclusion, because of its failure to generate a force which when necessary could have rendered low the dragon head of Race prejudice, whenever and wherever it raised its head. It is not too late, however, to begin to rectify and to reap the benefits of united effort. Only by unifying our forces in such a way as to force organized labor to realize that we can do lasting good or lasting evil, will they, with the assistance of those men and women already in their ranks fighting to change their erroneous way, understand and "come over into Macedonia and help us."

■ *Messenger*, July 1923, 759–60.

56

Solidarity—Black & White

William D. "Dan" Jones, a longtime leader in Local 8, wrote this very thoughtful analysis of race and unionism. A member of the organization since its founding strike in May 1913, Jones was among the most prominent black leaders in Local 8. In this essay, Jones laid out a vision for the Philadelphia Longshoremen's Union, for which he served as secretary, that paralleled IWW ideology: industrial unionism, absolute commitment to racial and ethnic equality and freedom, and anticapitalism. Jones highlighted the dangers of racial divisions within the working class, which ultimately served the employing class. Interestingly, he also castigated unions for waving the flag of "Americanism," noting that those unions celebrating "Americanism" actually were promoting white supremacy, equating "American" with being "white." He also cautioned black workers against the false if understandable response to racism—forming black-only unions. Here, Jones offered another veiled critique of Garveyism along the lines of Fletcher, Owen, and Randolph. Instead, Jones contended that black workers needed to recognize their common class interests with white workers in what he referred to as a "mixed union."

At this period and time when the world is in a condition of dissatisfaction and the cost of living is high, it is absolutely necessary that all workers, regardless of color, should join together in one solid union in order that they may obtain better living and working conditions and better support their families.

The Negro is a large factor in American industry. But the trade unions have been shortsighted in not admitting the Negro to membership, and by so doing have forced themselves into the conditions that exist at the present time—into the hands of the employers, who are forcing the open shop, and when necessary, using the Negro for that purpose.

The reason why the Negro has not been admitted to membership in the trade unions is on account of that distinguished slogan: Americanism. It is translated into what is better known as American race prejudice.

The merits of the mixed union are: that it eliminates the feeling of prejudice among the workers and establishes a congenial and most cordial feeling; it teaches each one that all have each other's interests in common; that they can maintain for themselves the best wages and working conditions only so long as they do not allow themselves to be divided. This equality has nothing to do with private social intercourse as has been stated by the employers to keep the workers divided. There is nothing to hinder an individual from selecting his or her social group or personal associates. The sooner the workers learn that they are workers, and that all workers are the same in the employers' eyes, the better off they will be. The sooner they learn this, the sooner will they attain a higher plane of living for themselves and families. There is no way to accomplish such an end as long as the workers are divided on national and racial lines.

It is an undeniable fact that the employers will use one race or one group of workers to defeat the other group. Whenever the employers are successful in destroying the benefits achieved by the most advanced group by using the other group, they also destroy the chances of both groups for advancement. In so doing they succeed in lowering the standard of the workers to a level of poverty.

As long as the workers allow themselves to be used one group against the other—preventing each other from maintaining a high standard of living—they will not be successful in accomplishing those high ideals and better things for which the human race craves. Not until all the workers are united into one union—and that union will see that each worker's rights are protected regardless of race or nationality—will the working class advance to that higher standard of living.

Mixed unions are the only kind for the workers in this country. They will frustrate the attempts of the employers to use one race against the other. The workers become more interested in each other, and in so doing establish the very key to the situation: Solidarity. Wherever solidarity exists the object, victory which is in view is sure to be accomplished. Having had personal experience in a mixed union for the past ten years, the writer is in a position to know that within that time the members succeeded in advancing their wages and bettering their working conditions to the point where they were the best paid of all unions that are in the same industry in this country. This was on account of solidarity and proves the merits of the mixed union.

Now as to the demerits of the mixed union. In mixed unions there often arises internal controversy, especially when the epithet ("nigger") is used which is the pride of Americans. This usually occurs when they want to take advantage of the other fellow. For instance, if something occurs that is to the advantage of one group and not to the other, there is jealousy and dissatisfaction, with the less fortunate group contending that discrimination has been used. This will keep up an eternal controversy. The best way to overcome such a condition is to use a mixed working force. Especially in selecting officers should this be done.

The writer does not believe in any Negro union that is not part of some craft or industrial union, unless it is in some of those loving states that make it a crime for a Negro to look at a white man or sit beside him. The workers should learn that such laws are to keep them divided and are a special benefit to the capitalist class. Wherever such laws exist the workers themselves should remove the condition by a joint committee composed of both races, if possible. There is no advantage to the Negro in being in a separate union. It is true that he would do his own bidding, and, should he receive the largest percentage of the work, there is no doubt that it would be the most laborious kind in the industry. He would be expected to produce more than the white unions and take a smaller wage.

One can readily see that would give the employer the opportunity to defeat both unions and in so doing would benefit only himself. The fact is that all Negro unions are failures, just the same as a craft union. The advancement of labor at this period must be along industrial lines if labor is to receive a fair percentage of the industrial product. In order that the Negro, who is a strong factor in the industrial market to-day, may receive a fair consideration for his labor, he must be in mixed unions. Wherever a Negro union exists there should be efforts made to work in conjunction with the other unions to bring about energetic action to obtain higher wages and better working conditions for themselves.

Black and white labor to-day is learning more about their increased power when closely united to gain greater concessions under the present conditions. It is to be hoped that in the near future all labor will be united for one common cause. It is an undeniable fact that all labor has something in common: a desire for a higher standard of living. This can only be attainted through interracial solidarity in the mixed union.

■ *Messenger*, September 1923, 812.

Fletcher Speaks in Philadelphia

In the mid 1920s, Fletcher and other Philadelphia longshoremen committed to the IWW refused to give up on re-establishing Local 8's former power and glory. That the federal government was spying and reporting on Fletcher, in 1925, is further evidence of the fear that Fletcher continued to instill in the state and their allies in business and mainstream unions.

Agent: Redacted
Place report made: Philadelphia, Pa.
Date report made: 1/7/25
Period for which report made: 1/3/25

"Radical Activities—Philadelphia District: IWW"

On January 11th, 1925, BENJAMIN FLETCHER, well known colored agitator, recently released from Fort Leavenworth penitentiary, will speak in Philadelphia, Pa., at 928 E. Moyamensing Avenue; subject—"INDUSTRIAL UNIONISM IN THE MARINE INDUSTRY."

■ Bureau of Investigation, Department of Justice, obtained via Freedom of Information Act.

Fletcher Won't Give Up the Waterfront

After Local 8's domination of the waterfront ended in late 1922, the ILA sought to line up the longshoremen, most of whom were quite hesitant to join that union because it was well known for being undemocratic and racially segregated. Many ILA locals held no meetings, the union published no newspaper for its members, elections involved no competition, and the union leadership regularly deployed "muscle" to intimidate, beat, and even kill opponents of the existing power structure. All that said, it must be noted that the ILA did organize African American longshoremen—unlike many other unions in the era—though generally in segregated locals and with black members often getting fewer and worse jobs.

Agent: Redacted
Place report made: Philadelphia, Pa.
Date report made: 4/21/25
Period for which report made: 4/16/25

"Strike Marine Transport Workers Philadelphia and Threatened National Strike of Mine Workers"

Synopsis: Former Phila. IWW Local Marine Transport Workers reorganized by Ben Fletcher well known Negro ex-convict—have gone on strike—probabilities are ILA might do likewise—National Strike of United Mine Workers impending.

[Redacted portion] US Dept. of Labor, 132 So. 3rd St., Phila., reported today that the well known IWW agitator BENJAMIN FLETCHER has reorganized the Phila. Branch of the Marine Transport Workers Industrial Union—#510 headquarters 928 E. Moymanesing [sic] Ave., about 2 weeks ago and has called a strike of its members, numbering about 100 according to figures of the International Longshoremens [sic] Union which is affiliated with the American Federation of Labor and which is at loggerheads with the IWW local. BEN. FLETCHER is the well known IWW agitator paroled about 2 years ago from a 10-year term at FT. LEAVENWORTH resulting from his conviction in Chicago in 1917 [actually 1918] and arrested in Philadelphia by Agent. As a result of their differences [redacted] said the ILA would probably call a strike of their members in Philadelphia which if done would make a complete tie up of the port. The calling of the ILA strike depends largely upon the outcome of a conference now being held at the Hotel Hanover, Philadelphia, between the officers of the ILA, and the boss stevedores—the latter according to [redacted] apparently being in sympathy with the IWW. The Police have been notified of the impending trouble and have detailed about 500 men to hold themselves in readiness.

[final paragraph redacted]

■ Bureau of Investigation, Department of Justice, obtained via Freedom of Information Act.

59

Communist Praises Wobbly

This article is fascinating for several reasons, not least of which that Browder knew Fletcher before the former became the leader of the CPUSA during the 1930s and early 1940s. Browder also had served time in Leavenworth for his opposition to World War I, where he apparently became friends with Fletcher. Browder also insightfully noted how the mainstream (i.e., white-dominated) press reinforced racist stereotypes by highlighting black crime, a problem still. It might surprise some that Fletcher, a Wobbly, received such praise from Browder, given the fierce split between communists and anarcho-syndicalists like those in the IWW. Yet earlier in his life, Browder had belonged to the Socialist Party and then worked closely with IWW members James Cannon and William Z. Foster, both of whom were committed to syndicalism and then joined the CP. Considering how racist America was in 1925, Browder, who was white, expressed quite progressive views on race relations.

"A Negro Labor Organizer [Ben Fletcher]"

News of the stevedores' strike in Philadelphia brings the interesting item that Ben Fletcher, Negro labor organizer who went to Leavenworth prison with the IWW boys in 1918, is again on the job leading the struggle of the workers against the capitalists.

Fletcher is a living symbol of the possibilities of unity between white and black workers. He proves the ability of the Negro to organize. He demonstrates the class-consciousness, loyalty, and capacity for self-sacrifice of the Negro workers.

It was my pleasure to become acquainted with Fletcher while I was in Leavenworth with him. It is significant that among the political prisoners there, almost all workers, Fletcher was held in high respect. Any suggestion of racial prejudice between the white and black political prisoners would have been hooted down as ridiculous. We were all comrades in prison together.

In the March issue of the *Workers Monthly*, Maurice Becker portrays in his splendid lithographs some of the tortures that the political prisoners had to undergo. Among these was one which carried a line underneath describing it: "Guards Urge Negro Murderer to Attack IWW Prisoners," based upon an actual occurrence in Leavenworth. Some attempt has been made to interpret this is a sign that the political prisoners harbored race prejudice against the Negroes. Nothing could be further from reality, nor from Becker's intentions in writing this line. And no one who had been in prison during that period could make such a suggestion. While one Negro, a degenerate, was being used as a tool by the prison officials, another Negro, Ben Fletcher, was a leading figure among the political prisoners who stood up heroically under their persecution.

The reason that is has been possible for anyone to criticize Maurice Becker's cartoons and the line beneath it is because the capitalist press continually carries on a vicious and malicious campaign, in which they use the trick of continually stressing the word "Negro" as applied to criminals of that race, while no Negro ever receives favorable mention from them unless for abasing himself before his capitalist overlords.

The Communist attitude toward the Negro and his problems differs from that of the bourgeois-sentimentalist who proclaims himself a "friend of the Negro," as it does from the dastardly capitalist propaganda of race hatred. The Communists meet the Negroes as comrades, unite with them to close organizational co-operation to realize our common tasks, and wage war upon bourgeois-cultivated prejudices. We greet and offer our co-operation to the Fletchers, Whittmans, Dotys and Phillips, who are undertaking the gigantic task of organizing Negro workers for common struggle with the white workers, and for their common emancipation from capitalist exploitation.

Earl R. Browder

■ *The Workers Monthly*, May 1925, 294.

60

Defy the Blacklist

Fletcher's article below came at the moment when old-time Wobblies, Fletcher included, had one last hope that Philadelphia's longshoremen might return to the IWW fold. The rival ILA had wrested control of the docks, in 1927, in no small measure due to the active assistance of the federal government's Shipping Board, then headed by a former president of the ILA who had pressured local employers into granting an eight-hour day, a longtime worker demand. Though the local ILA chapter was integrated—another concession to what the IWW had sown and in contrast to all other ILA locals—the antidemocratic and strongarm tendencies of the ILA ruffled many former Wobblies' feathers, who were used to a fighting and fiercely democratic union. Despite these efforts, the ILA managed to hold on to the Philadelphia waterfront, which soon followed the model of the ILA in New York City: controlled by goons who did not have the best interests of the local members at heart let alone a vision for building a new society.

MARINE TRANSPORT DRIVE NEEDS YOUR SOLIDARITY
PHILADELPHIA CAMPAIGN MUST BE WON BY THE IMMEDIATE AID OF
ENTIRE IWW MEMBERSHIP
Crisis in Drive Has Been Reached, with Victory Just Ahead, but Depending on the Financial Response Our Members Give to This Stirring Appeal; Failure Is Impossible Unless Decreed by the General Membership; Rush Funds to Port of Philadelphia at Once!

PHILADELPHIA, Pa.—The organization campaign of the IWW here has reached a crisis, the International Longshoremen's Association is staggering from the onslaught of IWW agitation and internal disruption, provoked by repeated exposure of the ILA agreement as a proposition that supports and upholds the employing stevedores and steamship interests of the Port of Philadelphia.

The ILA membership has decreased from 3,800 to 2,900 since the first of January 1927, when the agreement went into effect. And to date, March 12, less than 50 per cent of the 2,900 in good standing on February 1 have secured their job buttons for March. It will be impossible for the

ILA to have more than 1,800 members in good standing by March 15, the expiration date for the February job buttons. The ILA officials are meeting with open defiance both on the job and off of it. Gunmen approached by one of the agents with a bank roll of $500 to "bump off those God damned IWW (bastards) denounced the scheme in the parlance of the underworld, saying "The IWW's are regular guys."

Lining Up Most Influential

From 25 to 50 longshoremen daily demonstrate their defiance to the supposed power of the ILA to blacklist them on the job, by coming to our hall and proclaiming their allegiance to the IWW. Our policy is to select one or two of the "heavyweights" among them that are the most influential ones for membership. This selective preliminary organizing tactic of course means that while we have fifty or sixty active members we have to date fully 20 times that many announced adherents.

The fight to get the Philadelphia longshoremen to redeem themselves from the base betrayal of the ILA is even being carried into the ILA business meetings. Their regular business meeting of March 1 almost resulted in a riot when Jas. [Joseph] Ryan, first vice-president of the ILA, and president of the North Atlantic district jurisdiction, was required to appear before Philadelphia Local No. 1116 of the ILA and explain why he decided against the local's contention for the IWW out of town rates on oil and other cargo, which was referred as a dispute to the "Committee of Four." (This committee is an arbitration board consisting of two representatives of the steamship and stevedoring interests and two representatives of the ILA local.)

ILA Faker Denounced

The committee, becoming deadlocked on the dispute in question, called in Ryan, who was acceptable to both sides and he, of course, decided against his members.

He was roundly denounced by speaker after speaker, and told point blank that the IWW was coming back. About one-third of the finances that are necessary to put the IWW across in the Port of Philadelphia has materialized to date, despite the generous amount of publicity that has been given in nearly every issue of our press since January 15.

Personally, and likewise for all others associated in this attempt to "carry on" this organizing campaign of the Philadelphia longshoremen, it is heartbreaking to have our efforts to accomplish something tangible for the IWW-and with results worthwhile and lasting just ahead—fail because of lack of support from other jurisdictions of the IWW. It is heartbreaking to anticipate another failure because of lack of concern of the membership generally and lack of their determination to put it over, whether the cost is great or small.

Funds Must Be Sent
The ILA spent $25,000 to get this port in its labor faking line up. Less than ten per cent of this amount is all that is required for the IWW to rout them.

Raise funds and rush them to A. L. Nurse, 702 So. 2nd St. (MTW Hall, Philadelphia, Pa. is the receiver). The MTW Hall is being rapidly shaped up with suitable appointments, $200 to date having been spent on that score. The ILA agreement, the confusion, double crossing lies, betrayal, etc., attendant thereto, which stampeded the longshoremen is rapidly being dissipated and the realization of the need and only hope, the IWW, is breaking through in the minds of Philadelphia's longshoremen like the rising dawn of day. Heed this call and remember that we cannot fail unless the IWW membership generally so decrees.

Benjamin H. Fletcher,
G.O.C. Member, MTWIU No. 510 of the IWW

■ *Industrial Solidarity*, March 23, 1927.

61

Speaking Tour

This announcement of Fletcher's speeches highlights a subject of central concern to Fletcher throughout his organizing career, radically inclusive unionism.

**WORKING MEN! WORKING WOMEN!
ATTENTION!**

DETROIT MASS MEETING
Come and Hear Fellow Worker
BENJAMIN FLETCHER

Orator and organizer for Industrial Workers of the World, and official Representative of the Marine Transport Workers Union No. 510,
who will speak at the following places:
TUESDAY, SEPT. 27,
at 7:30 P.M.
1618 EAST DAVISON AVE.
SATURDAY, OCTOBER 1,
at 7:30 P.M.
1423 FARNSWORTH AVE.
SATURDAY, OCTOBER 8,
at 7:30 P.M.
MCDOUGALL and GRATIOT AVE.

ON THE SUBJECT
"Can and Shall Workers of All Races, Sexes, Colors,
Creeds, and Nationalities Organize Together and
Build One Big Union Of The IWW?"

All Working Men and Working Women Are Cordially Invited to Attend!
ADMISSION FREE!

Auspices: INDUSTRIAL WORKERS OF THE WORLD

■ *Industrial Solidarity*, October 12, 1927.

62

Hello, Detroit

These articles confirm Fletcher's activism in and commitment to the IWW in the late 1920s. While Local 8 no longer held power on the Philadelphia water-front, Fletcher's speaking abilities remained both powerful and in demand. In an incredibly rare coincidence, this article was corroborated—forty years later—in the reminiscences of Nick DiGaetano, an immigrant from Palermo, Sicily, who worked for Chrysler in the 1920s and later became an organizer for the United Auto Workers (UAW). In his 1968 interview, DiGaetano recalled seeing Fletcher speak in Detroit, which also was advertised in the handbill (Document 61). This story also demonstrated that an active Wobbly scene existed in late 1920s Detroit, committed to the IWW and hoping for a return to its former heights.

Fletcher Meetings Waken A New Interest

DETROIT Mich.—Fellow Worker Ben Fletcher, IWW speaker touring the country for the W.I.E.S. [Workers (Incorporated) Educational Society], made two very impressive speeches here on September 24th and 27th, and his meetings are having a very good effect on the members. He spoke on October 1st, and is scheduled to address another meeting in this city on the 8th.

The meetings are educating the workers who are crowding into them, and there is an awakening of good sentiment among the old-timers, and also a stir among ex-members who are realizing that the IWW is going strong and just needs the help of active members to make it grow greater than ever before. The ex-members are lining up, and those who were getting behind in dues are stamping up. Then there are the new line-ups, all of which looks very good for a real membership drive here.

Other meetings for Fletcher are being arranged, and there is a possibility that Detroit will awaken to the IWW message and respond as in 1919 when there were eleven branches here. What the future holds for us depends upon what the Detroit membership does in the matter.

Fellow Worker Fletcher is a very clear and convincing speaker and it is very instructive to hear him. No member should fail to take in his meetings, and to bring other workers along.

Martin L. Sperling, Del. T 7-62

■ *Industrial Solidarity*, October 12, 1927, 3.

The hall was at capacity, perhaps five hundred. I don't remember seeing any Negroes in the audience, perhaps there were some. Ben Fletcher was a good speaker.

■ Nick DiGaetano, interviewed by Jim Kenney and Herbert Hill, Detroit, June 17, 1968.

63

Speaking to Finnish Workers in Canada

From Detroit, Fletcher crossed the northern border into Ontario, Canada, where he delivered a series of talks. One possible reason for the smaller crowds, in some locations, could be that the tour was organized at a time of the year when large numbers of loggers, including many Finnish immigrants, cut and hauled lumber in remote logging camps. This article, translated from Finnish, also is interesting for its description of how the tour was organized and its self-critical tone and commonsensical proposal for drawing bigger crowds to "dry" (alcohol-free) speaking events. Importantly, the newspaper that carried this story, *Industrialisti*, was the only daily IWW newspaper ever published in North America. As historian Saku Pinta, himself a Finnish Canadian, noted, "Given the union's multiethnic composition, it's so fitting that the Wobbly newspaper of record would be published in a language different from that of the dominant language [English]."

The readers of this newspaper will have previously noticed fellow worker Ben Fletcher's touring schedule. Now we will devote a few words towards taking a look at these speaking engagements. They were not successful when considering audience numbers. The reason for this is likely because the organizers probably did not have enough time. On the other hand, fellow workers in all locations did not take a sufficiently serious approach and neglected the organizing of these educational events. Why was this done? For this each locality may provide their best explanation.

It is disappointing that some localities allow inactivity and indolence to go so far. The Port Arthur branch of Industrial Union 120 (which first received notice of the speaker's tour) did everything possible to assist comrades in other localities. One thousand posters were printed, which were sent to several locations. A circular was even distributed informing all those Canadian Industrial Union Finnish Association locals, located in the vicinity of the speaker's tour, that they are to organize venues for these speaking engagements. But not every locality gave the issue the appropriate amount of attention. In some instances this organizing was left up until the speaker had already arrived in their community.

The first speaking engagement was in Sault Ste. Marie, Ontario. From there the speakers was to travel to Sudbury. A speaking engagement had not been organized there. An event was organized at the Workers Hall in Copper Cliff, but the officious police of the city arrested the event flyposter. They were brought to the police station, questioned, but nonetheless released after they promised to leave the township where the nickel barons rule with unlimited power. When the speaking engagement was set to begin, the small size of the audience was such that it did not justify proceeding with the event.

It is no wonder. The English-speaking population of the aforementioned township are entirely in the fetters of the Catholic Church. Since there are no actual worksites in Sudbury the majority of the English-language population there are "business people" who have no interest in hearing a speaker that does not give advice on business affairs, but rather speaks directly only on behalf of the interests of the poor and wage workers.

The next speaking engagement was intended to be held in Kirkland Lake. Local fellow workers themselves may best explain the reasons why this was not organized. In Timmins there were two speaking engagements. The hope is that something from Fletcher's clearly understandable speech will sprout in the minds of those miners who previously, for one reason or another, have not yet grasped that industrial unionism in the only hope and liberator of the wage slave.

Fletcher spoke on four separate occasions in the District of Thunder Bay. One evening at a trade union hall in Fort William, once in the large Lyceum Theatre, and twice in the industrial unionist-controlled Finnish Labour Temple.

Without exaggeration it can be stated that Ben Fletcher is a good speaker. He clearly and thoroughly illustrated that neither trade unionism nor political action can liberate the working class from wage slavery, but rather industrial unionism as represented by the Industrial Workers of the World, is the only hope for wage slaves, capable of carrying out the social revolution.

Attendance at the speaking engagements in these twin cities was not as big as expected considering the fervent demands on the organization that an English-language speaker be acquired.

At the meeting of the event organizing committee, held at the Labour Temple on the evening of November 30, these speaking engagements were thoroughly discussed. In general we came to the previously held conviction, gained through experience, that speaking engagements alone do not draw sufficient audiences. It was decided that speakers would be included in other programs. Specifically, we are of the opinion that large audiences consider speaking engagements alone to be to "dry." Music, singing, recitals etc. should be organized alongside these events which would diversify the program to the satisfaction of a lighter crowd.

It was unanimously decided that some tactical changes are to be implemented in organizing speaking engagements in the future, if we intend to draw bigger audiences to them.

—Canadian News Service

■ *Industrialisti*, December 9, 1927. Translated by Saku Pinta.

64

Fletcher Visits Work People's College

Not only were many Finns active in radical politics in Canada, so, too, in the United States. In the Upper Peninsula of Michigan, northern Minnesota, and Pacific Northwest, Finnish loggers and miners played conspicuous roles. In Duluth, Wobblies, many of whom were Finns, created the Work People's College, a working-class institution to educate workers in the liberal arts, socialism, and labor organizing. This Finnish newspaper first was published in New York City, then in Chicago during the 1920s, before moving to Duluth in 1929 where it published into the late 1930s.

15th of November was stormy. It seemed as if nature was tearing up everything and everyone who wasn't prepared for winter's storms. Workers' life is like a journey amidst oppression. But despite all the oppression we have a bright image of future before us. Without it our lives would be too horrible to bear.

A worker has two periods of miserableness in a year. Winter is the most horrible, which is why one always ties to prepare for it. Only few workers can save themselves from the worst ordeals.

Now, on the 15th of this month, some twenty workers in a peaceful state of mind, but still determined, are smiling as they watched how nature and capitalism tried to threaten them, without effect. These lucky twenty came from different parts of the country. Some were tired for having jumped out of a freight train. Some had driven cars, some had traveled with gentlemen on the trains, some had even walked. No matter how they had gotten here, they were now gathered at the reading hall of the Work People's College, where the rules of the College were read to them. Curriculum was also introduced and it was hoped that their enthusiasm would continue. They were also made aware of their responsibilities at the College.

So this is how the 20th term year of the College begun.

We were surprised how small the group was. We thought about the societal situation and the need for organization and preparedness. Only twenty! Only twenty worker comrades had been able to save themselves from the grinding stones of capitalism? Or was it because there were among us only 20 workers who were prepared to devote themselves to study the basic principles of our society, its causes and effects, and to develop themselves as proper servants of their class?—And we are supposed to "take control of the means of production and to abolish the wage system!"

All in all, there have been 44 students at the College this year.

The student body is now somewhat different than before, because four students came from Canada this year. There representatives of the British world power are good folks. Not only Canada and England, but all nations of the British commonwealth, black and white, can be proud of them. This can have some diplomatic effects, because our psychology teacher had such an effect on one of the students that he/she switched his/her allegiance and became a United States subject. In this way, perhaps for the first time in history, British foreign affairs were dealt with on a psychological footing.

We have had many visitors during this winter. The first was Ben Fletcher, the IWW organizer, who during his tour visited us a couple of times, lecturing to the comrades, speaking about how education was necessary in advancing the cause of the labor movement. . . .

We have no fear that we will forget our proletarian character. When we want to have a change, we go to Duluth pool halls and breathe in the nutritional spirit of bottom strata of society. Then we can go and breathe the fresh air of the Michigan street slave market and Duluth Point, where we can curse off in a real proletarian way the camps and camp bosses with the unemployed. In midst of these unemployed, who have been poisoned by alcohol and their environment, we can feel like we are among our own kind. This makes us feel at home.

We sleep until 7 in the morning, we eat two times a day and have a few coffee breaks. Who could claim that our studying does not have an economic base!

—a College Student

■ "Among Books," Tie Vapauteen [The Road to Freedom] 10, no. 4 (April 1928): 5–8. Translated by Aleksi Huhta.

Drawing by Ralph Chaplin. Designed as a stickerette (now, "sticker"), ca. 1916. Stickerettes also were called "silent agitators."

65

Fifteen Hundred Have Listened, Spellbound

Fletcher's talks in Canada were remarkably well documented. One only wished that other of his speaking tours, earlier ones, had commanded such media exposure. Despite years in prison and the near destruction of the IWW, Fletcher remained committed to the Wobbly ideals of industrial unionism, antiracism, and socialism. He also continued to impress audiences, so much that one took the time and effort to write a letter from Ontario to Philadelphia.

The motto invoked, "An injury to one is the concern of all," actually was from the much-older Knights of Labor. The IWW adapted the original by replacing "the concern" with "an injury."

The *Philadelphia Tribune* was, and remains, that city's main black newspaper. Alas, it never reported on Ben Fletcher (or Local 8) except in this letter and its brief obituary in 1949.

Port Arthur, Ontario, Canada
December 1, 1927

Editor of the *Philadelphia Tribune*
16th and Rodman Streets
Philadelphia, Pa.

Dear Sir:

While this purports to be a letter relating to the lecture tour of one of your Philadelphia citizens of color, Benjamin H. Fletcher, I am requesting that you publish it as an article dealing with his tour generally in Canada.

Mr. Fletcher, under the auspices of the Workers Educational Society (Incorporated) of Chicago, Ill., USA, began his lecture tour at Sault Ste Marie, Canada. His subject was "Industrial Unionism, the Only Hope of Labor."

At his several meetings about fifteen hundred have listened, spellbound, as he masterly marshalled facts and figures, that left no doubt as to the ineffectiveness of the craft unions and so-called Political Parties of

Labor, as weapons of 'labor in their struggles against capital." Mr. Fletcher pointed out, and oh! So clearly, that labor must organize regardless of race, color or craft differences, on a basis of working-class consciousness, and assemble themselves together in one big union, just as they are assembled in the industries, and inscribe on their banner, "An injury to one is the concern of all." And further, train and disciplines themselves in the everyday struggle, with capital, not only to win more wages, shorter hours and better working conditions, but also to carry on production when capitalism collapses, by and through their industrial unions, as proposed by the Industrial Workers of the World.

Never will I forget this labor apostle of color and hundreds like me. I learned something of your struggles as a working race in America and more, I saw more clearly that we who labor must organize as a class throughout industry. You should be proud of Ben Fletcher, who in thunderous tones with clarion ring so capably espouses labor's cause. He is endeared to our hearts and lasting memories.

Yours sincerely for Labor,

Hilya Laurri [a.k.a. Hilja Lauri]

■ "Ben Fletcher in Canada," *Philadelphia Tribune*, December 29, 1927, 16.

66

Claude McKay on Local 8

Jake Brown was the African American protagonist in a legendary novel by the author and activist, Claude McKay. Born in Jamaica, McKay already was an accomplished poet by the time he moved to New York City in 1914, where he wrote his legendary poem, "If We Must Die" (1919) and most well-known novels, *Home to Harlem* (1928) and *Banjo* (1929). In addition to being influenced by Marcus Garvey, McKay also was committed to socialism, first as a member of the IWW and, later, the CP. While some speculate that Fletcher and McKay knew each, which would not be surprising, no definitive proof exists. Nevertheless, this excerpt from *Home to Harlem* demonstrates that McKay knew well about Local 8, which is to say he knew about Fletcher. Set on a pier in lower Manhattan, long the country's busiest port, this passage also confirms McKay's insights into labor and race in Progressive Era America. This remains the only known reference to Local 8 in a fictional work.

A note on the manner in which McKay composed dialogue: his use of writing black oral dialect has been criticized by some and praised by others. Here, it remains unedited.

"Jake was working longshore. Hooking barrels and boxes, wrestling with chains and cranes. He didn't have a little-boss job this time. But that didn't worry him. He was one blackamoor that nourished a perfect contempt for place. There were times when he divided his days between Rose and Uncle Doc's saloon and Dixie Red's pool-room."

One week when they were not working, Zeddy came to Jake with wonderful news. Men were wanted at a certain pier to unload pineapples at eight dollars a day. Eight dollars was exceptional wages, but the fruit was spoiling.

Jake went with Zeddy and worked the first day with a group of Negroes and a few white men. The white men were not regular dock workers. The only thing that seemed strange to Jake was that all the men ate inside and were not allowed outside the gate for lunch. But, on the second day, his primitive passion for going against regulation urged him to out in the street after lunch.

"Heaving casually along West Street, he was hailed by a white man. 'Hello, fellow-worker'!"

"'Hello, there! What's up?' Jake asked.

"'You working in there'?"

"'Sure I is. Since yestidday'."

"The man told Jake that there was a strike on and he was scabbing. Jake asked him why there were no pickets if there was a strike. The man replied that there were no pickets because the union leaders were against the strike, and had connived with the police to beat up and jail the pickets.

"Well, pardner,' Jake said, 'I've done worked through a tur'ble assortaments o' jobs in mah lifetime, but I ain't nevah yet scabbed it on any man. I done weak in this heah country, and I works good and hard over there in France. I works in London and I nevay was a blackleg, although I been the only black man in mah gang.'

"'Fine, fellow-worker; that's a real man's talk,' said the white man. He took a little red book out of his pocket and asked Jake to let him sign up in his union.

"'It's the only one in the country for a redblooded worker, no matter what race or nation he belongs to.'

"Nope, I won't scab, but I ain't a joiner kind of a fellah,' said Jake. 'I ain't no white folks' nigger and I ain't no poah white's fool. When I longshored in Philly I was a good union man. But when I made New York I done finds out that they give the colored mens the worser piers and holds the bes'n a' them foh the Irishmen. No pardner, keep you' card. I take the best I k'n get as I goes mah way. But I tells you, things ain't none at all lovely between white and black in this heah Gawd's own country."

■ Claude McKay, *Home to Harlem*.

67

Fletcher Thrills Crowd
in Philadelphia

Fletcher was respected by African American radicals well beyond the membership of the IWW and Local 8's heyday. In 1929, he spoke before the American Negro Labor Congress, a CP-affiliated organization led by the former Wobbly Lovett Fort-Whiteman. In this speech, Fletcher repeated the standard IWW ideology: industrial unionism, anticapitalism, creating a society based upon people rather than profit, an egalitarian society free of racism, sexism, and other prejudices. Still only thirty-nine years old, Fletcher continued delivering rousing speeches on the horrors of capitalism, in this instance just months before the onset of the Great Depression.

Addressing the Forum of the American Negro Labor Congress, Sunday, February 3rd, 610 South 16th Street, Benjamin Fletcher, noted militant of the glorious IWW brought the audience to its feet, when he told them that industrial unionism, as expounded by the IWW, is the hope of the suffering and exploited Negro workers in his struggles for real freedom. Fellow Worker Fletcher pointed out the heroic attempt of the IWW to organize the workers into one big union, based on industry, regardless of race, sex or nationality, pointing out the fact that the bosses are well organized nationally and internationally, and if the workers are to cope with the mighty industrial problems confronting them, they too, must be well organized into industrial unions of their class to struggle for their class, in the interest of their class. The speaker pointed out the marvelous industrial machine, and said, if industry was organized for use rather than for profit, and if all those who are able to work, were put to work for a few hours each day for about five days, we could produce all that is necessary to make life happy and contented, eliminating unemployment, hunger, poverty, and the many other evils which is the common lot of the toiling millions. Pointing out the mighty combination of capital, the speed-up system, etc., the speaker said, the hope of the working class lies in the organization of industrial unions of all those who work nationally and internationally; pointing out that a Negro employer is as ruthless as a white employer, or a Chinese, or Japanese, that the question confronting

the workers is not race. That we are in the midst of an intense class struggle, and the workers must organize as a class and prepare to take over the
management and operation of industry in the interest of suffering society,
as the solution of the vexing problems confronting society. Ben was in
the best of good form, in the discussion that followed. It was pointed out
that, if the IWW would begin the organization of Philadelphia they could
sweep the city. This was one of the best talks that has graced the Forum
in a long time, the audience showed their appreciation by demanding
his early return.

—A. Warreno

■ *Industrial Worker*, February 16, 1929.

68

Industrial Unionism & Black Workers

In 1929 Ben Fletcher engaged in extensive correspondence with Abram Lincoln Harris, the radical black historian and economist of Howard University. Along with scholar Sterling Spero, Harris was writing what remains one of the best histories of African American labor, *The Black Worker* (1931). During their research, they contacted numerous black labor leaders. Fletcher seemed pleased that Harris wanted Fletcher's thoughts and took pains to detail his experiences and beliefs. In 1929 Fletcher remained a Wobbly organizer and speaker albeit without a local.

In this first letter, Fletcher staked his claim as a true believer in industrial unionism as well as the necessity for any viable labor union to be fully inclusive of all workers, regardless of creed or color. He contended the IWW could create economic equality for African Americans and eliminate racism. Fletcher also saw Spero and Harris's book as an opportunity to organize black workers and, as such, should be used to highlight how the AFL was useless as a fighting organization. Finally, he took a jab at the far-better-known A. Philip Randolph, head of the Brotherhood of Sleeping Car Porters, for affiliating with the AFL.

Fletcher to Abram L. Harris, July 22, 1929
Phone, Bell, Evergreen 7549
3322 Wallace St. (Res)
Philadelphia, Pa.
July 22nd '29

Mr. Abram L. Harris
405 Edgecombe Ave.
New York, N.Y.

Dear Mr. Harris:
    Yours of the 16th is before me and the contents of same has been fully noted. In response will state that I will endeavor to have the requested information, and data, together with my personal observation on the subject matter, in your hands, by Friday or Saturday morning.

I will spare neither time nor patience in getting the matter together, and you may compensate for same as your judgement dictates.

Needless to state I am glad to note that you are developing that theory of Industrial Unionism and Negro workers' fortunes are bound up therein. I have been identified with the Labor Movement—twenty years, and I am at a safe distance from forty yet. Nineteen of those years have been spent in the ranks of the IWW and this long ago I have come to know that, the Industrial Unionism as proposed and practiced by the IWW is all sufficient for the teeming millions who must labor for others in order to stay on this planet, and more, it is the economic vehicle that will enable the Negro Workers to burst every bond of Racial Prejudice, Industrial and political inequalities and social ostracism.

We are living in a machine age of Industrialism that reveals the utter folly of the negro worker even contemplating of advancing his class interests with Socialist, Communist or Trade Union programs.

The why and the wherefore I'll cover with facts indisputable in the matter I'll submit to you. Am glad that you are giving this angle serious consideration, and if you hew to that line throughout, the book will be a winner. Those of us in on the know *know*, that the AFL is committed to preserving the status quo between Capital and Labor, and to act as a bulwark against working class dictation to capital. Every one of its Executive Council is interested in protecting business and espousing patriotism, many of its official membership are business people and members of various Capitalist organizations, such as the Chamber of Commerce who are committed to the Open Shop and yet despite all, we note Phil Randolph freeing this drivel off his chest. Wm. Green, another Lincoln, it is to laugh—No you couldn't have expected me take otherwise your suggestion if entertaining any doubts. To referentially inquire of him Dabney left here about a year ago is teaching in the South, Virginia I believe. With best wishes,

Am yours truly,

Benjamin H. Fletcher

■ Abram Lincoln Harris Papers, Moorland-Spingarn Archives, Howard University.

69

The IWW & Negro Wage Workers

This essay by Fletcher, part of his correspondence with Abram Harris, is really a partial history of Local 8, with only a few references to black members in other branches of the IWW. With the notable exception of the Brotherhood of Timber Workers, Local 8 was the only IWW branch with a significant black presence. Unfortunately, Fletcher did not discuss his own early involvement with the IWW or Local 8 prior to 1920. Rather, he focused upon the 1920 strike, Philadelphia Controversy, 1922 strike, role of communism in Local 8 and the IWW, rival ILA, and schisms created by these competitors—the multiple factors explaining Local 8's demise.

Worth considering further is that Fletcher made numerous references to the destructive role that Communists played in Local 8, a vital subject difficult to reconstruct with limited evidence. Clearly, the Communists wanted to increase their power in the United States. In 1919 and early 1920s, the Wobblies were the obvious group to recruit from. Thus began a bitter battle between those Wobblies who wanted to join the Communists and those who did not; similar splits occurred in every other industrialized country among different Left tendencies. Like most other Wobblies, anarchists, and syndicalists, Fletcher fiercely opposed the Communists albeit in no small part because the CP actively worked to undermine Local 8, once Lenin ordered the CPs to focus on "boring from within" the AFL instead. On a related subject, there is no evidence that members of Local 8 loaded ammunition for anti-Bolshevik forces in the Russian Civil War. In fact, it is conceivable and possible that Communists in the MTW and IWW fabricated this story to disrupt Local 8 in what became the "Philadelphia Controversy." In the last section, Fletcher discussed how the IWW fought Jim Crow segregation that hindered BTW organizing efforts. He might have learned this history firsthand from E.F. Doree or Bill Haywood, both of whom were active in that campaign. Perhaps they even reminisced about such efforts while languishing in Leavenworth.

The IWW Marine Transport Workers' Strike of six weeks duration, ending on July 7th 1920, involved Longshoremen (Deep-water and Coastwise, Checkers and Grain Ceilers). Fully 5,500 workers tied up the Port so far as shipping was concerned tight as a drum, and 3,200 Sympathizing workers working in and about the Harbor lined up in the Unions of the Phila IWW Jurisdiction during the duration of that memorial struggle.

The continued Rising Cost of Living and the desire of the IWW— membership to tighten up their ranks numerically in order to get in position to battle for an increase in wages and 8 hour day (44 hour week was the cause of the 1920 strike. The port throughout the war period and up to that time was on a 50 hour week basis. The Philadelphia Marine Transport Workers Branch occupied a peculiar and unique position. In all other Atlantic and Gulf Ports during the War and up to the time of the 1920 strike, the organized Longshoremen were identified with the International Longshoremen's Association whose parent organization is the AFL.

The ILA had right at the beginning of the war used the influence of their former president T.V. O'Connor (now Chairman of the US Shipping Board and then a member of that Board) to alienate the Phila. Marine Transport Workers from the IWW and identify themselves with the ILA.

Insincere local IWWs conspire with T.V. O'Connor and his ILA official cohorts, the Press and a few local stevedoring and steamship Interests to no avail. The IWW squelched all maneuvers in this direction and captured all Government stevedoring—work both at the US Navy Yard where an IWW-MTW monthly job button was tantamount to a pass or procuring of one, and Dupont's ammunition plants on the Delaware from Wilmington to Phila.

This situation obtained despite the fact that the Phila MTW was alone in their organized affiliation, so far as Job control was concerned with this group of Marine Transport Workers. The demands of the 1920 strike was $1 per hour basic scale, 8 Hr. day, time and a half overtime with a differential scale and scales of pay running from 10 to 25% on varied cargoes Coast wise Longshoremen 65 cents per hour basic scale 8 hour Day $1 overtime. Same to be retroactive to about Jan. when Coast wise shipping companies cut the Coast wise Longshoremen 30% and on June 10th 1920, during the strike asked the Interstate Commerce Commission for a 31% increase in freight rates.

The strike ended in partial victory, the Grain Ceilers, received 12 1/2% increase in wages and the Checkers Union recognition. Just about the time the Communist element issued their order from Moscow to American agents to initiate a campaign looking forward to control of the IWW forthwith, and in conformity with that order throughout the IWW, Communist activities were begun to take the IWW into camp.

I. W. W. LONGSHOREMEN TIE UP SHIPPING IN PHILADELPHIA

"HOLD FAST, BUDDIE, WE GOT 'EM"

E.F. Doree, *One Big Union Monthly*, July 1920.

Solidarity—the official organ of the IWW was at this time June, 1920 manifestly being edited by one of the Communist agents. The General Executive Board had at least three agents of Moscow. The General Secretary-Treasurer was a Communist and the Secretary Treasurer of the National Office of Marine Transport Workers was a Communist also. This state of affairs precipitated a crisis which about the summary suspension of the Phila. Br of the MTW in August 1920, by the Communist controlled GEB (General Executive Board) on the flimsy charge and pretext that members of that organization were loading ammunition that was going to Wrangel who was then conducting a military expedition against Soviet Russia (Read—Phila. Controversy *etc* pamphlets already forwarded).

The suspension wasn't lifted and the organization reinstated as a Unit of the IWW until the Spring of 1922. During the Suspension Period of about 18 months the Phila. MTW organization continued as an IWW organization, refusing to recognize the Communist controlled GEB's suspension order.

During this period the ILA redoubled their efforts to "capture the Port" and when by Sept 1922 the Communist element saw that they couldn't control the IWW, they in compliance with another order from Moscow initiated what is known as the "Liquidating Program." So on or about Sept. 30th 1922 they were successful in stampeding the Phila

Longshoremen into another strike for the 44 Hour week at a Rump mass meeting, after a Regular Business meeting had decided to hold the strike in abeyance 1st, because 1,300 new members had been taken into the Union just a month before 2nd, It was well known that the ILA had secured the two card affiliation of about 1500 Longshoremen, who were pledged to scab on the IWW in case of a strike 3rd and, it was known that the 48 Hr. week which obtained in N.Y. Harbor could be gotten by negotiations to that end. The strike occurred or rather disruption by Jan. 1923 three unions were in the field, IWW Phila Longshoremen's Union and ILA (Note: The Philadelphia Longshoremen's Union was organized in Jan. 1923 by those IWW members who refused to go along with the Communist stampeded IWW element, who seceded and opened another Hall etc. this schism and breach could and would have been averted and the IWW yet maintained.) If in Oct 1923, when Walter T Nef, Ed. F. Doree and Ben Fletcher had of been in position to step into the fray and help to get order out of chaos, but this had been wisely circumvented by insincere local officials of the IWW who had come under the influence of the ILA and communist teaching together to bring about the expulsion of these three members and ex-officials of the Marine Transport Workers, in Sept 1922, just before the strike fiasco and while they were serving time in the US Penitentiary at Leavenworth, Kansas; on the grounds and false charges that they had made applications for pardons to the president of the US and agreed not to have anything else to do with the IWW. The part that Race prejudice played in the defeat of the BTW was a minimum one. Because of the widespread discontent of the Lumber workers, its use generally by the Lumber Interests had a negative effect to illustrate:

In order to offset union juices among the Negro element the Employers resorted to the use of Negro detectives and spies who spied and informed on whites as well as blacks. Further, as I previously pointed out when race prejudice was resorted to at Alexandria, La. To prevent the meeting of the 1912 Convention of the BTW it failed, the community and delegates alike had deaf ears for such appeals. So, consequently when Haywood got there and told them that the IWW way and only way to get labor solidarity was to assemble all together as one, they understood and acted accordingly and that sentiment was so dominant that open warfare would have resulted if that convention had of been interfered with. Of course Race prejudice was played up—and mob rule resorted to wipe out the Union what was successful only because of the previously mentioned causes.

In the Lumber Industry as in all others the Negro element's employed is restricted generally to certain jobs and this obtains to a lesser degree of course with all other race groups—it is one of those social contradictions of capitalism. It is depended upon to maintain division in the ranks of labor.

It disappears as the concentration and mechanization of industry with its manifold makeshifts and readjustments and finally and fully when the Industrially organized working class with their economic mechanism—the Industrial Unions, frees the Social producing agency industry—from the antisocial or undemocratic control and administration of the capitalist class.

1929

■ Abram Lincoln Harris Papers, Moorland-Spingarn Archives, Howard University.

70

Race Consciousness

Fletcher clearly was excited about Harris' project so took great pains to provide Harris with IWW documents and share personal thoughts. The section most revealing of Fletcher's personal ideological views came in the postscript, in asserting that the motivations of black and white Wobblies were identical: black workers, like white ones, wanted to improve their working conditions, raise their wages, reduce their hours, etc. According to Fletcher, however, more whites joined the IWW because whites had a longer history of wage work in an industrial economy. Fletcher saw blacks "passing through a period of Race Consciousness," be it membership in Marcus Garvey's Universal Negro Improvement Association or embracing the New Negro identity embodied by Harlem Renaissance artists. Fletcher, though, saw class consciousness as a later, more "advanced" state of awareness that blacks would enter as their experiences with industrial capitalism educated them about its realities. Fletcher seemed quite confident of this eventuality.

Fletcher also gave a tiny glimpse into his current life: unemployed and barely managing to pay the rent. In fact, his residence has changed from the letter he sent just one week prior.

Fletcher to Abram Harris, July 29, 1929
332 W. Girard Ave.
Philadelphia, Pa.
July 29th, 1929

Mr. Abram Harris
405 Edgecombe Ave.
New York, NY

Dear Mr. Harris:

Am enclosing herewith the promised material. Delay in forwarding same was unavoidable. It occurred that Thursday when I began assembling some of the data it was missing from my trunk and I lost time track it down, eventually locating it in the possession of a friend who had borrowed same. I particularly refer to article enclosure by the late Wm. D. Haywood [who died in Moscow in 1928] captioned, "Timber Workers and Timber Wolves."

Then further, I was compelled to perform the task under harassing circumstances, of unemployment and the plaguing annoyances of gouging parasitic rent chasers. Of such is the making of the class struggle.

Advise me of your earliest opportunity of your receipt of this letter and enclosures, and whether same suffices.

Needless to state, I am hoping that you have success in getting the book across. If there is anything else in the way of information, dates, etc. that you may desire and I have, it's yours for the asking. With best wishes, I am,

Yours Sincerely,

Benjamin H. Fletcher
P.S. Will look Dabney's address up for you.
P.S. In reading over your letter I note some omissions on my part, in response, to your last of questions, 1st, There never was any conflict in the unknown between the Negroes and whites of the IWW. It is my knowledge and observation that as a general theory the Negroes who join the IWW *are no different in their motives for doing so than the whites, those motives are such as desires to secure better working conditions, higher wages, shorter hours, and the like but the whites of course register a higher percentage of those, who possess the idealism of the IWW* and the whole gamut of its revolutionary purpose. And this disparity can be explained by the simple fact that the whites have had on the whole a longer experience with Industrialism (wage slavery), and further the Negro is passing through the period of Race Consciousness, for the most part.

But Race Consciousness with the Negro is rapidly being displaced with Class Consciousness, as Economic Pressure of capitalism cuts off all escape for all the Negroes except a few, by way of Race Consciousness. It follows therefore that the Negro worker place as prominent factor in the Revolutionary ranks of the IWW is assured. I have been identified with the IWW 19 years and actively so, and I note an increase in the number of Negro wage workers who stand at a street meeting or attend a Hall meeting or line up on the job.

B.H.F.

■ Abram Lincoln Harris Papers, Moorland-Spingarn Archives, Howard University.

71

Heartache

This short letter reveals Fletcher's interest in and respect for Harris for undertaking the task of writing a book. Fletcher's mention of a beloved niece who had passed away recently is an all-too rare piece of family history. Child mortality was quite high in this era, especially for the working class and particularly for people of color.

Fletcher to Abram Harris, October 1, 1929
332 W. Girard Ave.
Phila, Pa. 10/1/29

Dear friend Harris:

I hope you will share with me some understanding of the difficulty that attends the attempt to commit to one through the written word the details, meat and substance of such a subject as commands your attention. And when such a task is undertaking under circumstances far from ideal—know that it becomes a monumental one. Yours of the 16th return reached me at the moment of the funeral dirge's last echo over the bier of my beloved little niece Alice, who passed on to peace and rest after an illness of two years and my heart though well nigh riveted over with tarts of sorrow and pain in a long, long struggle that summarily leads no where, it was well nigh at the breaking point when your letter came. So, until today I have waited until time and lessening of heartaches would permit the writing of the requested material, enclosed herewith. I am hopeful that we meet shortly in N.Y.C. preferably—to discourse at length about continuing with each other upon the subject matter of our correspondence until far in the night.

Warmly yours,

Benjamin H. Fletcher

■ Abram Lincoln Harris Papers, Moorland-Spingarn Archives, Howard University.

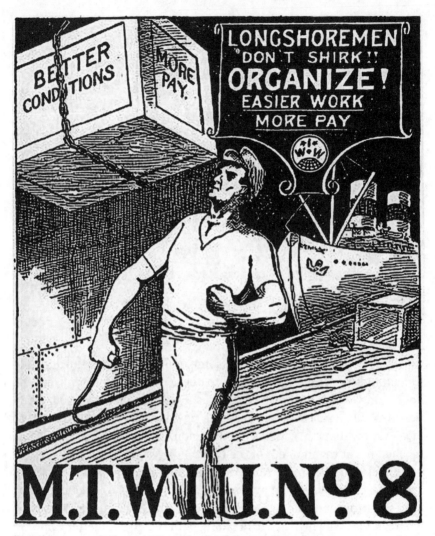

"Longshoremen don't shirk!! Organize!" A "silent agitator," poster, 1920.

72

A Thousand Join in One Day!

Here Fletcher offered estimates of IWW membership as well as for the Marine Transport Workers Industrial Union. When he discussed the number of African Americans in the MTW and IWW it is vital to note that—overwhelmingly—they belonged to Local 8. Other than among Philadelphia longshoremen, black Wobblies were relatively few. The 1920 strike that Fletcher discussed is noteworthy for its size, duration, community support, and effects. As had many other unions in postwar America, Local 8 pushed for an eight-hour day and wage increases to keep up with runaway inflation. Though Local 8 mobilized nearly all of the city's waterfront workers, including many nonunion workers, ultimately the strike was a draw at best, a defeat at worst. Employers did not concede to the union's demands. More damaging, the swelling of Local 8's ranks resulted in thousands of new members, many recent Southern black migrants, with little industrial or union experience. Further, Local 8's efforts to control the waterfront labor surplus caused a split with the national organization a few months afterwards, the Philadelphia Controversy.

Fletcher to Abram Harris, August 8, 1929
3322 Wallace St.
Philadelphia, Pa.
Aug. 8th, 1929

Dear friend Harris:

Yours of the fifth with M.O. enclosed therein for Ted Dole and for submitted material on Industrial Unionism and the IWW and Negro came duly to hand many thanks for same. Writing now, on the omitted information: The IWW membership to date is approximately between ten and fifteen thousand the Negro membership is between two and three hundred; during our "balmy days," the Negro constituted from ten to fifteen percent, and during the aforementioned period, the IWW membership generally hovered between fifteen and one hundred thousand and one half of those totals in bad standing. The best year—periods for the IWW in the Marine Transport Industry, were as follows, 1913-14—when its membership averaged about 5,000 all told, Negro constituting—about 25%. 1916–17, when its membership averaged about 10,000, the Negro membership constituting about 30%; 1920–21, when its membership averaged about 25,000, the Negro constituting about: 20%. During 1920, Here in the Port of Phila, in the month of May, the Marine Transport Workers Industrial Union #8, lined up 8,200 workers of various Industries within 30 days, fully 5,000 Negroes, 1,000 joining in one day. The IWW button was a passport every where's hereabout. The town was electrified. If you were operating a Restaurant, Saloon Club, or other whatnot, where Longshoremen and Marine Transport Workers and their allies frequented, you were outspoken in your support of the IWW or you couldn't play. The Harbor was tied up for 6 weeks over a hundred deep Sea Vessels were anchored in the stream. Fifty-million Dollar loss inflicted on the Business element, attempts to scab were vigorously suppressed. Politicians actually fought to effect release of our members, where strike picketing activities ended in arrest. Am hoping to be able to see you before the year is over and as I stated before anything in the way of information that you feel I might be able to convey is yours for the asking. With best wishes,

I am your sincerely,

Benjamin H. Fletcher

■ Abram Lincoln Harris Papers, Moorland-Spingarn Archives, Howard University.

73

Fletcher Recalls Nearly
Being Lynched

This is the only known interview with Fletcher and is a jewel. It reveals so much about Fletcher but especially his experiences just prior to the big trial in 1918, unwavering commitment to the IWW and, more broadly, ongoing commitment to revolutionary industrial unionism. He made clear how much he saw the Communist Party as disruptive and manipulative, including in the decline of the IWW. In 1931, the CP only had started to rise as a potent force in the United States, beginning in the spring of 1930 when it helped organize and lead protests, in cities across the land, to push the federal government to assist Americans in desperate need due to the depression. Also in 1931, despite Fletcher's vitriol, the CP started to make a concerted effort to reach out to and advocate on behalf of African Americans. Earlier in 1931, the CP helped save the lives of the so-called Scottsboro boys, a group of nine black teens and young men who had been falsely accused of raping two white girls. Without Communist assistance, those nine black males surely would have been executed by the state of Alabama. Regardless of Fletcher's viewpoint, the CP became the premier force on the American Left in the 1930s and 1940s.

Sadly, the author of this article is unknown. Founded in 1909, the *Amsterdam News* is a weekly newspaper geared to the black community of New York City and among the older still-operating black newspapers in the United States. Named after Amsterdam Avenue, a major street in Harlem, the paper long has been a voice for equal rights and power and none other than Malcolm X wrote a column in the paper. Its workforce unionized in 1936 and remains so.

Old IWW Organizer Tries to Rebuild the Machine

"and then they let me into the courtroom and finally into Leavenworth."

Ben Fletcher, long time IWW organizer, drew a deep puff of his cigar and looked placidly out of the window as he concluded the reminiscences of his radical activities which led to his imprisonment in 1918 along with 100 other members of the Industrial Workers of the World in the Federal

Some People Are Taken to Jail, But Ben Fletcher Just 'Went in'

Old I. W. W. Organizer Tries to Rebuild the Machine

"—— and then they let me into the courtroom and finally into Leavenworth."

Ben Fletcher, long time I. W. W. organizer, drew a deep puff of his cigar and looked placidly out of the window as he concluded the reminiscences of his radical activities which led to his imprisonment in 1918 along with 100 other members of the Industrial Workers of World in the Federal Penitentiary at Leavenworth on indictments returned against them by a Government possessed of a wartime hysteria.

A simple tale he told. The story of his life as a class-conscious worker. The story of how he had been turned to I. W. W. by the discriminatory practices and craft limitations of the American Federation of Labor unions; of how he had organized longshoremen along the coast from Boston to Norfolk; of how he had been smuggled out of the latter city by friends after the shipping interests had threatened him with lynching; of how he had been trailed by Federal operatives; of how he had to force himself into that Federal courtroom in Chicago, where for nineteen weeks he and 112 other leaders of the syndicalist movement stood trial on charges of espionage and obstructing the Government's war program, and finally of the two years and six months of the ten-year sentence he served in the Federal penitentiary.

"I was preparing the longshoremen of Baltimore for a strike in 1917 for higher wages, shorter hours and better working conditions when I received instructions from headquarters to proceed to Norfolk where the dock workers were becoming restless and asking that an organizer be sent them," Fletcher began.

"I found the men responsive and eager for a union. But I had not been in town long before word was circulated that I represented a dangerous element set on the destruction of property and the overthrow of the Government. Then I began receiving messages of a threatening character. I would be lynched if I spread that doctrine around Norfolk, I was told. One night friends, fearing that my life was in danger, smuggled me aboard a northbound ship to Boston.

"By this time the Government spurred on by the lumber and copper interests of the West had set about a deliberate plan to eradicate the I. W. W., which was growing rapidly in numbers, gaining control of certain important industries, and threatening the supremacy of the A. F. of L. which the Government consistently favored throughout the war period.

"It was while I was working in Boston that I received a tip that I was in line for indictment by a Federal Grand Jury. Accepting the tip as authentic I returned to my home in Philadelphia, where I preferred to be placed under arrest. The next week I read in the paper that indictments had been returned against 166 of us and that we were to be arrested on sight."

Ben Fletcher paused long enough to relight his cigar and to glance reflectively about the room; to think again of the days when his organization was a rallying ground for the revolutionary workers of the country; when it constituted enough of a threat to compel the attention of the Government; when it had cards issued to a million workers including 100,000 black men and women whose membership was discouraged or barred by the A. F. of L. unions. Times have changed and now with its scant

BEN FLETCHER.

3,000 dues paying members it is little more than a proletarian sect.

"For five months," he said, taking up the thread of his narrative, "I remained in Philadelphia, a fugitive from justice yet going about my work with no effort to conceal my identity. During this period I was working in a roundhouse of the Pennsylvania Railroad.

"One day—it was February 9, 1918—two strangers appeared at my door. They were special agents of the Government. They placed me under arrest and I was held in $10,000 bail. After being imprisoned for two weeks bail was reduced to $1,500 by the Federal district attorney. This was secured by the I. W. W. local and I was released.

"Summoned to appear in court in Chicago on April 1, I arrived two hours late due to a train wreck. Making my way through the Federal agents and police who swarmed the corridors I was blocked at the courtroom door by the chief bailiff, who inquired:

" 'What do you want in here?' "

" 'I belong in here.' "

" 'Oh, a wise boy from the South side want to see the show?' "

" 'No, I'm one of the actors.' "

" 'Take that stuff away. You can't get in here.' "

"Insisting that I belonged there I pulled out my card and told him to go in and see if Ben Fletcher's name wasn't on the indictment. He left the door in charge of assistants, went in and returning announced: 'He's Ben Fletcher, all right. Let him in.'

"And then I walked into the courtroom and into the Federal penitentiary."

Asked the cause of the decline of the I. W. W. Fletcher pointed out two factors: Lack of comprehension among the workers of the length to which the employing class will go to maintain its control, and the "disruptive influence of the Communists."

"Up until the time of the war it was believed that because of the hetrogenity of the population and certain democratic ideals that this country would never resort to such harsh practices in suppressing revolutionary movements as we witnessed during and since the war."

The Communists, Fletcher charged, set about deliberately to wreck all locals of the I. W. W. which they could not capture and use for their own ends.

"Inevitably, the I. W. W. will be revived," he said, "with the full exposure of the insincerity of the American Communists and the continued rationalization of industry which oblivates craft lines, making the trades unions of the A. F. of L. obsolete and necessitating the building of industrial unions such as those of the Industrial Workers of the World."

Today Ben Fletcher is one of the faithful few remaining active in the once powerful I. W. W. Since his release from Leavenworth in October, 1922, he has carried on propaganda for the organization, speaking to small sectarian groups of anarchists, syndicalists and other non-Communist radicals, but no longer to the great body of unskilled and unorganized workers to whom the I. W. W. once appealed. Today Ben Fletcher sits at his desk in the dingy quarters of the district recruiting office at 90 East Tenth street and lives again the days when the I. W. W. was a growing mass movement threatening to challenge American capitalism on its own grounds.

Amsterdam News (New York City), December 30, 1931.

Penitentiary at Leavenworth on indictments returned against them by a Government possessed of a wartime hysteria.

A simple tale he told. The story of his life as a class-conscious worker. The story of how he had been turned to IWW by the discriminatory practices and craft limitations of the American Federation of Labor unions; of how he had organized longshoremen along the coast from Boston to Norfolk; of how he had been smuggled out of the latter city by friends after the shipping interests had threatened him with lynching; of how he had to force himself into that Federal courtroom in Chicago, where for nineteen weeks he and 112 other leaders of the syndicalist movement stood trial on charges of espionage and obstructing the Government's war program, and finally of the two years and six months of the ten-year sentence he served in the Federal penitentiary.

"I was preparing the longshoremen of Baltimore for a strike in 1917 for higher wages, shorter hours and better working conditions when I received instructions from headquarters to proceed to Norfolk where the dock workers were becoming restless and asking that an organizer be sent them," Fletcher began.

"I found the men responsive and eager for a union. But I had not been in town long before word was circulated that I represented a dangerous element set on the destruction of property and the overthrow of the Government. Then I began receiving messages of a threatening character. I would be lynched if I spread that doctrine around Norfolk, I was told. One night friends, fearing that my life was in danger, smuggled me aboard a northbound ship to Boston.

"By this time the Government spurred on by the lumber and copper interests of the West had set about a deliberate plan to eradicate the IWW, which was growing rapidly in numbers, gaining control of certain important industries, and threatening the supremacy of the AF of L, which the Government consistently favored throughout the war period.

"It was while I was working in Boston that I received a tip that I was in line for indictment by a Federal Grand Jury. Accepting this tip as authentic I returned to my home in Philadelphia, where I preferred to be placed under arrest. The next week I read in the paper that indictments had been returned against 166 of us and that we were to be arrested on sight."

Ben Fletcher paused long enough to relight his cigar and to glance reflectively about the room; to think again of the days when his organization was a rallying ground for the revolutionary workers of the country; when it constituted enough of a threat to compel the attention of the

Government; when it had cards issued to a million workers including 100,000 black men and women whose membership was discouraged or barred by the AF of L unions. Times have changed and now with its scant 3,000 dues paying members it is little more than a proletarian sect.

"For more than months," he said, taking up the thread of his narrative, "I remained in Philadelphia, a fugitive from justice yet going about my work with no effort to conceal my identity. During this period I was working in a roundhouse [locomotive maintenance shed built around a turntable] of the Pennsylvania Railroad.

"One day—it was February 9, 1918—two strangers appeared at my door. They were special agents of the Government. They placed me under arrest and I was held in $10,000 bail. After being imprisoned for two weeks bail was reduced to $1,500 by the Federal district attorney. This was secured by the IWW local and I was released.

"Summoned to appear in court in Chicago on April 1, I arrived two hours late due to a train wreck. Making my way through the Federal agents and police who swarmed the corridors I was blocked at the courtroom door by the chief bailiff, who inquired:

"'What do you want in here'?"

"'I belong in here'."

"'Oh, a wise boy from the South side want to see the show'?"

"'No, I'm one of the actors'."

"'Take that stuff away. You can't get in here'."

"Insisting that I belonged there I pulled out my card and told him to go in and see if Ben Fletcher's name wasn't on the indictment. He left the door in charge of assistants, went in and returning announced: 'He's Ben Fletcher, all right. Let him in.'

"And then I walked into the courtroom and into the Federal penitentiary'."

Asked about the cause of the decline of the IWW Fletcher pointed out two factors: Lack of comprehension among the workers of the length to which the employing class will go to maintain its control and the "disruptive influence of the Communists."

"Up until the time of the war it was believed that because of the heterogeneity of the population and certain democratic ideals that this country would never resort to such harsh practices in suppressing revolutionary movements as we witnessed during and since the war."

The Communists, Fletcher charged, set about deliberately to wreck all locals of the IWW which they could not capture and use for their own ends.

"Inevitably, the IWW will be revived," he said, "with the full exposure of the insincerity of the American Communists and the continued rationalization of industry which [obviates] craft lines, making the trade unions of the AF of L obsolete and necessitating the building of industrial unions such as those of the Industrial Workers of the World."

Today Ben Fletcher is one of the faithful few remaining active in the once powerful IWW. Since his release from Leavenworth in October, 1922, he has carried on propaganda for the organization, speaking to small sectarian groups of anarchists, syndicalists and other non-Communist radicals, but no longer to the great body of workers to whom the IWW once appealed. Today Ben Fletcher sits at his desk in the dingy quarters of the district recruiting office at 90 East Tenth street and lives again the days when the IWW was a growing mass movement threatening to challenge American capitalism on its own grounds.

■ "Some People Are Taken to Jail, But Ben Fletcher Just 'Went In,'" *Amsterdam News* December 30, 1931, 16.

74

Cuts to the Bone of
Capitalist Pretension

The last detailed account of a Fletcher speech. As with others, it celebrated Fletcher's speaking abilities in that most tricky of venues: the street corner. Almost a decade after ceasing to play a central role on the Philadelphia waterfront, and twenty-one years after joining the IWW, he continued to support its principles and worked to grow the organization. Notably, it was an organizer for the AFL—the IWW's bitter rival—who praised Fletcher. Around 1931, Fletcher moved from Philadelphia to New York City, where he lived for the rest of his life.

The editor is in receipt of a letter from E.S. Marlin, an AF of L officer, who said he stopped at a New York City street meeting intending to listen for just a few minutes. It was an IWW meeting, addressed by Fellow Worker Benjamin J. Fletcher. "I stayed for an hour until he finished," wrote Marlin.

"I have heard all the big shots of the labor movement over a period of 25 years," he went on, "from coast to coast and it is no exaggeration when I state that this colored man, Ben Fletcher, is the only one I ever heard who cut right through to the bone of capitalist pretensions, to being an everlasting ruling class, with a concrete constructive working class union argument."

This correspondent said he learned more about the AF of L from Fletcher's talk than he had ever known and predicated a great future for our organization if only we have more of the type of speakers that Ben Fletcher is.

■ *Industrial Solidarity*, August 11, 1931.

75

Fletcher Knows Which Side He's On

For much of the 1930s, Harlan County was synonymous with working-class radicalism and union organizing. Coal miners in that eastern Kentucky region, affiliated with the United Mine Workers of America and some of whom later joined the Communist-affiliated National Miners' Union, and other groups, engaged in a ferocious struggle against rabidly anti-union mine owners and law enforcement officials. The classic labor song "Which Side Are You On," written by Florence Reece, described the "Harlan County War" or, more pointedly, "Bloody Harlan."

The roster of prominent speakers included Fletcher along with Roger Baldwin, founding director of the American Civil Liberties Union; legendary theologian Reinhold Niebuhr, and Norman Thomas, nicknamed "Mr. Socialism," and the public face of the Socialist Party in the generation after Eugene Debs. Along with longtime Italian activist Arturo Giovannitti, Fletcher presumably represented the IWW. James Price, an attorney working on murder cases in Evarts, Kentucky, earlier had aided the IWW General Defense Committee, created to defend Fletcher and other Wobblies during World War I. It is quite doubtful that Fletcher traveled to Harlan County, but another Wobbly whom Fletcher knew well, Herb Mahler, spent time there and became a stalwart activist on behalf of Harlan's miners.

This story was published in the *New Yorker Volkszeitung* (*New York People's Newspaper*), the longest-running German language daily labor newspaper in US history, 1878–1932. The Socialist Party of America and Social Democratic Party of Germany both endorsed this paper.

Joe Cawood, a Harlan County miner and a former city clerk in Evart [Evarts], Ky., himself one of the 47 workers who have been charged with murder and conspiracy in connection with the major strike in the Black Mountain area for defending their most elementary human rights, will come to New York later this month to report firsthand to local workers.

Cawood will be the main speaker at the rally arranged by the Kentucky Miners Defense and Relief Conference for Friday, January 29, 8:00 P.M. The mass gathering will take place at Irving Plaza Hall, Irving

Place and 15 St., and in addition to Cawood there will be a number of notable speakers representing all currents of the progressive workforce, including Roger Baldwin, Louis F. Budnez, Ben Fletcher, Arturo Giovannitti, Jacob Panken, Jas. Price, Reinhold Niebuhr, Norman Thomas.

The aid conference for the accused miners, of whom, as is generally known, two—President [William] Hightower and Secretary [William B.] Jones of the Harlan Co. miners' union—have already been sentenced to life in prison, is bound to expect of New York's progressive workforce that the intolerable situation in Kentucky become widely known.

■ "Kentucky Miner, in Mt. Sterling, charged with murder, speaks at mass gathering here," *New Yorker Volkszeitung*, January 16, 1932. Translated by Max Henninger.

76

IWW Attempts a Comeback

Due to more than three years of capitalist-induced horror, also known as the Great Depression, a huge number of Americans turned leftward, electing Franklin D. Roosevelt in a landslide in 1932 and wildly supporting the New Deal legislation soon thereafter. Millions of Americans were further radicalized, and some veteran Wobbly organizers thought the time was ripe for an IWW resurgence. Among the impressive list of "astute organizers," not surprisingly, was Fletcher.

However, the IWW proved unable to harness the surging energy of the Left and did not expand in the 1930s. Instead, the primary beneficiary of such discontent was the Communist Party. That does not mean to suggest that the IWW was not influential—far from it. Many new industrial unions, which far more fully rejected racism and sexism (along the lines that the IWW pioneered) formed and counted more than five million members by the late 1930s. Mostly, these unions belonged to the Congress of Industrial Organizations (CIO), founded in 1935. Importantly, former Wobblies populated many CIO unions and Wobbly ideals shaped many of those new unions.

This article, sadly with no reporter attributed, is impressive in detail if not entirely accurate. Almost all IWW leaders imprisoned in 1918 had been released from prisons by the mid 1920s. What did happen in 1933 was that FDR pardoned Fletcher and the other imprisoned Wobblies.

This article's repeated mention of the IWW's antifascism also is of interest. The Wobblies were—once more—far ahead of many of their peers because, in 1933, this issue was not on most Americans' radar. Yet, in January 1933, Adolf Hitler had been made the German chancellor, beginning the Nazis' rein of power. Going back to 1919 and the 1920s, the IWW had battled fascists in the American Legion and Ku Klux Klan, as it continues to do.

War-Time Organizers Released From Prisons, Convening for New Drive

The remnants of the old war-time IWW forces, scattered for sixteen years in isolated groups about the docks of the great ports, in distant mining fields and in the more radical districts of the manufacturing cities are attempting for the first time since the World War to pull themselves together and once again are planning 'to take the war path' in the American scene. The surviving leaders of the old IWW aggression, free now from prisons, are on their way to New York from various parts of the country, coming to attend a congress scheduled to convene here at 8 o'clock Friday night among the faded velvet hangings and crystal chandeliers of Irving Plaza Hall, Irving Place and Fifteenth Street.

Either already arrived or on their way to this meeting are James P. Thompson, who led the picketers in the 1912 textile strike at Lawrence, Mass.; James Price, who once was kidnapped and beaten during trouble in the Kentucky mines; Herbert Mahler, for years active in Northwestern lumber camps; Arthur Boose, organizer of agricultural workers; Peo Monoldi, from the Western metal mines; F. Leigh Bearce, organizer in the building trades; Andrew Leporati, of the hotel and foodstuff workers; Jack Walsh, who has spread the 'one big union doctrine' among sailors on all the oceans, and Ben H. Fletcher, Negro organizer of waterfront workers in Philadelphia.

Would Plan "Lines of Action"

Their purpose this time is the same as it was before 1917, 'to organize the nation's workers into industries and eventually to have these workers take over the whole machinery of production.' The particular concern of this New York congress is to 'plan lines of action to avert the growing menace of Fascism in the United States, and to take advantage of the widespread resentment of the workers against exploitation of employers under the cloak of the NRA [National Recovery Administration, part of the New Deal].

In addition to opposing Fascism, the Roosevelt administration and the NRA, the IWW's still are against the American Federation of Labor, 'which has sold out to the Administration," and are bitter enemies of "the damned Communists." They are going to fight for the same cause for which President Wilson, their wartime enemy, said the United States fought the World War, "for democracy."

These strange words were uttered yesterday in the new headquarters of the organization, 94 Fifth Avenue, by Herbert Mahler, who was among the group arrested after the explosion of the bomb in the Chicago post office. Mahler afterward was sent to Leavenworth as were Thompson, Boose, Walsh and Fletcher. Price, another of the old timers on his way here, served a prison sentence in California, convicted of criminal syndicalism for membership in the IWW.

Use "Astute Organizers"

Mahler said yesterday the tactics of the IWW remnants in late years had been to work where they could quietly, "to send astute organizers into the big industries to line up new members without advertising their presence to employers." They had not "dissipated their energies in exhausting strikes."

Gone was their old "thousand-mile picket line," the freight trains of the West on which the IWW's used to attempt the organization of workers beating rides to and from the Kansas and Nebraska wheat harvests. Gone was at least 75,000 of their 1917 membership of 100,000, but the organizers had been busy lately, said Mahler, enrolling "new blood and new steam" along the New Orleans, Philadelphia, Galveston, and Houston waterfronts, the Northwest lumber woods, the Western grain fields, the fruit orchards of the Yakima Valley in Washington, and big construction projects on the Pacific Coast. New York still is a "tough spot." They plan to attack it next, according to Mahler.

■ "IWW Leaders Called Here to Rebuild Forces," *New York Herald Tribune*, September 27, 1933, 15.

77

A Communist Cynically Exploits Fletcher's Story

This excerpt, part of an essay, was written by Herbert Aptheker, an important historian long affiliated with the Communist Party. During the Cold War, Aptheker suffered persecution so never found a secure teaching position despite writing dozens of books, his most important being *American Negro Slave Revolts* (1943). He also worked closely with, and as an assistant to, W.E.B. Du Bois in the years after World War II.

In this essay, Aptheker argued African Americans should be highly skeptical of US involvement in World War II, to wit the article's subtitle: "Powers-that-Be Failed to Keep Promises Last Time: How Race Called on When Dying to Be Done, Granted No Democracy, Shown." The context is key: in April 1941, Germany had not yet invaded the Soviet Union. At that moment, the CPUSA fiercely criticized President Roosevelt's vocal support for the Allies as symbolized by his turning the US into "an arsenal for democracy" and delivering his legendary "Four Freedoms" speech, earlier that year. Then, in June 1941 Germany invaded the Soviet Union and, in a nanosecond, Soviet supporters, including in the US, reversed course, condemned the fascists, and clamored for the US to join the fight against the Nazis.

There are many layers of irony in Aptheker's use of Fletcher as a symbol. First, a Communist used a Wobbly to support his claim that blacks opposed World War I when, in fact, Fletcher did not openly oppose the war. Second, Fletcher despised the Communists to his dying days (for fabricating the Philadelphia Controversy and more) so would have bristled at being used as an example by Aptheker. Lastly and as noted, less than two months after he wrote this essay, Aptheker and other Communists flipped 180 degrees and loudly called for the United States to enter the war against Germany.

This essay was published in *New Masses*, a monthly literary magazine published by the CPUSA. Interestingly, the *Norfolk Journal and Guide* (now *New Journal and Guide*), which has served the black community since 1900, reprinted it. In the 1940s, it had the highest circulation of any black newspaper based in the South.

Even President Wilson deigned to comment on the situation. In a letter written April 19, 1917, he professed amazement that 'many of the members of the colored race were not enthusiastic in their support of the government in this crisis.' He saw to it that one Negro, who showed a marked lack of enthusiasm and whose speeches denouncing the war makers were gaining increasing sympathy, was imprisoned and silenced. Thus it was that Ben Fletcher, a Negro official of the Industrial Workers of the World, was sent in 1918 to Leavenworth to make the acquaintance of a certain Mr. Browder [Document 59].

■ Herbert Aptheker, "Status of 'Negroes in Wartime' Revealed," *Norfolk Journal and Guide*, April 26, 1941, 9.

78

Fletcher Corresponds with Anarchist Archivist

Agnes Inglis was a social worker, Wobbly, and anarchist who became the first curator of and driving force behind the Labadie Collection, at the University of Michigan, which has become a leading archive for the history of anarchist and other radical movements. In that capacity, for decades Inglis wrote to Fletcher and many other Wobblies (e.g., Doree and Nef) and radicals, soliciting information and donations for the Labadie.

Among other points of interest in their brief correspondence, Fletcher noted his serious health troubles that began with a major stroke in 1933—at the age of forty-two. Fletcher lived just two blocks from Walter Nef's widow, in Bedford Stuyvesant, Brooklyn. The mandatory registration card Fletcher filled out, in 1942, indicated that he was unemployed [see p. 57].

The paper referred to in Fletcher's letter was written by Allen A. Holland Jr. and entitled "The Negro and the Industrial Workers of the World," a seminar paper for Professor Vandervelde, presumably at the University of Michigan. Inglis sent copies of this paper to Fletcher and Covington Hall, an important white organizer in the Brotherhood of Timber Workers.

The third letter was to George Carey, an activist in the IWW and Socialist Party from 1917 into the 1930s. Like Fletcher, Carey engaged in solidarity work with imprisoned coal miners in Harlan County. Fletcher's pessimism, in 1944, contrasted with his hopefulness in mid 1942. Quite possibly, Fletcher's own health woes, which he discussed, are part of the explanation. The letter to Carey is the last-known writing by Fletcher, who lived another five years albeit in increasingly poor health.

191 Bainbridge St.
Brooklyn, NY
May 21, 1942

Dear Miss Inglis—

Yours of the 15th of Feb. relative to Mr. Holland's historical research came duly to hand [?]. I forwarded Mr. Holland some information, but it was very meagre [sic] and I fear disappointing, because it occurs that for nearly 10 yrs I have been very inactive in my union, [illegible words] of so my disabilities—by a stroke 1/21/33.

Hypertension + Blood Pressure was the cause. I was on a [illegible word] so sorry, I couldn't give Mr. Holland the desired information and data. It was so kind of you to write me. You recalled to me a period in my life that I cherish beyond words to express. Yes, I remember your [illegible words] never forget your courageous interest in our battle a quarter century ago for the Industrial Freedom and a better world.

For some time I have contemplated writing my memoirs of the Labor movement [illegible words] my humble contributions to it.

Needless to state I will forward you whatever I compile. By the way, I mentioned to Mrs. Nef. I had heard from you last evening when I saw her that I heard from you, she expressed the desire of being remembered to you and sends her best wishes. Her address is 436 McDonough St. Brooklyn, NY.

The Industrial Workers of the World is not the virile dynamic union labor movement it was [illegible word]. The task to which it is dedicated must eventually become fait accompli, however, with my [illegible word] wishes for your continued good health, I am yours most sincerely,

Benjamin H. Fletcher

■ Correspondence to Fletcher, Benjamin H., Agnes Inglis Papers, Labadie Collection.

July 26, 1942

Dear Friend and Fellow Worker,

Yours of the 10th together with Mr. Holland's monograph on the IWW came duly to hand. I am much pleased with Mr. Holland's paper. It is well done and a worthwhile contribution to the literature pertaining to the IWW.

I am of course not unmindful of your—sympathetic—contribution. It is my recollection that you offered to forward me Ralph Chaplin's and Covington Hall's addresses so please do, I want to write both of them.

Aug 3rd, about a week ago I began this letter and had to forgo its completion until now. The IWW without question carried the ball further than any other labor movement and I am certain that it will be in there carrying the ball right now over the goal line for a touchdown.

You inquire of the Dorees. Mrs. Doree and her two children, Edward and Ellen, live here in Brooklyn. Mr. Doree died 15 yrs ago this sept or

October. Mrs. Nef no doubt will write you shortly. Mr. Keefer I think died years ago in London.

It is my fervent wish to be able to get myself a car and head westward, stopping en route to renew my old acquaintances it will take about six months.

Unlike many folks I am always certain that Humanity is on its way upward and I even have abiding faith in the ability of the American people to secure better rewards for their efforts and contributions to this thing we term Progress. A better understanding among the people is bound to show the realization of their ability to secure a better life [illegible word] closer to view. I am patient and [illegible word]. I've learned to Labor and to wait. The phone rings and if (the message) re [illegible word] me I am due to be at a friend's house 30 blocks away so, I conclude for the time being this note. Keep Cheerful and hopeful, and know I am, as ever, yours for a better world.

Benjamin H. Fletcher

■ Correspondence to Fletcher, Benjamin H., Agnes Inglis Papers, Labadie Collection.

191 Bainbridge Dr.
Brooklyn, NY
July 31, 1944

Dear George:

Yours of twenty-nine days ago together w/ enclosure photo in his Indian regalia was duly red'd and contents fully noted. Am in the midst of decorating and renovation of the house here, hence the delay—not to mention my painful feet. I will be over to see just as soon as I can navigate.

Haven't been able to get back to the point of production since Jan 21st nearly eight months ago, and of course that is bad luck but unavoidable as I got a severe cold the week after x-mas together with sciatic rheumatism. Am trying to hold [illegible word] for a couple of years or so. Thank you for the photo, I will write her one of these days. I am expecting no miracles after the cessation of the war. The Union idea doesn't exist any more, in sufficient account to assume a challenge worthy of consideration by the powers that are.

The post war days of returning to "normalcy" will record a few spasms of Organized Labor's part but they will be spasms of despair and defeat and no more. I have been getting aroused very little because it is too [illegible word]. I know that eventually complete retirement from the move [illegible words] activities of life must cease. Will ring off here until I see you if possible Sat. night. Until Cheerio.

Yours for a better world
Benjamin H. Fletcher

■ Correspondence to Fletcher, Benjamin H., George V. Carey Papers, Labadie Collection.

79

The IWW Celebrates Fletcher's Life

This touching obituary is taken from the IWW's newspaper and is therefore as "official" a last report as exists. Among those attending the funeral were Jack Walsh, who organized along the Delaware River with Fletcher and served time in Leavenworth with him, and Fanny Nef, widow of Walter. Fletcher was buried in Brooklyn in an unmarked grave that never has been located.

"Ben Fletcher's Funeral Showed High Regard for Old Rebel"

New York City Funeral services for Benjamin Harrison Fletcher, veteran IWW organizer and one of the 101 men who went to Leavenworth prison in the Chicago IWW war case, were held at the Farley Funeral Home, 1865 Fulton St., Brooklyn, on Wednesday evening, July 13. More than 100 men and women attended, among them IWW members and ex-members active in historic battles on the industrial front.

Ill in recent months with a heart condition, Fletcher, 59 years old, died on July 10 at his home, 813 Hancock St., Brooklyn.

In 1917 he was indicted with William D. Haywood and 100 other IWW officers and organizers on the charge of conspiracy to violate the Espionage Act and the Selective Service Act, and on counts of leading strikes in war-time. Tried before US Judge Kenesaw M. Landis in Chicago, all were found guilty and sentenced to terms from one to 20 years. Fletcher, the only Negro convicted in such a case during that war, received a 10-year sentence.

Set Free by Harding

In 1922 President Harding gave him an immediate commutation, and in 1933 President Franklin D. Roosevelt granted him a full pardon. After his release Ben remained in the IWW and continued his work as a speaker and writer on industrial unionism until recently, when illness forced his retirement after 41 years of membership.

Tributes were paid to him at the funeral services by old associates and friends—Sam Weiner [Dolgoff], Harry Paxton Howard, Sam Kramer, Herbert Mahler, and John Nicholas Beffel.

They recalled his many years of valiant service as an industrial union organizer, his uncompromising attitude throughout the war trial, his realistic view of the racial conflict, his philosophical adjustment to prison life, his notable sense of humor, his effectiveness as a speaker, and his skill in parrying the questions of hecklers, even in Jim Crow territory in Virginia.

Sam Weiner, a younger champion of industrial freedom, said, "Ben, we won't forget the great part you played in the struggle to emancipate the workers, and we will carry on inspired by your example."

Had Greatness of Spirit

Harry Paxton Howard, author and lecturer, declared that Ben had "true greatness—greatness of spirit," and emphasized "how right Ben was in his contentions about Wilson's war—a war not to end war but to prevent peace and protect Morgan investments."

Herbert Mahler, also one of the ex-Leavenworth prisoners, cited Fletcher's argument that Negroes would be wise to avoid accentuating the racial conflict and to organize their own people into strong industrial unions and solidly grounded co-operatives, and his assertion among the world's various colored peoples the only ones really to be feared were green men—greenhorns. Sam Kramer, actor and roommate of Joe Hill shortly before Joe's arrest in the Salt Lake City murder case, spoke movingly in his memories of Ben, and read Chaplin's poem, "The Red Feast."

"Solidarity Forever" and the Workers Funeral Hymn were sung at the end of the services.

Those who attended included James Price, F.W. [Fellow Worker] Shaefer and his wife, and several others from Philadelphia; Oscar Sokal, treasurer of New York Local 8 of the IWW's General Defense Committee, and his wife; Robert McGinniss, secretary here of Marine Workers Industrial Union No. 510; James Holland, Jack Walsh, Joseph Mangano, John Shuskie, Ben Breenhut, Rose and Lawrence Seco, Minnie Federman Corder and son Ray, Meyer Friedkin, Fanny Nef, Chris Nelson, Paul Kikke, John Lynch, Adolph Laikauf, F.W. Smith.

Also Adelaide Schulkind, Becky Loomer, Rebecca Dempsey, Jennie Carliph Ebert, Josephine and Herbert Chalcroft, Ethel McGill, Bessie Mahler, John Feczko and wife and son Bill; F.W. Martin.

Carnations Farewell Token

At the burial in Evergreen Cemetery, Brooklyn, next day, Herbert Mahler spoke briefly. "Ben wouldn't want us to mourn," he said. "He has earned his rest. It is up to us who survive to go on with the work that he lived for and died for." Then Mrs. Sam (Esther) Weiner [Dolgoff], Adolph Laikauf, and Bill Feczko dropped red carnations into the grave, in token of farewell from the General Defense Committee.

Fletcher always contended that neither he nor his fellow-defendants had conspired to violate the Espionage and Selective Service Acts, but were really convicted because the Industrial Workers of the World insisted upon their right to conduct strikes in war-time. Later the US Circuit Court of Appeals in Chicago reversed the convictions on the strike charges, but let the Espionage and draft counts remain as being matters the jury alone could decide.

In the early months of the war Fletcher and many other longshoremen whom he had organized in the IWW on the Philadelphia waterfront, loaded munitions on ships sailing from that port, without any interruption, defense evidence at the Chicago trial showed.

Organ Tones in His Voice

Ben was a remarkable speaker, with deep organ tones in his powerful voice. Once he and I spoke at a protest meeting here in Union Square, in behalf of the Centralia (Wash.) IWW members who were still in prison for defending themselves against an American Legion mob. Our rostrum was a step-ladder, without any sound amplifier. My throat quickly went bad, straining against the traffic din, and I had to slow down. But when Ben got up to speak, he not only made himself heard above the regular traffic, but above the fire department going by.

I think of that incident as a symbol—of Ben's voice reaching out and sounding its vibrant message where other voices might not be heard.

Ben Fletcher was born in Philadelphia on April 13, 1890. Some of his ancestors were American Indians. Two sisters and a brother survive.

—John Nicholas Beffel

Many Tributes to Ben Fletcher

We regret it is impossible to publish all of the many tributes that have been received to Ben Fletcher on the occasion of his death. It seems to have moved many beside the hundred and fifty or more fellow workers who attended the funeral. A Chicago fellow worker who attended the trial of the 101 recalls Ben's very short speech to the Judge when he was asked what he had to say before sentence was imposed: "I would like to call attention to your grammar; your sentences are too long." Numerous poems and other expressions of esteem for the departed fighter, some read at the funeral, others from fellow workers not able to attend, attest the high regard in which Ben Fletcher was held.

The following tribute by Herbert Mahler was read at the funeral service:

> Rest, rest old fighter, rest,
> Scars of battle on your breast
> Prove that you have done your best,
> Rest, rest old fighter, rest.
>
> In the hands of eager Youth,
> Trust the crimson flag of Truth,
> That you carried all the way,
> They will guard it till the day,
> Of Freedom . . .
>
> Let no worry mar your sleep.
> Though the road be rough and steep,
> Fraught with danger, filled with pain,
> We will struggle on to gain,
> The Victory . . .
> While you rest, old fighter, rest.
>
> Rest, rest, old fighter, rest,
> Your noble deeds by Memory blest.
> Inspire us all in Freedom's quest.
> Rest, rest, old fighter, rest.

■ *Industrial Worker*, July 22, 1949, 4.

80

Fletcher's Obituary in the *New York Times*

That the nation's most well-respected mainstream newspaper ran an obituary of Ben Fletcher, more than a quarter of a century after he ceased being a prominent labor leader, attested to his importance. Oddly, this and other obituaries incorrectly identified him as leading the strikes in Lawrence and Paterson suggested how little care it gave to black radicals.

Labor Organizer Convicted Under Espionage Act in 1917 Dies

Benjamin Harrison Fletcher, veteran Negro labor organizer, died on Sunday in his home at 813 Hancock Street, Brooklyn. His age was 59. Mr. Fletcher was born in Philadelphia and in 1912 became associated with other left-wing leaders in the strikes led by the Industrial Workers of the World at Lawrence, Mass., Paterson, N.J., and other industrial centers.

In 1917 he was tried and found guilty of conspiracy to violate the Espionage and Selective Service Acts, on a count of leading strikes in wartime. He was sentenced to the penitentiary; his term was commuted later by President Harding, and, in 1933, a full pardon was granted by President Franklin D. Roosevelt.

■ *New York Times*, July 12, 1949, 27.

81

Philadelphia Tribune Obituary

The *Philadelphia Tribune* is that city's longtime black newspaper, founded in 1884 and still operating. Shockingly, this paper never published a single article on Local 8, an organization of thousands of African American Philadelphians, but then the *Tribune* typified many, if not all, in the black press in its quest for bourgeois respectability. Thus, it is disappointing but not surprising that the obituary neglected to mention Local 8 at all or that Fletcher led this powerful and important local union of black workers. The biographical information included on Fletcher is in question. In the early 1970s, historian William Seraile tried to find evidence of Fletcher's attendance at university but failed. Moreover, records from his time in Leavenworth make no mention of university or even high school graduation, nor did Fletcher refuse the "full pardon" as indicated.

Veteran Socialist Dies; Led Strike Against US Govt.
Brooklyn N.Y.—Funeral services were held here last week for Benjamin Harrison Fletcher, 59, formerly of Philadelphia, Pa., who died July 10 after a long illness.

Fletcher, who attended both Wilberforce and Virginia Union Universities, was the first Negro member of the National Socialist Party and a former organizer for the IWW, both of which he joined in 1911.

Just prior to the outbreak of World War I, Fletcher and 110 white IWW members were arrested in Philadelphia for leading workers in strikes against the Government. Tried in Chicago for violating the selective service and espionage acts, they were each sentenced to 5 to 10 years by the late Judge Kenesaw Mountain Landis, subsequent czar of baseball. All his fellow workers were granted a full pardon, which he refused. Subsequently President Harding commuted his sentence. Fletcher returned to the IWW and was made a member of the general national body, a position he retained until death. President Franklin D. Roosevelt granted him a full pardon.

Narrator for the funeral rites was Henry P. Howe, a life-long friend and author of "America's Role in Asia and the Future of the Far East." A message was read from Norman Thomas, perennial Socialist candidate for President of the United States.

His survivors are: Miss Clora [Clara] Fletcher [actually his wife] and Mrs. Helen Braxton of Brooklyn, and Mrs. Alice Fletcher, of Philadelphia, sisters; Edward, brother; four nephews, three nieces, and one grand-nephew, Mr. and Mrs. Benjamin B. Johns, Mr. and Mrs. Dennis, Alice Braxton, and son Ronald, of Philadelphia; Howard Johns, and Miss Faith Braxton, of Brooklyn; and Louis A. Johns, Associated Negro Press correspondent.

Interment was in Evergreen cemetery, here.

■ *Philadelphia Tribune*, July 19, 1949, 2.

82

Brooklyn Eagle Obituary

While Fletcher's age and hometown are correct, along with the fact that he was a longtime Wobbly activist, it is interesting to see how many details in such a short article are incorrect or, to put it more kindly, for which there is no evidence, The Lawrence "Bread and Roses" strike happened in 1912, not 1922, and there is no evidence of Fletcher's involvement in midwestern or western strikes—or that he ever traveled to the Mountain or Far West. There also is no evidence of his involvement in the Paterson silk strike of 1913, but he definitely knew about it and could have participated in some manner since Paterson is only about a hundred miles from Philadelphia.

The funeral parlor was located in Fletcher's Bedford-Stuyvesant neighborhood and the Evergreen Cemetery is nearby.

"Benjamin Fletcher, Labor Organizer"

Benjamin Harrison Fletcher, a labor organizer for more than 40 years for the Industrial workers of the World, died Sunday in his home, 813 Hancock. St. He was 59.

Mr. Fletcher, a native of Philadelphia, became associated with leftwing leaders while still in his 'teens. He took part in the IWW-led strikes at Lawrence, Mass. In 1922 and at Paterson in 1913. Later he participated in strikes in the Midwest and on the Pacific Coast.

Services will be held at 8:30 P.M. tomorrow in the Farley Funeral Home, 1865 Fulton St.

■ *Brooklyn Daily Eagle*, July 12, 1949, 9.

83

Atlanta Daily World Obituary

Although ostensibly somewhat conservative, according to historian Robin D.G. Kelley, the *Atlanta Daily World* printed quite a sympathetic obituary. Due to more than four hundred years of oppression, African Americans long have been suspicious of people persecuted by the government, black people in particular. Hence, though the US was in the midst of the second Red Scare, in the late 1940s, Fletcher, a victim of the first Red Scare, was depicted quite positively. It also is detailed if somewhat inaccurate. The use of the word "International" rather than "Industrial" in the union's name is an all-too-common mistake.

This story was issued by the Associated Negro Press (ANP), a national news service begun in Chicago by Claude Albert Barnett in 1919, served about 150 US-based newspapers and 100 newspapers in Africa in both English and French, making it the first and widest network of black media, worldwide.

New York—(ANP)—Benjamin Fletcher, 59, organizer for the International Workers of the World and one of the "Wobblies" sent to prison for impeding the war effort in 1917, died at his Brooklyn home Sunday.

Fletcher, born in Philadelphia, turned to the leftist organization when he was 17. He participated in several strikes, including the Lawrence, Mass., 1912 strike; Paterson, N.J. in 1913, and later strikes on the Atlantic seaboard, the Pacific coast and the mid-west.

In 1917, he was tried and found guilty of conspiracy to violate the Espionage and selective service acts and of leading strikes in wartime. He was given a long sentence in a Federal penitentiary, but his term was commuted by President Harding and later, in 1933, President Roosevelt granted Fletcher a full pardon.

Highly Respected

One of the most brilliant Negroes ever associated with a leftist organization, Ben Fletcher was highly respected for his scholastic ability and his oratorical efforts.

He was one of the first Negroes to be associated with the IWW in an organizational capacity and upon his release from penitentiary, found employment in the field he loved so well. Fletcher's life was adventurous and stormy, but in his later years, he lived very quietly and worked with a labor organization near Union Square.

At the time of Fletcher's arrest and conviction, mass hysteria swept the country and new laws, Criminal syndicalism made its appearance in California as a weapon to prosecute supposed subversives.

■ "Benjamin Fletcher Passes in New York," *Atlanta Daily World*, July 22, 1949, 6.

84

A Tribute to Fletcher

This tribute by a Finnish IWW member was originally written for the English-language page of the Finnish Wobbly paper, *Industrialisti*, in 1950 and reprinted in *Industrial Worker*, in 1960. She must have been visiting New York, on April 13, 1949, making her recounting the last documented memory of Fletcher's life. That Aakula had long heard about Fletcher suggests his visit to Duluth in 1927 continued to be remembered decades later.

I had often heard the name Ben Fletcher mentioned but had never met him until the night of his 59th birthday, at his home in New York.

Mrs. Fletcher, a lovely woman with an intelligent fine-featured face, met us at the door and led us in to meet Ben who was a semi-invalid, having suffered a[nother] stroke. I expected a tough strong fisted soap boxer, who had had to fight his way the ward way through life, but instead, found this kindly mannered man that life had mellowed into smooth velvet.

Ben Fletcher did not shrink from the duty of life. He fought not only for himself and his race, but for all the downtrodden. He carried no hate in his heart for the wielders of the blows that he had received.

It seemed as though he held the knowledge of all life in the palm of his hand, but knowing also that his duties on earth were just about ended, he went grandly, wearing his battle scars, towards the last journey where Mother Earth doesn't ask if you are black or white—just folds you into her bosom for a well-earned rest.

Tyne Aakula
Duluth, Minnesota

■ *Industrial Worker*, October 3, 1960, 4.

85

Brave Spirit

This beautiful recollection of Fletcher was written by Matilda Robbins approximately forty years after the events she described. Almost certainly, this strike was chronicled by Robbins, in 1913 still using her original name Rabinowitz, in Document 5. Rabinowitz first organized with the IWW during its legendary 1912 "Bread and Roses" strike in Lawrence, Massachusetts.

Tyne Aakula's reminiscence and tribute to Ben Fletcher stirred up my own memory of this sensitive, dedicated man, one of the best in the ranks of the IWW of the past.

On one of my organizing assignments which took me from the textile towns of the South to those of the North I stopped in Philadelphia where

Ralph Chaplin, "The Hand that Rules the World—One Big Union," *Solidarity*, June 30, 1917.

Ben was organizing longshoremen. I met him for the first time when I heard him speak one night at the IWW hall. I remember how strongly he held the attention of the grim-faced, work-marked men. How their faces brightened with understanding of the meaning of industrial unionism; the need for solidarity and resistance against the shipping companies who kept them divided. Ben won the confidence of both Negro and white workers by his exposition how they were being used against one another by the bosses to prevent organization.

Day after day and night after he night he covered the water front, twenty miles of it, repeatedly at the risk of his life. He took me to see the slums in the City of Brotherly Love where longshoremen and their families lived. He agonized over their degrading poverty. He was of them. He was with them.

He was soft-spoken and his eyes seemed to reflect the tragedy of his race. But he was tough-minded, too; courageous and dedicated to the emancipation of the working class. He was a brave spirit, one of the unsung heroes of labor.

I look back upon those few hours with Ben Fletcher, so far away and long ago, and the memory is rewarding.

Matilda Robbins

■ *Industrial Worker*, November 2, 1960, 2.

86

Fred Thompson on Meeting Fletcher

Fred Thompson was one of the most influential Wobblies after the IWW's so-called heyday, from the late 1920s and into the late 1980s. He served as the unofficial "house" historian of the IWW for most of the century. In that capacity he authored *The IWW: Its First Fifty Years (1905–1955)* and coauthored *The IWW: Its First Seventy Years (1905–1975)*. Born in 1900 in St. John, New Brunswick, Canada, he became a socialist in his teens and a strike leader in a shipyard of his hometown in 1920. He joined the One Big Union, a Canadian Wobbly offshoot, in 1920 and the IWW, while working in construction in San Francisco, in 1922. He spent several years in the California state prison, in San Quentin, on a criminal syndicalism charge. Along with Franklin and Penelope Rosemont and others, Thompson helped revive the Charles H. Kerr Publishing Co. in the early 1970s. He passed away in Chicago in 1987.

This excerpt, part of a much longer interview/discussion, began with a point that cannot be emphasized enough: at first, IWWs almost uniformly were thrilled by the Bolshevik Revolution. How could they not be? Yet within a few years, most Wobblies had soured on the Soviet Union. Along with many other anarchist organizations and syndicalist unions, most Wobblies and the US branch (officially) chose to not join the Communist International and Red International Labor Unions. They detested the authoritarian nature of the Communist Party and Soviet state, in no small part because Lenin cracked down on all anarchists and syndicalists inside the Soviet Union, very early in the revolution. Moreover, in his book *"Left-Wing Communism": An Infantile Disorder* (1920), Lenin condemned "dual unions," like the IWW, instead insisting that Communists "bore from within" mainstream unions. In the United States, that meant Communists should join AFL unions which the IWW rejected. Another impact of this rift was the "Philadelphia Controversy" discussed at length in this volume's introduction.

Thompson also placed Fletcher in Philadelphia in the "early 1930s" and offered quite a reasonable explanation for why Fletcher left the waterfront. However, Thompson was wrong about Polly Baker, who became a leader in Philadelphia's ILA local and, much later, a senior official in that union.

When the Bolshevik Revolution came [in 1917], all the Wobblies were as enthusiastic as I was. I thought a beautiful new world was being born here. I didn't think that in 1970 there would still be capitalism. I was very optimistic in those days. And I think almost everybody was very happy about this Bolshevik Revolution. Later on they had reasons to disagree. They didn't like the shooting down of striking street car workers and the other things of that sort. They hoped to get control over the World Federation of Unions they were building and things like that. So we had our disagreements. Some people said, "Let's play along with the Bolsheviks"; others said, "No, that's not the way to organize the American working class." You'll find a lot of words about that at this time.

The Communists didn't like our practical job control in Philadelphia, so they accused us of loading ammunition to go there to overthrow the Russian Revolution, which was a bunch of bullshit. They weren't loading any ammunition for anybody. We hadn't been loading any ammunition since the war was over. It was nonsense.

I went to Philadelphia in the early '30's, and talked to Polly Baker and Ben Fletcher and the other people who had been in that union and were still around and asked them was that the reason they left. Well, they didn't like that kind of thing, but that wasn't the reason why. They said it was because they liked to eat. That's why they dropped out. There wasn't very much shipping. There were alternative port facilities so that the ships coming into Philadelphia could have gone to various other places, and there was a connected drive telling the boys "If you insist on striking we're going to arrange that all these ships go to these other ports and you guys won't eat." The reason we lost them was because we weren't in the position to protect them against that kind of a threat. And yet the things the historians will practically all say, it was the quarrels, only peripheral things, when the actual thing was this practical bread and butter issue.

■ Fred Thompson, Speeches and Discussion with the Canadian Student Federation of Waterloo, Ontario, January 1970.

87

Esther Dolgoff
Remembering Fletcher

While her husband Sam Dolgoff was far better known, Esther also was a politically engaged anarchist. Both were Jewish but she was born in the States to Russian Jewish immigrants. She graduated from college and a master's program, in Cleveland, and might have been on route to a comfortable, "respectable" middle-class life when, around 1930, she fell in love with the Russian Jewish house painter then visiting Cleveland to deliver a lecture at the Anarchist Forum. They lived in New York City for many decades.

With Sam and their two sons, Esther developed a close friendship with Ben and Clara Fletcher in the 1930s and '40s. In this interview, she offered fascinating recollections. Ben Fletcher knew the printing trade, something not mentioned elsewhere. That an African American inmate, at Leavenworth, was used by the guards to harass Wobblies (and other political prisoners), a situation Earl Browder also alluded to, is interesting. While unconfirmed by other sources, that FBI agents continued surveilling Fletcher into the 1930s seems quite possible. Lastly, she noted Fletcher's very poor health "crippled" him, a quite common occurrence among working-class people who toiled for decades in a society that failed to provide adequate health care and food to the country's working people, especially its African American ones.

Ann Allen [interviewer]: "The Wobblies were one of the few unions with blacks in it."

Esther Dolgoff: "Oh yes. Down south they had some of the first meetings for blacks and whites; they had to have them in the open air."

Sam Dolgoff: "Did I ever tell you about Ben Fletcher in Norfolk, Virginia? Ben Fletcher was addressing a meeting in Norfolk, Virginia, and you know Ben Fletcher was very, very black. And he was talking about racial equality and so forth and so on. Some of the racists in the crowd, the white racists, wanted to embarrass him or get him to say something that would provoke a riot. So they asked him a question. They said, 'Ben, what do you think of a black man living with a white woman?' Ben looked around, he looked all around. He said, 'I don't see many people here that's any blacker than me'."

Esther Dolgoff: "When Ben Fletcher was in jail the trustee was a colored fellow but he made life miserable for him. Because everyone was against the IWW; called it the I 'trouble-u trouble-u,' and 'I won't work.' They were supposed to be criminal syndicalists. There was a great persecution of the IWW, And the jail, which is a reflection of the society outside, there's quite a few articles on that subject in the English *Anarchy* magazine, but that's another thing. But he was miserable to him. But when Ben Fletcher got out, he was walking along the street and this trustee had gotten out by that time and he met him. And the trustee, he said, black as he was, he turned white when he saw Ben. But Ben, he went up to him and said, 'How do you do? How do you feel?' And he was able to talk to him and start some ideas in his head. But that's the kind of man that he was. He was quite brilliant and he was a printer, in Philadelphia, Then he worked for the longshoremen. He organized thousands on the docks in Philadelphia. But what gets me is the things that they called for. It seems cruel that they would have to fight that hard. For instance, [as a longshoreman] to have grappling irons, not to grab the freight when it came in by the hands. You wouldn't think that they'd have to fight so hard for it. Now of course it's all mechanized [due to containerization] but not at that time. When he was so crippled the FBI still followed him around, fearing his powers to organize. He had beautiful English, beautiful diction. He was a printer and he started early [in his life] to be interested in social questions. And so he fought for the IWW. And I've often wondered, here is a bona fide, true blue hero. They have such characters that they choose as their symbols, the colored people. And no one hears of him. You know, when he was jailed against the first world war and they gave him ten years, they gave long sentences then. His turn came up and the judge said, 'Have you anything to say?' He says, 'Your grammar's very poor judge, and your sentences are too long.' He was a well-read man, He had a dignity, and he worked hard for his living. He was no pie card artist. As I told you, he was so crippled, he had to push the dolly. We [the IWW] had so many of these people, so devoted. And that's what an organization needs, very devoted and idealistic people."

■ Sam and Esther Dolgoff, interview with Ann Allen, New York City, June 15, 1972.

88

A Fellow Philadelphia
Longshoreman Remembers

Filmmaker Deborah Shaffer interviewed James Fair, an African American long-shoreman in Philadelphia, in 1978 as part of research for the documentary film *The Wobblies* (1979). Fair's recollections include the effective interracialism of IWW Local 8 and hostility of employers to the union.

Q: What about some of the leaders of the IWW?

JF: We had one, Fletcher, he was a Negro. And we had one, I don't remember his first name but it was Neff [Walter Nef]. He was white. I don't remember what nationality he was [German Swiss], but he was a very dedicated union man, both of these men. These men they did serve time in prison for something they trumped up on them to get rid of them while they were in prison, that was one of the ways that they had of breaking the IWW. The IWW was something for the working man, it didn't make any difference who you was, what kind of work you did, they was in to, out to organize all working people.

Q: What were the particular problems Negro workers had in those years getting into any unions, particularly the AF of L.

JF: Well it was, getting a job as far as a Negro, a black was concerned was pretty rough. And to my knowing at that time the IWW was the only thing that was accepting negro or black workers you know without, you know with, I mean freely. They would accept them and they did advocate just this thing, solidarity. IWW did that. We would have our pep talks and whatnot and Fletcher, after he made a speech or something or another, solidarity, all for one and one for all.

And he tried to demonstrate that, because we as negroes or blacks as you would call it today, we got along fairly good on the docks of Philadelphia. There was always somebody who was going to disagree but most of us you know got along pretty good with each other on the docks. Now when we left the job it was different. We worked on the

IWW poster, ca. 1910.

decks together, we worked on the wharves together, we worked in the hold together, a lot of my experience together, my experience beginning my advancement from the truck to the deck of the ship it was done . . .

Q: Why do you think the companies fought so hard against the IWW?

JF: The IWW was the best thing, best union, I think it portrayed just what it said. It was for laboring man, it was for the laboring man, not for just black or white or Negro, but it was for the working people and that was why it was so opposed by capitalists, and I'm not a radical, not by no means, but I do believe in moderation. I do believe in getting the most for my labor in all fairness.

Q: What did the IWW say about Negro workers and white workers working together, did Ben Fletcher have any specific things?

JF: Ben Fletcher would tell us that we had to live together, we must work together. And his pet word was, all for one and one for all, solidarity was the main thing. And it sank in with a lot of us. Not with all, and it paid off and it's paying off today.

Q: Were there other ports than had IWW organizations?

JF: Not that I know of, I only know Fletcher, but he was just, he was not only just in Philadelphia, he was a national organizer . . .

Q: How did the workers feel when Fletcher was arrested in 1917?

JF: Some of us were very hurt over it, because we knew that he was doing something for us to earn a livelihood to support ourselves and families and it was just like well, I would say it was to one who was interested in organized labor and improving our standards of life, it something near like Martin Luther King. Because some of us were very hurt, because the way it was done, just trumped up, just charges that was brought against us, it wasn't a local charge, they were charged with a federal offense. They didn't go to a state prison, they were sent to a federal prison.

Q: Do you remember the trial in Chicago?

JF: No, I don't remember anything about that, to tell you the truth. The only [thing] that I remember about it is I remember Fletcher and Nef going off to prison.

Q: How did it affect the union when Fletcher was in prison?

JF: When Fletcher and Nef were in prison it affected their natural health, because I did see them after they came out and they were very thin. How long they lasted after that, I just don't know, I don't recall. But after they came out of prison, their activities ceased. I mean [after they] went to prison the activities soon ceased here in Philadelphia. The IWW lingered on for several years after they had gone to prison, but it wasn't effective because we had several, you know, to come along to try and did what they could, but the opposition, the odds were just against us.

■ James Fair, interview with Deborah Shaffer, Philadelphia, December 21, 1978.

89

Ellen Doree Rosen
Remembers Fletcher

Ellen Doree Rosen's father was Edwin F. Doree, a child of Swedish immigrants, who organized for the IWW in the 1910s including Local 8. E.F. Doree and Walter Nef married sisters, Chiky and Feige, who were Jewish Lithuanian immigrants and working-class radicals. In a story one could not improve upon, Doree met his soon-to-be wife while speaking at an IWW rally in Rochester, New York, in 1914. Chiky then worked in a clothing factory and attended the rally where Doree spoke. Along with Fletcher, Nef, and Walsh, Doree were the Local 8 leaders found guilty in the 1918 trial of IWW members in Chicago. Tragically, only a few years after his release from Leavenworth, Doree died in a freak accident in Texas at just thirty-eight years of age. Doree's widow, daughter, and (second) son moved with the Nef family to Brooklyn sometime thereafter and lived in the same Bedford-Stuyvesant neighborhood as Fletcher and his wife who had moved up from Philadelphia. Rosen went on to earn a PhD and taught political science at John Jay College, in New York City. During her retirement, she published the letters that her mother preserved from her father while the latter was imprisoned; only his side of the correspondence survived. The letters, relevant excerpts included, as well as her reflections which begin this section, reveal that Doree was close with Fletcher, not surprisingly, during the years they were imprisoned together. Dr. Rosen's brief description of Clara Fletcher is among the few ever found.

Ellen Doree Rosen's recollections:
[Edward Frederick] Doree was certainly aware of the racial distinctions that marked US society and culture, but one of his best friends and a fellow Wobbly, Ben Fletcher, was coal black . . . when Doree died suddenly and unexpectedly in West Texas, his wife moved herself and two young children [Ellen being one] back East, to Brooklyn, New York, where they settled in a Bedford-Stuyvesant rooming house she ran in order to support the family. They were often visited by Ben Fletcher, and they remained there as the neighborhood turned black [during the 1940s]; they persisted as the last white family in an all-black block and an all-black community

When I was small [in the 1930s], my mother would take us to the annual Wobbly Ball in New York, where I would inevitably be pulled to the front of the room to lead the singing of songs from the "Little Red Songbook."

The other Wobbly lived nearby. Ben Fletcher was the blackest man I have ever met; his cherubic face gleamed like polished ebony. Unlike Walter [Nef, her uncle and neighbor], Ben smiled and found the humor in every situation: it was he who said Judge Landis used poor English because his sentences were too long. I adored Ben's wife, Clara, with her no-nonsense warmth and practical energy. My mother explained that I was to bear two things in mind about Clara. Firstly, although we knew that she was Ben's wife, for some reasons they passed as brother and sister. Secondly, although I could call her "Clara" at home, I was to call her "Miss Fletcher" in the street. Clara was sensitive that people might think, because she was colored, that I was summoning a servant.

Letters from E.F. Doree to his wife, Chiky:

October 31, 1921: "Now to our case. Nef, Fletcher, [Joseph] Graber and I will sign the applications for pardons if the committee think best. I have told you repeatedly that I will do whatever you ask in this matter. Walsh says that he will not sign. It puts things in a funny way for him as he is likely to change his mind later, when it is too late. He will answer personally so there is no need for me to go into details at all. [Manuel] Rey has his own committee and Weinberger is his lawyer. He is trying to get deported and told me that it is his desire now that the Philadelphia committee should do nothing on his behalf. He asks me to write this for him as he does not intend to answer personally." (p. 150)

December 14, 1921: "But if the committee think that it is best to proceed upon the lines which they have chosen, then Nef's case [for pardoning] is the best from the purely war standpoint. There is nothing against him and his 'proally-ism' is well-established. Fletcher's case is also a good one, in some ways better than Nef's. But there are no bad cases from Phila." (p. 160)

January 18, 1922: "I did say [in a previous letter] that 'personally I am unwilling to be a party to leaving the other boys behind.' I mean that, but—get me right, if any wish to stay, or can get any glory of self-satisfaction out of their petty heroics, I am the last who wishes to interfere with their foolishness. If [Jack] Walsh does not care to have friends act in his behalf, that's his business, not mine. In that case, he's the party to leave himself behind, I am surely that party. But, then, with Fletcher, for instance . . . he is willing to do all he can personally, in a case such as his, I feel that I am bound by every tenet of honor to be with him in his struggle." (p. 165; ellipses in original)

March 22, 1922: "I didn't know Fletcher had the 'flu.' I wouldn't know it now, if I hadn't heard it from you. I haven't seen him in several days, may be weeks, now that I come to think of it. You see, he eats on a different mess, cells in a different house, and unless we happen to meet in the yard on Sundays, we don't see one another at all. You must know that it's easy to miss one man among 2350. But I must confess, I had not heard of him being sick at all." (p. 180)

April 26, 1922: "Fletcher and Walsh received their clemency applications last night. Fletcher signed his and returned it today. I am told that Walsh returned his unsigned. That is as I expected. I have always felt that it was useless to send it on to him. He is a funny sort. He'll sign those papers some day, mark what I say, so please have them saved for him unless his brother or some one else signs them on his behalf. (p. 190)

April 28, 1922: "Oh, yes, I must tell you. Fletcher signed his papers, and returned them. Walsh returned his unsigned." (p. 191)

August 30, 1922: "Fortunately, Ben gets the [Philadelphia] 'Ledger' here and I saw that Saturday and Sunday stories [updates on the pardon cases and the health of Doree's young son, Bucky who, sadly, died in 1923]." (p. 219)

■ Ellen Doree Rosen, A Wobbly Life: IWW Organizer E.F. Doree.

90

Harry Haywood on Fletcher

Harry Haywood was one of the earliest and most prominent African Americans in the Communist Party of the United States. This passage reconfirmed that Fletcher was a force to be reckoned with among African Americans on the Left and that his speaking ability, organizational skills, and reputation were highly regarded in 1925, even after the IWW lost control of the Philadelphia waterfront. Fletcher was only thirty-five then, so could have been an active force for decades to come. In his foreword, Robin D.G. Kelley provides further, invaluable context.

Lovett Fort-Whiteman, on the other hand, was still an unknown quantity. My feelings about him were rather mixed. I was both repelled and fascinated by the excessive flamboyance of the man. But much later, I recalled overhearing a conversation between him and Robert Minor during the preparations for the American Negro Labor Congress. Minor informed Fort-Whittman that Ben Fletcher, the well-known Black IWW leader, had expressed a desire to participate in the congress. It was evident that Bob was pleased by the response of such an important Black labor leader. Fletcher, an IWW organizer, had played a leading role in the successful organization of Philadelphia longshoremen. His attendance would undoubtedly have attracted other Blacks in the labor movement.

Fort-Whittman, however, vehemently opposed the idea and exclaimed, "I don't want to work with him; I know him. He's the kind of fellow who'll try to take over the whole show." That ended the discussion; Fletcher was not invited.

I didn't know Fletcher at the time, but as I reflected back on the incident some time later, it was clear to me that had he been allowed to participate, Fort-Whittman would have been overshadowed. I was too new to pass judgment on Fort-Whittman's qualifications, but I did wonder why he was chosen over such stalwarts as Moore and Huiswood. Huiswood, as a delegate to the Fourth Congress of the Comintern in 1922, was the first Black American to attend a congress of that body. (Claude McKay was also a special fraternal delegate to that congress.) Together with the other delegates, Huiswood visited Lenin and became the first Black man to meet the great Bolshevik. He later became the first Black to serve as a candidate of the Executive Committee of the Communist International.

On the whole, I was very optimistic during my early years in the Party—confident we were building the kind of party that would eventually triumph over capitalism.

■ Harry Haywood, *Black Bolshevik: An Autobiography of an Afro-American Communist*, 146–47.

91

Fletcher Meets Joe Hill?

Franklin Rosemont was a celebrated surrealist poet, Wobbly, historian, and publisher whose most important contribution, perhaps, was helping revive and lead the Charles H. Kerr Company from the 1970s through his death in 2009. Among his many books of fiction and nonfiction, the imaginative, thoroughly researched six-hundred-plus-page tome on the life of Wobbly songwriter Joe Hill stands out. One short chapter considered Hill's relationship to black hoboes he may have met in his travels as well as the fragment of a story in which Ben Fletcher met Joe Hill in Philadelphia around 1910. This excerpt is suggestive of the careful thought and logic that historians must deploy, particularly in the absence of definite evidence, and despite great effort and research. Although it may never be certain if Fletcher and Hill met, this tantalizing story remains exciting to consider and serves as a powerful reminder that, as Rosemont concluded, "The history of the IWW remains a mystery."

Through the union's publications, Hill surely knew of at least one prominent African American Wobbly, Ben Fletcher . . .

A loyal Wobbly till his death in 1949, Fellow Worker Fletcher was the best known of the union's Black organizers. And he remembered seeing Joe Hill in Philadelphia, "sometime before 1911."

This astounding revelation was quietly announced to the public in 1969 in a note on page 214, column 2 of Gibbs M. Smith's biography of Hill, and to the best of my knowledge has never been mentioned anywhere else. The source of the information is a 1966 letter from the IWW's in-house historian, Fred Thompson, who got it from Fellow Worker Jack Sheridan, who in turn got it direct from Ben Fletcher himself.

I knew Jack Sheridan quite well in the 1960s when I was active in the Chicago branch of the IWW and editor of its magazine, *The Rebel Worker*. An old Dil [or Dill] Pickler, he was one of the "regulars" at Branch meetings, and the other old-timers considered him one of the union's best soapboxers. (It was Sheridan and Thompson who gave me my own first lessons in soapboxing at Bughouse Square in 1964.) I didn't always agree with Jack about everything, but I did find him to be scrupulously honest. If he told Thompson that Fletcher said he saw Hill, that's good enough for me.

Dick Brazier, for his part, vouched for Fellow Worker Fletcher's veracity. As he wrote to Thompson, the Fletcher/Hill meeting appeared "quite possible and plausible," for Fletcher was organizing longshoremen around that time, and besides, "Ben was not given to lying about things. If Ben told Jack Sheridan that he had met Joe Hill then Ben had met Joe Hill, without doubt" [January 7, 1967].

Curiously, just before Thompson wrote Brazier about Sheridan and the Fletcher/Hill meeting, Brazier had written Thompson noting that John Reed had told him that he (Reed) had met Hill—in Philadelphia in 1911 [December 21, 1966]. In other words, Brazier was offering an interesting piece of supporting evidence even before Thompson had raised the question [Thompson to Tynne and Vaino Konga, January 5, 1967].

In yet another letter, and hinting at yet another dimension in the mystery of Hill's biography, Thompson noted that "Jack Sheridan recalls Fletcher 'speaking as though Hill had a Swedish girl friend in Philadelphia, whose name he recalls as something like Thelma Erickson" [to Sam and Esther Dolgoff, January 6, 1967].

This is all we have in the way of facts: In the mid 1960s, in Chicago, Jack Sheridan told Fred Thompson that Ben Fletcher, during the late 1930s or early 40s in New York, told him that he (Fletcher) remembered seeing Joe Hill sometime around 1910-11, in Philadelphia. Beyond that, all we have in regard to this grand encounter between two legends-in-the-making— the man who became the IWW's most celebrated Black organizer and the man who would become the union's most famous bard and martyr—is conjecture. It makes us realize how much the history of the IWW remains a mystery.

■ Franklin Rosemont, *Joe Hill: The IWW & the Making of a Revolutionary Workingclass Counterculture*, 266–68.

92

Fletcher and T-Bone

In the 1930s and 1940s, Fletcher lived in New York City, where he became close friends with Sam Dolgoff (1902–1990), a Russian Jewish immigrant who became a prominent anarchist, Wobbly, and writer. The first two sections are excerpted from letters by Dolgoff to Franklin Rosemont. Dolgoff recalled Fletcher in his years after Local 8 including befriending T-Bone Slim. A child of Finnish immigrants, whose given name was Matti Valentin Huhta, T-Bone Slim was a famous Wobbly poet and hobo who died under mysterious circumstances in New York in 1942. Dolgoff also recalled Fletcher's second wife, Clara.

SAM DOLGOFF
Letter to Franklin Rosemont
June 10, 1987
Excerpt

Ben Fletcher certainly knew T-Bone [Slim]. They were very close. It may be interesting that Fletcher's wife—a registered nurse—ran a rooming house; Ben took care of the place (cleaning, other chores while she worked). I believe that the house was leased not owned. Anyhow, after Ben died, she lived with a man from Philadelphia, a swindler who took every cent she had and then left her flat.

Another thing: She complained about the way she was treated by some of the phony Wobblies who were racists. Ben himself also told me of some very distressing situations.

While Ben was a valiant Wobbly, he was also politically not much more than a Socialist Party sympathizer. This did not impair our friendship or detract from his dedication. He was above all a man of ACTION.

★

June 16, '87

T-Bone and Ben Fletcher were very intimate. [In the late 1930s and early 1940s] T-Bone played pinochle with quite a few FW's [Fellow Workers], seldom with Ben Fletcher who played very seldom.

93

Give Them a Chance

Ben Fletcher's hilarious, insightful response to Sam Dolgoff's fiercely anti-religious stance was typical of Fletcher: one part wisdom, one part toleration, and all Wobbly.

After serving five years in Leavenworth Federal Penitentiary with the 101 class-war prisoners labeled "subversives," [Herbert] Mahler became the Secretary-Treasurer of the IWW with headquarters in Chicago. Later he moved to New York, where he reorganized the General Recruiting Union branch of the IWW in a new hall at 94 Fifth Avenue. The front windows were emblazoned with the letters IWW looked out on Fifth Avenue, one of New York's most fashionable and heavily traveled streets. The walls of the new hall were decorated with an immense mural painted with the help of artistic members, by the artist Carlson who lived in his skylight studio on the top floor.

The mural, in the prevailing proletarian style, depicted in lurid colors the stages of the class struggle from the bloated greedy employers smoking a big cigar and the priest representing the clergy lording it over their victims, the women and children, and ended with the defiant workers waving red flags, chanting 'Solidarity Forever,' crushing the cringing capitalist and priest, with the radiant sun of the new day illuminating the scene.

Picturing the clergy as enemies of the workers aroused the antagonism of religiously minded sympathizers whom we were trying to reach. This reminds me of how the Newark branch lost a newly organized shop when the new members protested the inclusion of antireligious songs like "The Preacher and the Slave," a parody of "Onward Christian Soldiers," etc. in the wobbly *Little Red Songbook*.

When I discussed this question with Benjamin Fletcher, one of the 101 class war prisoners jailed in Leavenworth Penitentiary for opposing World War I, he chided me: "What the hell do you care if they go to church if they beat up scabs after the services and practice solidarity on the job? Don't interfere. Give them a chance to learn from their own experience."

■ Sam Dolgoff, *Fragments: A Memoir*, 132–33.

94

As Black as I Am

Sam Dolgoff recalled the fierce commitment and political acumen of his close friend Ben Fletcher. Also noteworthy was Dolgoff's very close friendship with Manuel Rey, a Spanish anarchist and Wobbly who organized sailors out of Philadelphia in the mid-1910s and also was tossed into Leavenworth with Fletcher and the other Wobblies. Hence, by the 1950s, Dolgoff likely knew more about Local 8 than nearly anyone else still alive. In his memoir, Dolgoff offered further evidence that Fletcher was a brilliant speaker and soapboxer, able to parry a racist heckler's taunts humorously but also insightfully. The intense drama of this moment—which potentially might have resulted in his being lynched—also was recounted by Fletcher in 1931. See Document 73.

According to Patrick Renshaw (*The Wobblies*, 140), between 1905 and 1924, the IWW issued 100,000 membership cards to negroes [Renshaw was citing Spero and Harris' figures, which most scholars consider to be too high]. The IWW pioneered the integration of white and black workers on the Philadelphia, Baltimore and Norfolk waterfronts. Over half the members were negroes. In promoting racial integration, the negro organizer Benjamin Fletcher, one of my closest friends, played a prominent part. Fletcher also was one of the 101 class-war prisoners. I knew Fletcher during the thirty years that elapsed from the time I first contacted the MTW. He vividly recalled an incident when he was organizing negro and white longshore workers on the Norfolk, Virginia waterfront: Fletcher, undoubtedly the most eloquent, humorous speaker I ever heard (his ringing voice needed no microphone), was addressing an open-air street meeting attended by white racists out to make trouble. They flung the sure-fire embarrassing question: "Do you approve of intermarriage or sexual intercourse between whites and blacks . . . have a nigger marry a white woman?" To show that the racist troublemakers were hypocrites when it was common knowledge that intercourse between white men and black women produced racially mixed, lighter skinned children, Fletcher remarked: "I don't see anyone as black as I am. But we all damn well know the reason." The meeting proceeded without further interruption.

When he moved to New York, Fletcher was one of the most popular and effective wobbly propagandists on the New York waterfront. He was unfortunately partially crippled by a major stroke. When he recovered some of the use of his limbs, he and his wife, a registered nurse, owned or rented a small rooming house in the Brooklyn negro Bedford-Stuyvesant district. Ben attended to the daily chores while his wife was at work. He died suddenly of a massive heart attack in the late 1940s or early 1950s [1949].

■ Sam Dolgoff, *Fragments*, 139–41.

95

Anatole Dolgoff Remembers Fletcher

Anatole Dolgoff was one of Sam and Esther Dolgoff's two sons. He was very close with his parents who introduced their young children to Wobbly and anarchist circles in New York City in the 1940s. Due to his father's close relationship with Fletcher, Anatole, as a young boy, spent much time with Fletcher. Their families lived in the same neighborhood, Bedford-Stuyvesant, as it transitioned to an increasingly African American population in the 1940s.

I remember my father, Sam Dolgoff, taking me with him to visit his friend and Fellow Worker Ben Fletcher. Fletcher was quite old then [late fifties], and no longer very active in IWW affairs. But my father always admired him and liked to keep in touch.

I would guess this was around 1947 or 48. I was nine or ten years old. Fletcher lived in a brownstone apartment building. I don't recall where it was—not even the street [Hancock St.]. But I remember going downstairs—a few steps down—into what I guess was a first-floor apartment. The venetian blinds were down tight and the room was dark, except for a bright television screen. And there was Ben Fletcher, watching Jackie Robinson in a baseball game on TV.

I don't remember what Fletcher and my father talked about—but I'd bet it was about world labor news, IWW news, what Fellow Worker so-and-so was doing now, and that sort of thing. That's what Wobblies always talked about: the working class, the ongoing struggle, and what to do next.

■ Phone call to Franklin Rosemont, October 3, 2004.

96

Sam Dolgoff's Children and Fletcher at the MTW Hall

In his seventies, while still teaching geography at various New York City universities, Anatole Dolgoff authored a loving, poignant memoir of his parents, Esther and Sam, and their radical milieu. This story, set in the late 1940s, featured Sam taking his two sons to the MTW hall located on Broad Street in lower Manhattan. In the twenty-first century, there remains no one alive who knew Fletcher better, albeit during his final years of life and when Anatole was a child. For decades after Fletcher passed, Anatole's parents recounted stories of Fletcher, a fitting close to this book.

I am five or six years of age at the Five-Ten Hall. While a small clutch of men, including my father, speak animatedly about things that buzz above me, my eyes are locked on one man in that group. I follow him wherever he steps, at a certain distance, too shy to approach. I am engrossed in the light that reflects purple and dark blue off his forehead and cheeks and by the contrast of his totally black skin and the whites of his eyes. No doubt such interest is not new to him. When our eyes meet he smiles at me in a kindly way. The name of this blackest of men was Benjamin Harrison Fletcher. He was among the greatest of IWW organizers and one of the pioneer civil rights leaders of the twentieth century: unsung and forgotten today.

Ben Fletcher was my first conscious knowledge of the black race. He appeared an old man whose health was shot when I knew him: a bit heavy with a paunch and with thick working man's shoulders that sloped oddly—the result of a stroke, my father told me years later. All in all, he did not cut the heroic figure of a black man white people of the 1940s found acceptable. He looked nothing like the relatively light skinned heavyweight champion Joe "a credit to his face" Louis, or, a generation later, like Sidney Poitier: handsome with ramrod straight posture, who wore his dignity as a suit of armor. Instead he projected good humor and decency—you wanted to be in his company—but there was something sad that seeped through. Matilda Robbins was a Wobbly organizer who Ben knew in the full bloom of his youth and power, at a time when he was responsible for the organization and welfare of ten thousand men. She remembered Ben as "soft spoken" and that "his eyes seemed to reflect the tragedy of his race."

Sam called Ben Fletcher "undoubtedly the most eloquent, humorous speaker I have ever heard (which is saying quite a lot). His ringing voice needed no microphone." He was fond of retelling the incident Ben had recounted to him of time his black skin saved his life.

It is 1912 or thereabout, and Ben is on the soapbox addressing a crowd of longshoremen on the Norfolk Virginia docks. Remember this is one-hundred years ago. Ten men, all white and all business join the audience. They are interested in nothing Ben has to say, save the answer to this single question that pierces the air: "Nigger! What do you think of miscegenation?" The crowd tightens around Ben like a noose; it is a classic lynching set up. For a full tense minute Ben's eyes size-up each and every member of the crowd. "Well," Ben says at last, "I see a whole lot of folks whiter than I am. And you damn well know how that happened!" It takes a moment to sink in. The tension is broken. The moment has passed. It is hard to work up whatever it takes to murder a man when you have just laughed at his joke.

I cannot imagine the courage of a man such as Ben Fletcher to stand exposed in front of a hostile crowd in the jaws of the Jim Crow South of 1912. Espousing revolutionary unionism and racial integration, no less, at a time when a black man in the South had to step out of the way of an approaching white man. When a black man faced prison or worse for the crime of pissing in the same pot as a white man. When a black man imprisoned for the most trivial offense—or no offense at all—could find himself in chains and on a plantation work gang. It was a time when an entire nation was whipped into a state of hysteria because a black heavyweight, Jack Johnson, defeated every last one of his white opponents. It was a time when a film extolling the virtues of the Ku Klux Klan, *The Birth of a Nation*, was a huge sensation. It was a time when a rabbi's son, Al Jolson, who as a boy roamed the same streets as my father, could make a fortune prancing on stage with black grease-paint smeared on his face.

I add that it was a time when the Great [Statesman]—you know, Woodrow Wilson—in one of the first acts of his first term, sought fit to protect the racial purity of the Civil Service by segregating the facilities of Federal employees: installing separate bathrooms and partitioned lunch rooms and the like. This, after our paragon of integrity had appealed to black voters for support in the campaign of 1912.

In the face of that gale of racial hatred, Fletcher and his fellow Wobblies, white and black, organized and led thousands of Philadelphia dock workers in what was surely the largest interracial union of its time.

In 1923, five years after the war ended [Judge] Kennsaw Mountain Landis referred to the Wobblies in Ben's trial as "scum," "filth," and slimy rate." The comment is noteworthy because Landis was the judge who presided over that Chicago trial. In his viciousness and vindictiveness, he was furious at Calvin Coolidge for commuting the sentences of the Wobblies in jail.

Ben, who rarely spoke of the trial, despised Landis. He saw the plantation owner, the man with the whip. "A cracker!" he spat out years later to Mother, which for him was strong language. Many of Ben's fellow Wobblies, naturally enough, sought to offer documents and testimony in their defense, hoping to get off or at least draw a lesser sentence. Not Ben. One glance at Landis and he knew the effort was hopeless.

Instead, he put energy into lightening the burden of his fellow prisoners. The only black man in the court room, he'd crack that he was glad to add a bit of color to the proceedings. When it was his turn to speak during the punishment phase of the trial, he commented to Judge Landis that his grammar was poor. "Your Honor, your sentences are too long." Landis chuckled and down went the gavel: ten years. Mother insisted Ben said this directly to Landis rather than to his fellow Wobblies, as Haywood recalled in his biography.

■ Anatole Dolgoff, *Left of the Left*, 381–85, 402–5.

APPENDIX

Çolored Workers of America
Why You Should Join the I. W. W.

Fellow Workers—

There is one question which, more than any other, presses upon the mind of the worker today, regardless of whether he be of one race or another, of one color or another—the question of how he can improve his conditions, raise his wages, shorten his hours of labor and gain something more of freedom from his master—the owners of the industry wherein he labors.

To the black race who, but recently, with the assistance of the white men of the northern states, broke their chains of bondage and ended chattel slavery, a prospect of further freedom, of REAL FREEDOM, should be most appealing.

For it is a fact that the Negro worker is no better off under the freedom he has gained than the slavery from which he has escaped. As chattel slaves we were the property of our masters and, as a piece of valuable property, our masters were considerate of us and careful of our health and welfare. Today, as wage workers, the boss may work us to death at the hardest and most hazardous labor, at the longest hours, at the lowest pay; we may quietly starve when out of work and the boss loses nothing by it and has no interest in us. To him the worker is but a machine for producing profits, and when you, as a slave who sells himself to the master on the installment plan, become old or broken in health or strength, or should you be killed while at work, the master merely gets another wage slave on the same terms.

We who have worked in the south know that conditions in lumber and turpentine camps, in the fields of cane, cotton and tobacco, in the mills and mines of Dixie, are such that the workers suffer a more miserable existence than ever prevailed among the chattel slaves before the great Civil War. Thousands of us have come and are coming northward, crossing the Mason and Dixon line, seeking better conditions. As wage slaves we have run away from the masters in the south only to become the wage slaves of the masters of the north. In the north we find that the hardest work and the poorest pay is our portion. We are driven while on the job and the high cost of living offsets any higher pay we might receive.

The white wage worker is little, if any, better off. He is a slave the same as we are and, like us, he is regarded by the boss only as a means of making profits. The working class as a whole grows poorer and more miserable year by year, while the employing class, who do not work at all, enjoy wealth and luxury beyond the dreams of titled lords and kings.

As we are both wage workers, we have a common interest in improving conditions of the wage work-

Colored Workers of America:
Why You Should Join the IWW

This four-page pamphlet was published by the IWW headquarters in Chicago and distributed nationwide in 1919. Though the author is unknown, the writing suggests it might have been written by a black person. The pamphlet noted that black workers suffered from intense racism in the Jim Crow South but also in the industrial cities outside that region. It proudly declared the IWW as "One Big Union" in which all workers, regardless of race or nationality, are welcome. It is true that, in the 1910s, no other union in the United States was as ideologically committed to racial equality. It also is true that there were multiple instances of the IWW organizing in multiethnic, multinational, and multiracial workplaces. But outside of Local 8 and timber workers in the South, few African Americans belonged to the IWW. Similarly, few African Americans belonged to other unions. Another difference was that the IWW actively sought to line up black and brown workers while the AFL and other unions steadfastly refused to do so or ignored workers of color.

Colored Workers of America: Why You Should Join the IWW

Fellow Workers—

There is one question which, more than any other, presses upon the mind of the worker today, regardless of whether he be of one race or another, of one color or another—the question of how he can improve his conditions, raise his wages, shorten his hours of labor and gain something more of freedom from his master—the owners of the industry wherein he labors.

To the black race who, but recently, with the assistance of the white men of the northern states, broke their chains of bondage and ended chattel slavery, a prospect of further freedom, of REAL FREEDOM, should be most appealing.

For it is a fact that the Negro worker is no better off under the freedom he has gained than the slavery from which he has escaped. As chattel slaves we were the property of our masters and, as a piece of valuable property, our masters were considerate of us and careful of our health and welfare. Today, as wage workers, the boss may work us to death at the hardest and most hazardous labor, at the longest hours, at the lowest pay; we may quietly starve when out of work and the boss loses nothing by it and has no interest in us. To him the worker is but a machine, for producing profits, and when you, as a slave who sells himself to the master on the installment plan, become old or broken in health or strength, or should you be killed while at work, the master merely gets another wage slave on the same terms.

We who have worked in the south know that conditions in lumber and turpentine camps, in the fields of cane, cotton and tobacco, in the mills and mines of Dixie, are such that the workers suffer a more miserable existence than ever prevailed among the chattel slaves before the great Civil War. Thousands of us have come and are coming northward, crossing the Mason and Dixon line, seeking better conditions. As wage slaves we have run away from the masters in the south only to become the wage slaves of the masters of the north. In the north we find that the hardest work and the poorest pay is our portion. We are driven while on the job and the high cost of living offsets any higher pay we might receive.

The white wage worker is little, if any, better off. He is a slave the same as we are and, like us, he is regarded by the boss only as a means of making profits. The working class as a whole grows poorer and more miserable year by year, while the employing class, who do not work at all, enjoy wealth and luxury beyond the dreams of titled lords and kings.

As we are both wage workers, we have a common interest in improving conditions of the wage working class. Understanding this, the employing class seeks to engender race hatred between the two. He sets the black worker against the white worker and the white worker against the black, and keeps them divided and enslaved. Our change from chattel slaves to wage slaves has benefited no one but the masters of industry. They have used us as wage slaves to beat down the wages of the white wage slaves, and by a continual talk of "race problems," "Negro questions," "segregation," etc., make an artificial race hatred and division by poisoning the minds of both whites and blacks in an effort to stop any movement of labor that threatens the dividends of the industrial kings. Race prejudice has no place in a labor organization. As Abraham Lincoln has said, "The strongest bond that should bind man to man in human society is that between the working people of all races and of all nations."

The only problem then which the Colored worker should consider as a worker is the problem of organizing with other working men in the labor organization that best expresses the interest of the whole working class against the slavery and oppression of the whole capitalist class. Such an organization is the IWW, the INDUSTRIAL WORKERS OF THE WORLD, the only labor union that has never, IN THEORY OR PRACTICE, since its beginning twelve years ago, barred the workers of any race or nation from membership. The following has stood as a principle of the IWW, embodied in its official constitution since its formation in 1905:

> "By-Laws—Article 1. Section 1. No working man or woman shall be excluded from membership in Unions because of creed or color."

If you are a wage worker you are welcome in the IWW halls, no matter what your color. By this you may see that the IWW is not a white man's union, not a black man's union, not a red or yellow man's union, but A WORKING MAN'S UNION. ALL OF THE WORKING CLASS IN ONE BIG UNION.

In the IWW all wage workers meet on common ground. No matter what language you may speak, whether you were born in Europe, in Asia or in any other part of the world, you will find a welcome as a fellow worker. In the harvest fields where the IWW controls, last summer saw white men, black men and Japanese working together as union men and raising the pay of all who gathered the grain. In the great strikes the IWW has conducted at Lawrence, Mass., In the woolen mills, in the iron mines of Minnesota and elsewhere, the IWW has brought the workers of many races, colors and tongues together in victorious battles for a better life.

Not only does the IWW differ from all organizations in regard to admission of all races, but there is a fundamental difference in form of organization from all other labor unions. You have seen other and house the world; a world where the words "master" and "slave" shall be forgotten; a world where peace and happiness shall reign and where the children of men shall live as brothers in a worldwide INDUSTRIAL DEMOCRACY.

The following is the preamble of the IWW constitution, showing the reason and form of its *organization*, the aims and purposes of its membership:

> The working class and the employing class have nothing in common. There can be no peace so long as hunger and want are found among millions of working people and the few, who make up the employing class, have all the good things of life.
>
> Between these two classes a struggle must go on until the workers of the world organize as a class, take possession of the earth and machinery of production and abolish the wage system.

We find that the centering of management of industries into fewer and fewer hands makes the trade unions unable to cope with the ever growing power of the employing class. The trade unions foster a state of affairs which allows one set of workers to be pitted against another set of workers in the same industry, thereby helping defeat one another in wage wars. Moreover, the trade unions aid the employing class to mislead the workers into the belief that the workers have interests in common with their employers.

These conditions can be changed and the interest of the working class upheld only by an organization formed in such a way that all its members, in any industry, or in all industries, if necessary, cease work whenever a strike or lockout is on in any department thereof, thus making an injury to one an injury to all.

Instead of the conservative motto, "A fair day's wage for a fair day's work," we must inscribe on our banner the revolutionary watchword, "Abolition of the wage system."

It is the historic mission of the working class to do awe, with capitalism. The army of production must be organized, not only for the every day struggle with capitalists, but to carry on production when capitalism shall have been overthrown. By organizing industrially we are forming the structure of the new society within the shell of the old.

The IWW welcomes you as a member, no matter in what industry you may work. The initiation fee is $2, the dues are 50 cents a month. After you once join you have the right of free transfer into any industry. All that is necessary to continue membership is the payment of dues, regardless of where you go or what your work may be.

For further information write to
GENERAL SECRETARY,
1001 W. Madison Street, Chicago, Illinois.
Printed by Printing and Publishing Workers' Industrial Union No. 1200.

Justice for the Negro:
How He Can Get It

This pamphlet also was published in 1919 and distributed by the national IWW. With great sympathy, it notes the intensity of racism, discrimination, and violence that African Americans suffered from in a country deeply committed to white supremacy since before the founding of the nation. Quite possibly, the author of this pamphlet was citing statistics from the Chicago-based journalist and civil rights activist Ida B. Wells. Notably, and unlike nearly every other predominantly white organization in the United States at that time, this pamphlet highlights the particular terror that white racist lynchings inflicted on African Americans. At the top of the pamphlet was a widely circulated photograph of Jesse Washington, brutally lynched by a mob in Waco, Texas in 1916.

Two lynchings a week—one every three or four days—that is the rate at which the people in this "land of the free and home of the brave" have been killing colored men and women for the past thirty years—3,224 Negroes known to have been put to death by mobs in this country since 1889, and put to death with every kind of torture that human fiends could invent.

Even during the war, while colored soldiers were being obliged to "fight for democracy" abroad, ninety-one of their race were lynched at home.

The wrongs of the Negro in the United States are not confined to lynchings, however. When allowed to live and work for the community, he is subjected to constant humiliation, injustice and discrimination. In the cities he is forced to live in the meanest districts, where his rent is doubled and tripled, while conditions of health and safety are neglected in favor of the white sections.[1] In many states he is obliged to ride in special "Jim Crow" cars, hardly fit for cattle. Almost everywhere all semblance of political rights is denied him.

---

1   The normal average death rate of males in a city is about 147.10 per 1,000; for negroes, 287.10 per 1,000." —*New York Times*, February 22, 1919.

N. B.—Workingmen have paid for this leaflet out of their earnings. When you have read it, pass it on.

Justice for the Negro

How He Can Get It

Actual Photograph of Charred Body of Jesse Washington, a Colored Lad Burned to Death by a Mob at Waco, Texas, May 15, 1916.

Two lynchings a week—one every three or four days—that is the rate at which the people in this "land of the free and home of the brave" have been killing colored men and women for the past thirty years—3,224 Negroes known to have been put to death by mobs in this country since 1889, and put to death with every kind of torture that human fiends could invent.

Even during the war, while colored soldiers were being obliged to "fight for democracy" abroad, ninety-one of their race were lynched at home.

The wrongs of the Negro in the United States are not confined to lynchings, however. When allowed to live and work for the community, he is subjected to constant humiliation, injustice and discrimination. In the cities he is forced to live in the meanest districts, where his rent is doubled and tripled, while conditions of health and safety are neglected in favor of the white sections.* In many states he is obliged to ride in special "Jim Crow" cars, hardly fit for cattle. Almost everywhere all semblance of political rights is denied him.

*The normal average death rate of males in a city is about 147.10 per 1,000; for negroes, 287.10 per 1,000."—New York Times, Feb. 22, 1919.

The Colored Worker Everywhere Unfairly Treated

When the Negro goes to look for work he meets with the same systematic discrimination. Thousands of jobs are closed to him solely on account of his color. He is considered only fit for the most menial occupations. It many cases, he has to accept a lower wage than is paid to white men for the same work.[2] *Everywhere the odds are against him in the struggle for existence.*

Throughout this land of liberty, so-called, the Negro worker is treated as an inferior; he is underpaid in his work and overcharged in his rent; he is kick about, cursed and spat upon; in short, he is treated, not as a human being, but as an animal, a beast of burden for the ruling class. When he tries to improve his condition, he is shoved back into the mire of degradation and poverty and told to "keep his place."

How can the Negro combat this widespread injustice? How can he not only put a stop to lynchings, but force the white race to grant him equal treatment? How can he get his rights as a human being?

Protests, petitions and resolutions will never accomplish anything. It is useless to waste time and money on them. The government is in the hands of the ruling class of white men and will do as they wish. No appeal to the political powers will ever secure justice for the Negro.

The Master Class Fears the Organized Worker

He has, however, one weapon that the master class fears—the power to fold his arms and refuse to work for the community until he is guaranteed fair treatment. Remember how alarmed the South became over the emigration of colored workers two years ago, what desperate means were used to try to keep them from leaving the mills and cotton fields? *The only power of the Negro is his power as a worker;* his one weapon is the strike. Only by organizing and refusing to work for those who abuse him can he put an end to the injustice and oppression he now endures.

The colored working men and women of the United States must organize in defense of their rights. The must join together in labor unions so as to be able to enforce their demand for an equal share of "life, liberty and the pursuit of happiness." When they are in a position to say to any community, "If you do not stop discrimination against the colored race, we will stop working for you," the hidden forces behind the government will see to it that lynchings cease and discrimination comes to an end.

---

2   The wages of colored kitchen workers in New York City average $20 a month lower than white employees.

Only by threatening to withdraw their labor power and thereby cripple industry and agriculture can the Negroes secure equal treatment with other workers.

The Workers of Every Race Must Join Together

But the Negroes cannot accomplish this alone; they must unite with the other workers in order to make their industrial power count to the utmost. If they form separate racial organizing they will only encourage race prejudice and help the master class in their effort to divide the workers along false lines of color and set one race against the other, in order to use both for their own selfish ends.

The workers of every race and nationality must join in one common group against their one common enemy—the employers—so as to be able to defend themselves and one another. Protection for the working class lies in complete solidarity of the workers, without regard to race, creed, sex or color. "One Enemy—One Union!" must be their watchword.

Trade Unions Do Not Want the Negro

Most American labor organizations, however, shut their doors to the colored worker. The American Federation of Labor excludes him from many of its unions.[3] In those to which he is admitted, he is treated as an inferior. *The Negro has no chance in the old-line trade unions.* They do not want him. The admit him only under compulsion and treat him with contempt. Their officials, who discourage strikes for higher wages or shorter hours, are always ready, as in the case of the Switchmen's Union, to permit a strike aimed to prevent the employment of colored men.

This narrow-minded policy of excluding the Negro from the trade unions often forces him to become a strike-breaker against his will by closing legitimate occupations to him. The consequence is racial conflicts such as the frightful tragedy in East St. Louis in 1917.

The IWW Admits Negro to Full Membership

There is one international labor organization in this country that admits the colored worker on a footing of absolute equality with the white—The Industrial Workers of the World. The first section of its By-Laws provides that "no working man or woman shall be excluded from membership

---

3   The constitution of the International Association of Machinists, for example, requires each member to agree "to introduce no one into the union but a sober, industrious WHITE man."

because of creed or color." This principle has been scrupulously lived up to since the organization was founded. In the IWW the colored worker, man or woman, is on an equal footing with every other worker. He has the same voice in determining the policies of the organization, and his interests are protected as zealously as those of any other member.

Not only does the IWW offer to the Negro worker union membership free from any taint or suggestion of racial inferiority, but in its form of organization it is far superior to the old-fashioned trade unions.

Industrial Unionism the Strongest Form of Organization

The IWW organizes the workers by industries, not trades. Instead of the American Federation of Labor plan of dividing the workers in any plant into ten or twenty separate craft unions, with separate meetings and separate sets of officials, the IWW unites *all the workers in each industry*, whatever their particular line of work may be, into One Big Industrial Union. In this way, the industrial power of the workers is combined and, when any of them have a disagreement with their employer, they are back by the united support of ALL the workers in that industry.

But the IWW does not limit its aim, as do the trade unions, to "less work and more pay." Its greatest object is *the complete emancipation of the working class*. As long as the workers hold their jobs only by permission of some employer, they are not free. As long as there is one class that lives in ease and idleness off their labor, they are industrial slaves. Freedom for the workers will come only when everybody does his share of the work of the world and when the workers take control of the industries and operate them, not as at present, for the benefit of the leisure class, but for the welfare of society as a whole.

Servants of Capitalism Lie about the IWW

Do not believe the lies being told about the IWW by the hired agents of the capitalists—the press, preachers and politicians. They are paid to deceive the workers and lead them astray. They are hired to throw dust in their eyes because the master class *does not dare to let them know the truth*.

Investigate the IWW for yourself and get the facts. We are confident that, when you learn the truth about it, you will realize that it is to your interest to join and help build up the organization.

Fellow workers of the colored race, do not expect justice or fair treatment as a gift from the ruling class. *You will get from them nothing but what you are strong enough to take*. "In union there is strength." The only power that workers of any race or nationality have is their power to act together as workers. We, therefore, urge you to join with your fellow workers of every race in the

ONE BIG UNION

of the

INDUSTRIAL WORKERS OF THE WORLD

1001 West Madison Street, Chicago, Illinois

Workers' Halls, with Reading Rooms, at 119 S. Throop St. and 951 W. Madison St.

NOTE—The IWW admits to membership every wage worker, man or woman, young or old, skilled or unskilled. Its plan of organization includes all workers. No matter what your occupation, if you work for wages, you can get a union card in the IWW.

N.B.—Workingmen have paid for this leaflet out of their earnings. When you have read it, pass it on.

The Negro Worker Falls into Line

This powerful article was written by Robert Hardoen, a young African American IWW member also active in Chicago's Dill Pickle Club. Founded in the 1910s and continuing into the 1930s, the Dill Pickle Club was located in what was, then, the working-class neighborhood of Tower Town (now, the expensive Gold Coast) and also was nicknamed "hobohemia." The Dill Pickle Club also operated around Jackson Park, on the city's South side, which was much more heavily African American. Founded by anarchists, Wobblies, and cultural radicals, the Dill Pickle welcomed everyone regardless of ethnicity, race, sexual preference, or politics. Here Hardoen deftly summarizes the various strains of political thought that different groups of black people held—by Du Bois and others in the NAACP, Marcus Garvey's UNIA, "New Negro" advocates, and African Blood Brotherhood—before explaining why capitalism was the root cause of black suffering and the IWW the ultimate solution. Hardoen went on to a career as a chemist, and at least some of his descendants continue the family tradition of radical politics.

The Negro Worker Falls Into Line
By Robert H. Hardoen

In accord with the historic tendency of a wide-spread group sentiment to crystallize into organized effort, it has long been expected that the general discontent among the American colored people would sooner or later express itself through militant bodies with the broad general object of emancipation by any or all of the means that other peoples have always employed to rid themselves of oppression.

The great danger attendant upon all the movements for group emancipation is that they may become purely nationalistic or racial in their aspects, rather than built along lines that take into consideration the economic foundations of society. This, as every class conscious worker knows, accounts for the strange anomaly that so many workers (most of them in the craft unions and some few in industrial unions too) have never lost their nationalistic tendencies, as witness the Polish workers who loaded ammunition for Wrangel, and that strange creature whom we encounter now and then, the Zionist radical.

Two points explain this anomaly: first, all of us have been thinking as races and nations for a hundred centuries, and only a very few are beginning to think as workers; secondly, the well known campaign of the capitalistic class to assiduously cultivate every line of working class division possible, which just now during the present economic crisis is being kindled into a fury of veritable nationalistic madness never known before, evidenced by anti-English, anti-Japanese, anti-Catholic, anti-foreigner, anti-Negro, anti-Russian, anti-Jew and especially anti-everything that portends social change.

Out of this pandemonium of shrieking, clawing class war, with its variegated false and real issues, from "white supremacy" in Tulsa, Oklahoma, to the miner's insurrection in West Virginia, have emerged three distinct types of Negro sentiment and lines of action. The oldest of these is represented by the National Association for the Advancement of Colored People. This is an organization comprised of Negro scholars and business men, together with quite a number of white journalists, liberals, philanthropists, etc. The official organ of the association is *The Crisis*, of which Dr. W.E.B. Du Bois is the editor. Its activities are confined largely to awakening a wide-spread sympathy for the Negro's problem. A well managed publicity bureau endeavors to investigate lynchings, riots, etc., and carries on a ceaseless campaign against Jim Crowism, and all legislation aimed at depriving the Negro of his rights as a citizen. Further than this, the Association does not attempt to go.

By far the greatest Negro organization in the world is the Universal Negro Improvement Association, at the head of which stands a full-blooded Negro publicist of the British West Indies, named Marcus Garvey. The aim of this society organized only three years ago and now numbering two million members is a free Africa. They have adopted a flag and racial emblem comprised of red, black and green stripes, running parallel. A steamship line, made up of six vessels, all named for colored writers or poets, and called the Black Star Line is already plying between New York, Liberia, Jamaica and the northern coast of South America.

Approached with a discussion of the class struggle, the members of the Universal Negro Improvement Association insist that no mere change of social structure can be expected to eradicate a century-old race hatred overnight in America and points to that almost solid wall of opposition which the Southland offers to every progressive idea, and Garvey himself, while recognizing that the race question is basically economic, maintains that an ethical superstition forms another important factor that no possible rearrangement of society can eliminate, not even education, that is conventional education, for educated folk and educators are often prejudiced.

Of course the flaw in this reasoning is not that they seek a free Africa; all peoples desiring freedom should have it and no one can dispute Mr. Garvey's reasoning that racial antipathy will, like every element of human consciousness, live somewhat longer than the conditions that gave rise to it and have kept it alive. But just as the decapitated serpent without its head must die and the engine that has exhausted its fuel must stop, just so the race problem bereft of its economic basis must vanish from American life.

The same danger lies hidden in the Garvey movement that is to be found in the Sinn Fein movement or the Zionist movement, namely, that in fleeing the claws of a lion in the form of foreign capitalists they may rush pell mell into the jaws of a tiger in the form of capitalists of their own group.

The third division of Negro sentiment, and by far the most prominent of all so far as vision and perspective of the true nature of their problem is concerned, is represented by a rapidly growing group who call themselves the "New Negro," in contradistinction to the black man with the vestigial slave psychology, whom they contemptuously designate as an "Uncle Tom" or an "Old Negro." This "New Negro" is at once the most interesting as well as the most intelligent of colored folk. The type is that of the awakening millions of toilers of the changing world, done in blacks and browns. The leading mouthpiece of this section of the race is the *Messenger*, a magazine published in New York City by two young Negro socialists, A. Chandler Owen and Philip Randolph who, in spite of the fact that they have gone far in putting the economic question before their people, have, nevertheless, all the shortcomings of political socialists of every race the world over.

A smaller but more dynamic force among the colored radicals is the *Crusader*, official organ of the African Blood Brotherhood, edited by a militant, class conscious man named Cyril Briggs. The African Blood Brotherhood is an organization that was originally formed to protect the race from armed attacks by its enemies and to prevent lynching, in accord with the world-old law of self defense. The Brotherhood educates its members in the class struggle and at the same time functions as an underground answer to the Ku Klux Klan. Their motto is, "Better a thousand race riots than a single lynching!"

Lest anyone think that this is only race-consciousness, we hasten to append the following from their manifesto issued at the last convention held in New York City, August 1921. "Negroes of the World, the day the European workers rise in armed insurrection against the capitalist exploiters of black and white toilers, we must see to it that Negro troops are not available as 'White Guards' to crush the rising power of the workers' revolution! On that day, Negro comrades, the cause of the white workers will be the cause of the black workers, the cause of a free Africa, the cause of a Europe freed from capitalist control."

In no organization is the colored worker made to feel more welcome or given a better chance than in the Industrial Workers of the World. Throughout the West and Southwest as well as the docks of Pennsylvania ports such as Philadelphia, great headway has been made in lining up the colored worker. The IWW tolerates no race lines, plays no politics, discriminates against no groups because of color or creed. The program is industrial organization of all the workers of a given industry into job or city branches which, in turn, are part of the One Big Union built to fight the battles of the present and so organized that at the collapse of the dilapidated old structure of capitalism the workers may assume control of industry and administer it to serve the needs of humanity and not for profit as at present.

In this program lies the greatest hope for the solution of the Negro problem, which is in reality only a special phase of the international labor problem. That this is the case cannot be disputed by any black man who will but reflect that wherever colored people live in small numbers as in France or Canada or New England, no race problem exists, but as soon as black men come in sufficient numbers to become a factor in the labor market, the race problem appears.

In conclusion, let us note this "New Negro" has completely exploded the ancient fallacious doctrine of Booker T. Washington, by showing their people, through practical demonstration, that merely getting educated, learning a trade, going into a profession or becoming a petty bourgeoisie would not solve the race problem, but on the contrary it only intensifies it. They do not hesitate to show their brethren that if the young colored medical graduate takes the patients of the white physician, the white man will not love him for it, but on the contrary is likely to join the Ku Klux Klan; that the white tradesman and white business man will hate him for taking away "their" job or patronage as long as the present competitive system stands.

They point out the folly of Du Bois' continual petitioning of Congress to pass an antilynching bill which must result in allowing the spirit of revolt to grow among the cotton workers and so curtail the profits of the Southern planter.

They point to the economic roots of the World War that centered around colonies, most of which lay in Africa, and try to tell the Garveyite that without the Social Revolution a few million poverty-stricken black men cannot hope to establish a free Africa with the combined armies of the whole capitalistic world waiting to crush them.

Indeed, this "New Negro" is a force to be reckoned with in the class struggle. Already he is causing those that have used him so long as a strike breaker many a sleepless night, and the authorities are steadily "investigating."

The writer who is one of them wishes to say to our white fellow workers: "Move over, fellow workers, move over. We're coming in. We've heard that the water's fine!"

■ *Industrial Pioneer*, October 1921, 13–19.

Bibliography

Speeches and Writings by and Interviews with Ben Fletcher (Alphabetical by Source)

"Some People Are Taken to Jail, but Ben Fletcher Just 'Went In,'" *Amsterdam News*, December 30, 1931, 16.

"Letter to Editor," *Baltimore Afro-American*, April 2, 1920, 4.

George V. Carey Papers, Joseph A. Labadie Collection, Special Collections Research Center, University of Michigan Library, Ann Arbor.

Abram Lincoln Harris Papers, Moorland-Spingarn Archives, Howard University, Washington, DC.

"Marine Transport Drive Needs Your Solidarity," *Industrial Solidarity*, March 23, 1927.

Agnes Inglis Papers, Joseph A. Labadie Collection, Special Collections Research Center, University of Michigan Library, Ann Arbor.

Stenographic Report of IWW's Eighth Convention, 1913, 110, 147, 160–61.

"Philadelphia's Waterfront Unionism," *Messenger* 5, no. 6 (June 1923): 740–41.

"The Negro and Organized Labor," *Messenger* 5, no. 7 (July 1923): 759–60.

"Philadelphia Workers Listen to Matilda Rabinowitz's Eloquent Appeal in Behalf of Little Falls Victims," *Solidarity*, March 1, 1913.

"Break This Conspiracy of the Shipping Trust, *Solidarity*, February 28, 1914.

"Solidarity Wins in Philadelphia," *Solidarity*, March 14, 1914.

"Ford and Suhr Protest Meeting in Philadelphia," *Solidarity*, April 11, 1914, 4.

"Transport Workers Strike in Philadelphia," *Solidarity*, February 13, 1915, 1.

"Philadelphia Strike Off," *Solidarity*, February 20, 1915, 1.

"Growth of IWW in Baltimore" and "Providence MTW," *Solidarity*, February 10, 1917, 4.

"Marine Transport Workers Line-Up in Boston," *Solidarity*, April 14, 1917, 4.

Reflections and Writings about Ben Fletcher

"A List of Class Warriors," *Ahjo* [*The Forge*] 3, no. 4 (December 1918): 55.

"Among Books," *Tie Vapauteen* [*The Road to Freedom*], April 1928, 5–8.

"Announcement of speaking engagement by Fletcher in Detroit," *Industrial Solidarity*, October 12, 1927.

"Ben Fletcher," *Messenger* 2 (August 1919): 28–29.

"Ben Fletcher in Canada," *Philadelphia Tribune*, December 29, 1927, 16.

"Ben Fletcher's Funeral Showed High Regard for Old Rebel," *Industrial Worker*, July 22, 1949, 4.

"Benjamin Fletcher, Labor Organizer," *Brooklyn Daily Eagle*, July 12, 1949, 9.

"Benjamin H. Fletcher: Labor Organizer Convicted Under Espionage Act in 1917 Dies," *New York Times*, July 12, 1949, 27.

"A Call to Solidarity!!" *Messenger*, February 1922, 360, and April 1922, 396.

"Colored and White Workers Solving the Race Problem for Philadelphia," *Messenger*, July 1921, 214–15.

"Fletcher's Speaking Engagements in Canada," *Industrialisti*, December 9, 1927.

"The Forum of Local 8," *Messenger*, July 1921, 234.

"Free 38 IWWs on Bail: Haywood and Others to Leave Prison Pending Court Review," *New York Times*, April 2, 1919, 21.

"Haywood Given 20 Year Term; 93 Sentenced," *Chicago Tribune*, August 31, 1918, 5.

"IWW Caught in the Act—On Trial," *Chicago Tribune*, April 5, 1918, 5.

"IWW Leaders Called Here to Rebuild Forces," *New York Herald Tribune*, September 27, 1933, 15.

"James P. Thompson's Report: As General Organizer, to the Seventh IWW Convention," *Solidarity*, October 26, 1912, 3.

"Kentucky Miner, in Mt. Sterling, charged with murder, speaks at mass gathering here," *New Yorker Volkszeitung*, January 16, 1932.

"Likes Lecture of Ben J. Fletcher," *Industrial Solidarity*, August 11, 1931.

"Longshoremen Fighting for Life," *Messenger*, December 1922, 538.

"Many Tributes to Ben Fletcher," *Industrial Worker*, July 22, 1949, 4.

"Marine Transport Workers Industrial Union No. 8, April 15th, 1920: Organization Plans for Spring 1920," *One Big Union Monthly*, May 2, 1920, 54.

"Marine Transport Workers Industrial Union No. 8, IWW," *One Big Union Monthly*, June 2, 1920, 57.

"A Miscarriage of Justice," *Messenger*, November 1921, 282–83.

"Seventh Convention," *Solidarity*, September 28, 1912, 1.

"Shaven IWWs Kiss as Trial Is Postponed," *Chicago Tribune*, April 2, 1918, 7.

"The Task of Local 8—The Marine Transport Workers of Philadelphia," *Messenger*, October 1921, 262–63.

"To the President of the United States," *Messenger*, March 1922, 377.

"Veteran Socialist Dies; Led Strike Against US Govt.," *Philadelphia Tribune*, July 19, 1949, 2.

"Why Should These Men Be Released?" *Messenger*, May 1922, 404–5.

Aakula, Tyne. "To Ben Fletcher—A Tribute," *Industrial Worker*, October 3, 1960, 4.

Aptheker, Herbert. "Status of 'Negroes in Wartime' Revealed," *Norfolk Journal and Guide*, April 26, 1941, 9.

Browder, Earl R. "A Negro Labor Organizer," *Workers Monthly*, May 1925, 294.

DiGaetano, Nick. Interviewed by Jim Kenney and Herbert Hill, Detroit, June 17, 1968. Blacks in the Labor Movement Oral Histories, Walter P. Reuther Library Archives of Labor and Urban Affairs, Wayne State University, Detroit.

Dolgoff, Anatole. Letter to Franklin Rosemont, October 3, 2004.

———— *Left of the Left: My Memories of Sam Dolgoff*. Chico: AK Press, 2016.

Dolgoff, Sam. Letter to Franklin Rosemont, June 10 and 16, 1987.

———— *Fragments: A Memoir*. Cambridge: Refract, 1986.

Dolgoff, Sam and Esther. Interview with Ann Allen, June 15, 1972, New York City, NY, Roosevelt University Oral History Project in Labor History, 20–21. https://libguides.roosevelt.edu/ld.php?content_id=38668329.

Fair, James. Interview with Deborah Shaffer, December 21, 1978, 3–4, Deborah Shaffer Papers, Box 3, State Historical Society of Wisconsin, Madison.

Flynn, Elizabeth Gurley. *The Rebel Girl: An Autobiography, My First Life (1906–1926)*. New York: International Publishers, 1955, 233.

Hardoen, Robert H. "The Negro Worker Falls into Line," *Industrial Pioneer*, October 1921, 13–19.

Harrison, George. "The Prison Story of the Wobblies," *Workers Monthly*, March 1925, 209–13.

Haywood, William D. *Bill Haywood's Book: The Autobiography of William D. Haywood.* New York: International Publishers, 1929, 324–25.

Jones, William D. "The Mixed Union: Merits and Demerits," *Messenger*, September 1923, 812.

Karsner, David. "The War and the IWW: The Extent of its Opposition to the Draft," *New York Call Magazine*, September 5, 1920, 6–8.

Lever, Jack. "Come to Baltimore," *Solidarity*, December 16, 1916, 1.

Marston, H. *Solidarity*, July 22, 1912, 4.

McKay, Claude. *Home to Harlem.* New York: Harper & Brothers, 1928, 43–46.

Robbins, Matilda. Letter to editor, *Industrial Worker*, November 2, 1960, 2.

Rosen, Ellen Doree. *A Wobbly Life: IWW Organizer E.F. Doree.* Detroit: Wayne State University Press, 2004, xx, xxv, 150, 160, 165, 180, 190–91, and 219.

Seraile, William. correspondence with Minkah B. Kamau (Benjamin B. Johns Jr.), March 28, 2001. In possession of the author.

Sperling, Martin L. "Fletcher Meetings in Detroit Waken a New Interest," *Industrial Solidarity*, October 12, 1927, 3.

Thompson, Fred. Speeches and discussion taped by the Canadian Student Federation of Waterloo, Ontario, January 1970, Roosevelt University Oral History Project in Labor History, 103–5. https://libguides.roosevelt.edu/ld.php?content_id=38688315.

Warreno, A. "Benj. Fletcher Thrills Crowds in Philadelphia," *Industrial Worker*, February 16, 1929.

IWW Pamphlets

"Colored Workers of America: Why You Should Join the IWW." 1919. Box 158, Industrial Workers of the World Collection, Walter P. Reuther Library Archives of Labor and Urban Affairs, Wayne State University, Detroit.

"Justice for the Negro: How He Can Get It." 1919. Box 166, Industrial Workers of the World Collection, Walter P. Reuther Library Archives of Labor and Urban Affairs, Wayne State University, Detroit.

Government Records

Fletcher, Ben H. Case Number 29434, Investigative Case Files of the Bureau of Investigation 1908–1922, Old German Files, 1909–21, National Archives and Record Administration.

Fletcher, Benjamin Harrison. Inmate 13126, Department of Justice, Bureau of Prisons. US Penitentiary, Leavenworth. Series: Inmate Case Files, July 3, 1895—November 5, 1957. Record Group 129: Records of the Bureau of Prisons, 1870–2009, National Archives and Record Administration at Kansas City.

Office Chief of Staff, War College Division. War Department, found in *US Military Intelligence Reports: Surveillance of Radicals in the United States 1917–1941*, ed. by Randolph Boehm and guide compiled by Randolph Boehm and Robert Lester. Frederick, MD: University Publications of America, 1984.

US Pardon Attorney, "Memorandum for Mr. Burns, Chief, Bureau of Investigation," April 8, 1922, JAF-CZC, Record Group 204, File no. 37-479, Box 985, 1853–1946. Record Group 204: Records of the Office of the US Pardon Attorney, National Archives and Record Administration, Suitland, MD.

US v. Haywood et al. File 188032, Straight Numerical Files, Record Group 60: Records of the Department of Justice, National Archives and Record Administration.

Sources Consulted and Recommended for Further Reading

Benson, Sara M. *The Prison of Democracy: Race, Leavenworth, and the Culture of Law.* Berkeley: University of California Press, 2019.

Buhle, Paul, and Nicole Schulman, eds. *Wobblies! A Graphic History of the Industrial Workers of the World.* New York: Verso, 2005.

Cameron, Ardis. *Radicals of the Worst Sort: Laboring Women in Lawrence, Massachusetts, 1860–1912.* Urbana: University of Illinois Press, 1995.

Chaplin, Ralph. *Wobbly: The Rough-and-Tumble Story of an American Radical.* Chicago: University of Chicago Press, 1948.

Chester, Eric. *The Wobblies in their Heyday: The Rise and Destruction of the Industrial Workers of the World during the World War I Era.* Santa Barbara, CA: Praeger, 2014.

Cole, Peter. *Wobblies on the Waterfront: Interracial Unionism in Progressive-Era Philadelphia.* Urbana: University of Illinois Press, 2007.

Cole, Peter, David Struthers, and Kenyon Zimmer, eds., *Wobblies of the World: A Global History of the IWW.* London: Pluto Press, 2017.

Dubofsky, Melvyn. *We Shall Be All: A History of the Industrial Workers of the World,* 2nd ed. Urbana: University of Illinois Press, 1988.

Foner, Philip S. *Fellow Workers and Friends: IWW Free-Speech Fights as Told by Participants.* Westport, CT: Greenwood Press, 1981.

———. The IWW and the Black Worker," *Journal of Negro History* 55, no. 1 (1970): 45–64.

Foner, Philip S., and Ronald L. Lewis. *The Black Worker,* vol. 5: *The Black Worker from 1900 to 1919.* Philadelphia: Temple University Press, 1980. Part VII: "Socialism, The Industrial Workers of the World, and the Black Worker."

Hall, Greg. *Harvest Wobblies: The Industrial Workers of the World and Agricultural Laborers in the American West, 1905–1930.* Corvallis: Oregon State University Press, 2001.

Heatherton, Christina. "University of Radicalism: Ricardo Flores Magón and the Leavenworth Penitentiary," *American Quarterly* 66, no. 3 (2014): 557–81.

Industrial Workers of the World. *IWW Historical Archives:* https://archive.iww.org/history/

Kohn, Stephen M. *American Political Prisoners: Prosecutions under the Espionage and Sedition Acts.* Westport, CT: Praeger, 1994.

Mayer, Heather. *Beyond the Rebel Girl: Women and the Industrial Workers of the World in the Pacific Northwest, 1905–1924.* Corvallis: Oregon State University Press, 2018.

Preston, William, Jr. *Aliens and Dissenters: Federal Suppression of Radicals, 1903–1933.* New York: Harper & Row, 1963.

Rosemont, Franklin. *Joe Hill: The IWW and The Making of a Revolutionary Workingclass Counterculture.* Oakland: PM Press, 2015.

Salerno, Salvatore. *Red November, Black November: Culture and Community in the Industrial Workers of the World.* New York: State University of New York Press, 1989.

Thompson, Fred, and Jon Bekken. *The Industrial Workers of the World: Its First One Hundred Years.* Cincinnati: Industrial Workers of the World, 2006.

University of Washington. *IWW History Project: Industrial Workers of the World 1905–1935:* https://depts.washington.edu/iww/

Weber, Devra Anne. "Wobblies of the Partido Liberal Mexicano: Reenvisioning Internationalist and Transnational Movements through Mexican Lenses," *Pacific Historical Review* 85, no. 2 (2016): 188–226.

Acknowledgments

It's always a pleasure to publicly thank folks who have helped me. No one writes a book alone, and this one is no exception. First thanks go to Franklin and Penelope Rosemont, who ran Charles H. Kerr Press for decades. I worked with them in 2005–2006 to create the first edition of this book. That was when I got the chance to meet the incredible artist Carlos Cortez whose woodcut of Fletcher served as the book's original cover. Thanks also to Tammy Smith, who now runs the legendary press. Although both Franklin and Carlos have "crossed the bar," I'm so appreciative of Penelope and others who keep the flame burning at Kerr.

My second thank you goes to Ramsey Kanaan, publisher of PM Press, for suggesting the idea of creating a new edition! Honestly, that was not on my radar. I was aware that the first edition was almost impossible to find, which was really frustrating. Plus, I had learned much more about Ben Fletcher since the first edition was published, so I'm grateful to have the opportunity to craft a book more worthy of his incredible life.

Over the course of several decades, literally, a great many people have provided me advice, material, and suggestions about this subject. At the risk of forgetting to include someone, thanks much to Jon Bekken, Alexis Buss, Aaron Goings, Daniel Gross, Julie Herrada, Ned Kihn, William Seraile, Jeff Stein, Dave Struthers, Dave Roediger, and Kenyon Zimmer. I want to give Bob Helms a special shout-out for finding a copy of Fletcher's prison photo, featured on the cover of this edition. Thanks also to the many archivists, librarians, historians (professional and "amateur") whom I have not individually named, as well as the wonderful PM team.

Although many people helped me, some went above and beyond. Evan Wolfson, who I've never met in the flesh but who is a genealogical researching ace, responded to countless emails from me with assistance about Fletcher's family. Matt White has been quite generous with his time and knowledge. FW Saku Pinta and Aleksi Huhta translated documents from Finnish into English. Max Henninger translated an article from German into English.

It's an honor and a pleasure that Robin D.G. Kelley made the time to write a foreword. Only after I requested he do so did I learn that his first labor history paper, in graduate school, was on Fletcher.

I am lucky that Anatole Dolgoff found me after my two books on Fletcher and Local 8 were published. Since then he has become a dear friend. It's so special to know someone who knew Ben Fletcher personally. Anatole's wonderful memories are, to my knowledge, the last direct, living link to Fletcher.

Final thanks go, as always, to my partner, Wendy Pearlman. Any author knows that those closest to them are subject to endless discussions about a project. In ways large and small, visible and invisible, she made the book better—just as she makes me a better human being.

Honestly, it's a bit odd to devote so much of one's life and energy to a person one never had the good fortune to meet. I feel like I know Ben Fletcher even though he passed away twenty years before I was born. I thank him for his incredible commitment and activism to achieve a better world! He understood how tortuous and unfair life is for people living in a country and world built on the foundations of capitalism and white supremacy. He understood, deep in his bones, that we need revolutionary changes so devoted his life to the struggle. That he—and we—have yet to achieve that vision is proof of the powerful forces arrayed against us. But he—and we—have no choice but to keep on keeping on. A new day will come, hopefully sooner than later. Ben Fletcher, presente!

Index

Page numbers in *italic* refer to illustrations. "Passim" (literally "scattered") indicates intermittent discussion of a topic over a cluster of pages.

About the authors

Peter Cole is a professor of history at Western Illinois University in Macomb and a research associate in the Society, Work and Development Institute at the University of the Witwatersrand in Johannesburg, South Africa. Cole is the author of the award-winning *Dockworker Power: Race and Activism in Durban and the San Francisco Bay Area* and *Wobblies on the Waterfront: Interracial Unionism in Progressive-Era Philadelphia*. He coedited *Wobblies of the World: A Global History of the IWW*. He is the founder and codirector of the Chicago Race Riot of 1919 Commemoration Project.

Robin D.G. Kelley is an American historian and academic and is the Gary B. Nash Professor of American History at UCLA. He is the author of *Freedom Dreams: The Black Radical Imagination; Hammer and Hoe: Alabama Communists During the Great Depression; Race Rebels: Culture, Politics, and the Black Working Class; Imagining Home: Class, Culture, and Nationalism in the African Diaspora; Into the Fire: African Americans Since 1970; Yo' Mama's DisFunktional!: Fighting the Culture Wars in Urban America; Three Strikes: The Fighting Spirit of Labor's Last Century;* and *Thelonious Monk: The Life and Times of an American Original.*

ABOUT PM PRESS

PM Press is an independent, radical publisher of books and
media to educate, entertain, and inspire. Founded in 2007
by a small group of people with decades of publishing,
media, and organizing experience, PM Press amplifies the
voices of radical authors, artists, and activists. Our aim is to
deliver bold political ideas and vital stories to all walks of life and arm the dreamers
to demand the impossible. We have sold millions of copies of our books, most
often one at a time, face to face. We're old enough to know what we're doing and
young enough to know what's at stake. Join us to create a better world.

PM Press
PO Box 23912
Oakland, CA 94623
www.pmpress.org

PM Press in Europe
europe@pmpress.org
www.pmpress.org.uk

FRIENDS OF PM PRESS

These are indisputably momentous times—the financial system is melting down globally and the Empire is stumbling. Now more than ever there is a vital need for radical ideas.

In the years since its founding—and on a mere shoestring— PM Press has risen to the formidable challenge of publishing and distributing knowledge and entertainment for the struggles ahead. With over 450 releases to date, we have published an impressive and stimulating array of literature, art, music, politics, and culture. Using every available medium, we've succeeded in connecting those hungry for ideas and information to those putting them into practice.

Friends of PM allows you to directly help impact, amplify, and revitalize the discourse and actions of radical writers, filmmakers, and artists. It provides us with a stable foundation from which we can build upon our early successes and provides a much-needed subsidy for the materials that can't necessarily pay their own way. You can help make that happen—and receive every new title automatically delivered to your door once a month—by joining as a Friend of PM Press. And, we'll throw in a free T-shirt when you sign up.

Here are your options:

- **$30 a month** Get all books and pamphlets plus 50% discount on all webstore purchases

- **$40 a month** Get all PM Press releases (including CDs and DVDs) plus 50% discount on all webstore purchases

- **$100 a month** Superstar—Everything plus PM merchandise, free downloads, and 50% discount on all webstore purchases

For those who can't afford $30 or more a month, we have **Sustainer Rates** at $15, $10, and $5. Sustainers get a free PM Press T-shirt and a 50% discount on all purchases from our website.

Your Visa or Mastercard will be billed once a month, until you tell us to stop. Or until our efforts succeed in bringing the revolution around. Or the financial meltdown of Capital makes plastic redundant. Whichever comes first.

Rebel Voices:
An IWW Anthology

Edited by Joyce L. Kornbluh with
a Preface by Daniel Gross and an
Introduction by Fred Thompson

ISBN: 978-1-60486-483-0
$27.95   472 pages

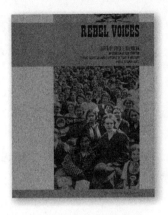

Welcoming women, Blacks, and immigrants long
before most other unions, the Wobblies from
the start were labor's outstanding pioneers and
innovators, unionizing hundreds of thousands of workers previously regarded as
"unorganizable." Wobblies organized the first sit-down strike (at General Electric,
Schenectady, 1906), the first major auto strike (6,000 Studebaker workers, Detroit,
1911), the first strike to shut down all three coalfields in Colorado (1927), and the
first "no-fare" transit-workers' job-action (Cleveland, 1944). With their imaginative,
colorful, and world-famous strikes and free-speech fights, the IWW wrote many
of the brightest pages in the annals of working class emancipation. Wobblies also
made immense and invaluable contributions to workers' culture. All but a few of
America's most popular labor songs are Wobbly songs. IWW cartoons have long
been recognized as labor's finest and funniest.

The impact of the IWW has reverberated far beyond the ranks of organized labor.
An important influence on the 1960s New Left, the Wobbly theory and practice of
direct action, solidarity, and "class-war" humor have inspired several generations
of civil rights and antiwar activists, and are a major source of ideas and inspiration
for today's radicals. Indeed, virtually every movement seeking to "make this planet
a good place to live" (to quote an old Wobbly slogan), has drawn on the IWW's
incomparable experience.

Originally published in 1964 and long out of print, *Rebel Voices* remains by far the
biggest and best source on IWW history, fiction, songs, art, and lore. This new
edition includes 40 pages of additional material from the 1998 Charles H. Kerr
edition from Fred Thompson and Franklin Rosemont, and a new preface by Wobbly
organizer Daniel Gross.

"Not even the doughtiest of capitalism's defenders can read these pages without
understanding how much glory and nobility there was in the IWW story, and how
much shame for the nation that treated the Wobblies so shabbily."
—*New York Times Book Review*, on the 1964 edition.

"The IWW blazed a path in industrial history and its influence is still felt today.
Joyce Kornbluh has performed a valuable service to unionism by compiling this
comprehensive anthology on the more militant side of labor history."
—*Southwest Labor*

The Big Red Songbook: 250+ IWW Songs!

Edited by Archie Green, David Roediger, Franklin Rosemont, and Salvatore Salerno with a Foreword by Tom Morello and an Afterword by Utah Phillips

ISBN: 978-1-62963-129-5
$29.95   560 pages

In 1905, representatives from dozens of radical labor groups came together in Chicago to form One Big Union—the Industrial Workers of the World (IWW), known as the Wobblies. The union was a big presence in the labor movement, leading strikes, walkouts, and rallies across the nation. And everywhere its members went, they sang.

Their songs were sung in mining camps and textile mills, hobo jungles and flop houses, and anywhere workers might be recruited to the Wobblies' cause. The songs were published in a pocketsize tome called the *Little Red Songbook*, which was so successful that it's been published continuously since 1909. In *The Big Red Songbook*, the editors have gathered songs from over three dozen editions, plus additional songs, rare artwork, personal recollections, discographies, and more into one big all-embracing book.

IWW poets/composers strove to nurture revolutionary consciousness. Each piece, whether topical, hortatory, elegiac, or comic served to educate, agitate, and emancipate workers. A handful of Wobbly numbers have become classics, still sung by labor groups and folk singers. They include Joe Hill's sardonic "The Preacher and the Slave" (sometimes known by its famous phrase "Pie in the Sky") and Ralph Chaplin's "Solidarity Forever." Songs lost or found, sacred or irreverent, touted or neglected, serious or zany, singable or not, are here. The Wobblies and their friends have been singing for a century. May this comprehensive gathering simultaneously celebrate past battles and chart future goals.

In addition to the 250+ songs, writings are included from Archie Green, Franklin Rosemont, David Roediger, Salvatore Salerno, Judy Branfman, Richard Brazier, James Connell, Carlos Cortez, Bill Friedland, Virginia Martin, Harry McClintock, Fred Thompson, Adam Machado, and many more.

"This engaging anthology features the lyrics to 250 or so Wobbly songs, rich with references to job sharks, shovel stiffs, capitalist tools, and plutocratic parasites. Wobbly wordsmiths such as the fabled Joe Hill, T-Bone Slim, Haywire Mac, and Richard Brazier set their fighting words to popular tunes of the day, gospel hymns, old ballads and patriotic anthems."
—*San Francisco Chronicle*

Joe Hill: The IWW & the Making of a Revolutionary Workingclass Counterculture, Second Edition

Franklin Rosemont with an Introduction by David Roediger

ISBN: 978-1-62963-119-6
$29.95   656 pages

A monumental work, expansive in scope, covering the life, times, and culture of that most famous of the Wobblies—songwriter, poet, hobo, thinker, humorist, martyr—Joe Hill. It is a journey into the Wobbly culture that made Hill and the capitalist culture that killed him. Many aspects of the life and lore of Joe Hill receive their first and only discussion in IWW historian Franklin Rosemont's opus.

In great detail, the issues that Joe Hill raised and grappled with in his life: capitalism, white supremacy, gender, religion, wilderness, law, prison, and industrial unionism are shown in both the context of Hill's life and for their enduring relevance in the century since his death.

Collected too is Joe Hill's art, plus scores of other images featuring Hill-inspired art by IWW illustrators from Ralph Chaplin to Carlos Cortez, as well as contributions from many other labor artists.

As Rosemont suggests in this remarkable book, Joe Hill never really died. He lives in the minds of young (and old) rebels as long as his songs are sung, his ideas are circulated, and his political descendants keep fighting for a better day.

"Joe Hill has finally found a chronicler worthy of his revolutionary spirit, sense of humor, and poetic imagination."
—Robin D.G. Kelley, author of *Freedom Dreams*

"Rosemont's treatment of Joe Hill is passionate, polemical, and downright entertaining. What he gives us is an extended and detailed argument for considering both Hill and the IWW for their contributions toward creating an autonomous and uncompromising alternative culture."
—Gordon Simmons, *Labor Studies Journal*

"Magnificent, practical, irreverent and (as one might say) magisterial, written in a direct, passionate, sometimes funny, deeply searching style."
—Peter Linebaugh, author of *Stop, Thief!*

Direct Action & Sabotage: Three Classic IWW Pamphlets from the 1910s

Elizabeth Gurley Flynn, Walker C. Smith, and William E. Trautmann

Edited by Salvatore Salerno

ISBN: 978-1-60486-482-3
$14.95   128 pages

The pamphlets reprinted here were first published in the 1910s amid great controversy. Even then, the tactics of direct action and sabotage were often associated with the cartoonists' image of the disheveled, wild-eyed anarchist armed with stiletto, handgun, or bomb—the clandestine activity of a militant minority or the desperate acts of the unorganized.

The activist authors of the texts in this collection challenged the prevailing stereotypes. As they point out, the practices of direct action and sabotage are as old as class society itself and have been an integral part of the everyday work life of wage-earners in all times and places. To the Industrial Workers of the World (IWW) belongs the distinction of being the first workers' organization in the U.S. to discuss these common practices openly, and to recognize their place in working-class struggle. Viewing direct action and sabotage in the spirit of creative nonviolence, Wobblies readily integrated these tactics into their struggle to build industrial unions.

Direct action is recognized as a valuable and effective tactic by many movements around the globe and remains a cutting-edge tool for social change. Whenever communities in struggle find more conventional methods of resistance closed to them, direct action and sabotage will be employed.

This new edition from the Charles H. Kerr Library contains "Direct Action and Sabotage" (1912) by William E. Trautmann, "Sabotage: Its History, Philosophy & Function" (1913) by Walker C. Smith, and Elizabeth Gurley Flynn's "Sabotage: The Conscious Withdrawal of the Workers' Industrial Efficiency" (1916), edited and with an introduction by Salvatore Salerno.

Organize! Building from the Local for Global Justice

Edited by Aziz Choudry, Jill Hanley & Eric Shragge

ISBN: 978-1-60486-433-5
$24.95   352 pages

What are the ways forward for organizing for progressive social change in an era of unprecedented economic, social and ecological crises? How do political activists build power and critical analysis in their daily work for change?

Grounded in struggles in Canada, the USA, Aotearoa/New Zealand, as well as transnational activist networks, *Organize! Building from the Local for Global Justice* links local organizing with global struggles to make a better world. In over twenty chapters written by a diverse range of organizers, activists, academics, lawyers, artists and researchers, this book weaves a rich and varied tapestry of dynamic strategies for struggle. From community-based labor organizing strategies among immigrant workers to mobilizing psychiatric survivors, from arts and activism for Palestine to organizing in support of Indigenous Peoples, the authors reflect critically on the tensions, problems, limits and gains inherent in a diverse range of organizing contexts and practices. The book also places these processes in historical perspective, encouraging us to use history to shed light on contemporary injustices and how they can be overcome. Written in accessible language, *Organize!* will appeal to college and university students, activists, organizers and the wider public.

Contributors include: Aziz Choudry, Jill Hanley, Eric Shragge, Devlin Kuyek, Kezia Speirs, Evelyn Calugay, Anne Petermann, Alex Law, Jared Will, Radha D'Souza, Edward Ou Jin Lee, Norman Nawrocki, Rafeef Ziadah, Maria Bargh, Dave Bleakney, Abdi Hagi Yusef, Mostafa Henaway, Emilie Breton, Sandra Jeppesen, Anna Kruzynski, Rachel Sarrasin, Dolores Chew, David Reville, Kathryn Church, Brian Aboud, Joey Calugay, Gada Mahrouse, Harsha Walia, Mary Foster, Martha Stiegman, Robert Fisher, Yuseph Katiya, and Christopher Reid.

"This superb collection needs to find its way into the hands of every activist and organizer for social justice. In a series of dazzling essays, an amazing group of radical organizers reflect on what it means to build movements in which people extend control over their lives. These analyses are jam-packed with insights about anti-racist, anti-colonial, working-class, and anti-capitalist organizing. Perhaps most crucially, the authors lay down a key challenge for all activists for social justice: to take seriously the need to build mass movements for social change. Don't just read this exceptionally timely and important work—use it too."
—David McNally, author of *Global Slump: The Economics and Politics of Crisis and Resistance*

Wobblies and Zapatistas: Conversations on Anarchism, Marxism and Radical History

Staughton Lynd and Andrej Grubačić

ISBN: 978-1-60486-041-2
$20.00   300 pages

Wobblies and Zapatistas offers the reader an encounter between two generations and two traditions. Andrej Grubačić is an anarchist from the Balkans. Staughton Lynd is a lifelong pacifist, influenced by Marxism. They meet in dialogue in an effort to bring together the anarchist and Marxist traditions, to discuss the writing of history by those who make it, and to remind us of the idea that "my country is the world." Encompassing a Left libertarian perspective and an emphatically activist standpoint, these conversations are meant to be read in the clubs and affinity groups of the new Movement.

The authors accompany us on a journey through modern revolutions, direct actions, anti-globalist counter summits, Freedom Schools, Zapatista cooperatives, Haymarket and Petrograd, Hanoi and Belgrade, 'intentional' communities, wildcat strikes, early Protestant communities, Native American democratic practices, the Workers' Solidarity Club of Youngstown, occupied factories, self-organized councils and soviets, the lives of forgotten revolutionaries, Quaker meetings, antiwar movements, and prison rebellions. Neglected and forgotten moments of interracial self-activity are brought to light. The book invites the attention of readers who believe that a better world, on the other side of capitalism and state bureaucracy, may indeed be possible.

"There's no doubt that we've lost much of our history. It's also very clear that those in power in this country like it that way. Here's a book that shows us why. It demonstrates not only that another world is possible, but that it already exists, has existed, and shows an endless potential to burst through the artificial walls and divisions that currently imprison us. An exquisite contribution to the literature of human freedom, and coming not a moment too soon."
—David Graeber, author of *Fragments of an Anarchist Anthropology* and *Direct Action: An Ethnography*

"I have been in regular contact with Andrej Grubačić for many years, and have been most impressed by his searching intelligence, broad knowledge, lucid judgment, and penetrating commentary on contemporary affairs and their historical roots. He is an original thinker and dedicated activist, who brings deep understanding and outstanding personal qualities to everything he does."
—Noam Chomsky

A History of Pan-African Revolt

C.L.R. James with an Introduction
by Robin D.G. Kelley

ISBN: 978-1-60486-095-5
$16.95   160 pages

Originally published in England in 1938 (the same year
as his magnum opus *The Black Jacobins*) and expanded
in 1969, this work remains the classic account of
global black resistance. Robin D.G. Kelley's substantial
introduction contextualizes the work in the history and
ferment of the times, and explores its ongoing relevance today.

"*A History of Pan-African Revolt* is one of those rare books that continues to strike
a chord of urgency, even half a century after it was first published. Time and
time again, its lessons have proven to be valuable and relevant for understanding
liberation movements in Africa and the diaspora. Each generation who has had the
opportunity to read this small book finds new insights, new lessons, new visions for
their own age . . . . No piece of literature can substitute for a crystal ball, and only
religious fundamentalists believe that a book can provide comprehensive answers
to all questions. But if nothing else, *A History of Pan-African Revolt* leaves us with
two incontrovertible facts. First, as long as black people are denied freedom,
humanity and a decent standard of living, they will continue to revolt. Second,
unless these revolts involve the ordinary masses and take place on their own terms,
they have no hope of succeeding." —Robin D.G. Kelley, from the Introduction

"I wish my readers to understand the history of Pan-African Revolt. They fought,
they suffered—they are still fighting. Once we understand that, we can tackle our
problems with the necessary mental equilibrium." —C.L.R. James

"*Kudos for reissuing C.L.R. James's pioneering work on black resistance. Many brilliant
embryonic ideas articulated in* A History of Pan-African Revolt *twenty years later
became the way to study black social movements. Robin Kelley's introduction superbly
situates James and his thought in the world of Pan-African and Marxist intellectuals.*"
—Sundiata Cha-Jua, Penn State University

"*A mine of ideas advancing far ahead of its time.*"
—Walter Rodney

"*When one looks back over the last twenty years to those men who were most far-
sighted, who first began to tease out the muddle of ideology in our times, who were
at the same time Marxists with a hard theoretical basis, and close students of society,
humanists with a tremendous response to and understanding of human culture,
Comrade James is one of the first one thinks of.*"
—E.P. Thompson

A Soldier's Story: Revolutionary Writings by a New Afrikan Anarchist, Third Edition

Kuwasi Balagoon, edited by Matt Meyer and Karl Kersplebedeb

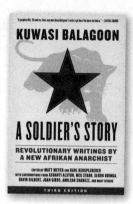

ISBN: 978-1-62963-377-0
$19.95   272 pages

Kuwasi Balagoon was a participant in the Black Liberation struggle from the 1960s until his death in prison in 1986. A member of the Black Panther Party and defendant in the infamous Panther 21 case, Balagoon went underground with the Black Liberation Army (BLA). Captured and convicted of various crimes against the State, he spent much of the 1970s in prison, escaping twice. After each escape, he went underground and resumed BLA activity.

Balagoon was unusual for his time in several ways. He combined anarchism with Black nationalism, he broke the rules of sexual and political conformity that surrounded him, he took up arms against the white-supremacist state—all the while never shying away from developing his own criticisms of the weaknesses within the movements. His eloquent trial statements and political writings, as much as his poetry and excerpts from his prison letters, are all testimony to a sharp and iconoclastic revolutionary who was willing to make hard choices and fully accept the consequences.

Balagoon was captured for the last time in December 1981, charged with participating in an armored truck expropriation in West Nyack, New York, an action in which two police officers and a money courier were killed. Convicted and sentenced to life imprisonment, he died of an AIDS-related illness on December 13, 1986.

The first part of this book consists of contributions by those who knew or were touched by Balagoon. The second section consists of court statements and essays by Balagoon himself, including several documents that were absent from previous editions and have never been published before. The third consists of excerpts from letters Balagoon wrote from prison. A final fourth section consists of a historical essay by Akinyele Umoja and an extensive intergenerational roundtable discussion of the significance of Balagoon's life and thoughts today.

"We have to get our jewels where we can, for this is how we carry on from one generation to the next—it's revolutionary cross-pollination. To paraphrase Che, we need one, two, three, many more Kuwasi Balagoons in order to get free of the chains that bind us."
—Sanyika Shakur, author of *Stand Up, Struggle Forward*